THE DEVELOPMENT OF YOUNG CHILDREN'S SOCIAL-COGNITIVE SKILLS

The Development of Young Children's Social-cognitive Skills

Michael A. Forrester
*Institute of Social and Applied
Psychology
University of Kent, U.K.*

LAWRENCE ERLBAUM ASSOCIATES, PUBLISHERS
Hove (UK)   Hillsdale (USA)

Lawrence Erlbaum Associates Ltd., Publishers
27 Palmeira Mansions
Church Road
Hove
East Sussex, BN3 2FA
U.K.

British Library Cataloguing in Publication Data

Forrester, Michael A.
    The development of young children's social-cognitive skills. -
    (Essays in developmental psychology. ISSN 0959-3977)
    I. Title II. Series
    155.413

    ISBN 0-86377-232-3 (Hbk)
    ISSN 0959-3977 (Essays in Developmental Psychology)

Cover by Joyce Chester
Printed and bound in the United Kingdom by Redwood Press Ltd., Melksham, Wiltshire

Contents

Acknowledgements

Thanks to many who provided the necessary support and stimulus for this book. In particular Glyn Collis, Sue Leekham and David Reason for encouragement, argument and prolonged discussion. Most of all my gratitute to the children, their mothers and caregivers who made this work possible.

Extracts on the following pages were reprinted with permission:

pages 2 and 6
from: Forgas, J. (1981). *Social cognition: Perspectives on everyday understanding.* London: Academic Press. Reprinted with permission of Academic Press and the author.

page 26
from: Olson, D. (1988). On the origins of beliefs and other intentional states in children. In J.W. Astington, P.L. Harris, & D. Olson (Eds.), *Developing theories of mind.* Cambridge: Cambridge University Press. Reprinted with permission.

page 74
from: Drew, P. & Wootton, A. (Eds.). (1988). *Ervin Goffman: Exploring the interaction order.* Cambridge: Polity Press. Reprinted with permission of Basil Blackwell Publishers.

page 78
from: Goffman, E. (1963). *Behavior in public places: Notes on the social organization of gatherings.* New York: Free Press. Copyright ©1963 by The Free Press, a division of Macmillan, Inc. Reprinted by permission of the publisher.

page 78
from: Goffman, E. (1967). *Interaction ritual: Essays on face-to-face behavior.* Harmondsworth: Penguin/New York: Doubleday Anchor. (Allen Lane The Penguin Press, 1972), copyright Erwin Goffman, 1967. Reprinted with permission.

page 82
from: Collins, R. (1988). Theoretical continuities in Goffman's work. In P. Drew & A. Wootton (Eds.). *Ervin Goffman: Exploring the interaction order.* Cambridge: Polity Press. Reprinted with permission of Basil Blackwell Publishers.

page 87
from: Ryan, J. (1974). Early language development: Towards a communicational analysis. In M.P.M. Richards (Ed.), *The integration of a child into the social world.* Cambridge: Cambridge University Press. Reprinted with permission.

page 92
from: Goffman, E. (1981). *Forms of talk.* Hillsdale, N.J.: Lawrence Erlbaum Associates Inc. Reprinted with permission.

CHAPTER ONE

Social-cognitive Development

INTRODUCTION

Investigating how infants and young children begin to participate in and understand the social world has become a major research paradigm within developmental psychology. Social-cognitive development or developmental social cognition has emerged as an important sub-discipline for a number of reasons. First, there is the intrinsic value of a field which concerns itself with understanding and seeking to explain how children become competent social beings; second, social-cognitive development research constitutes an important source of evidence for complementary areas of developmental psychology (e.g. developmental psycholinguistics, moral development) and third, such research seeks to provide 'baseline' developmental data on social-cognitive abilities for a range of specific problems within applied and clinical developmental fields (e.g. autism and learning impairment).

As adult social cognition research gained prominence (Eiser & Stroebe, 1972) calls for a developmental perspective increased (Forgas, 1981), particularly given the attractiveness of an approach which might fulfil demands for developmental psychology to be more ecologically valid and relevant (Bronfenbrenner, 1979; Neisser, 1976). The promise is that if we can only uncover how young children begin to take part in and cognise the social world, we will not only gain insights into developmental processes, but also into the very structure, function, and processing form of social cognition itself.

The term social cognition began to appear in social psychology and developmental psychology textbooks in the late 1970s and early 1980s in the U.S.A.(Shantz, 1975) and Europe (Forgas, 1981), and over the last 10–15 years boundary conditions for various nuances of the phrase have become established along one or other dichotomies, for example, European/American; rational/affective; cognitive/social; Piagetian/ Vygotskian and so on. Thus a cognitive view of social cognition:

'... an approach that stresses understanding of cognitive processes as a key to understanding complex, purposive, social behaviour' (Isen & Hastorf, 1982, p.2),

can be contrasted with a social outlook:

'... not merely the information processing analysis of social domains, but [as] a field genuinely devoted to the study of everyday knowledge and understanding ... the joint product of socio-cultural forces and individual cognitive processes' (Forgas, 1981, p.259).

And as an example of a European/American dichotomy, Durkin (1986) notes the European approach as being concerned with social social cognition:

'... cognition is seen as an achievement promoted and regulated via social interaction'

while the American view emphasises individual social cognition:

'social cognition ... thoughts and reasoning about people, their mental and physical attributes, their personalities, behaviour and viewpoints' (pp.206–207).

We can also note definitions that attempt to negotiate a position somewhere between individual/social extremes, by articulating what is to be taken as social and what as individual, for example:

'... All the ways in which the child exchanges, receives and processes information from others. These ways include some general cognitive processes, such as attention and memory as well as some that are strictly social, such as communication and perspective taking' (Damon, 1981, p.82).

During the 1970s and early 1980s a number of books and review articles began to mark out a series of research issues which were to form the basis for much of current developmental social-cognitive research (Garvey, 1977; Higgins, Ruble, & Hartup, 1983; Mugny & Doise, 1978; Perret-Clermont, 1980; Schaffer, 1977; Shantz, 1975; Shatz & Gelman, 1973; Turiel, 1982). The emergence of developmental social cognition as a distinct field of inquiry can be traced to a range of interests, some theoretically inspired, such as the cross-fertilisation of models from cognitive psychology; some methodological, for instance driven by the concerns of educationalists and clinicians, and others simply pragmatic (e.g. moral development researchers seeking to incorporate a somewhat marginalised area within a broader theme).

The enthusiasm that this research engendered was related to the growing dissatisfaction for some researchers with Piagetian logico-mathematical accounts of development. Although theoretically sophisticated this approach tended in practice to emphasise what the child couldn't do rather than on her abilities at any given age (Donaldson, 1978; McGarrigle, Grieve, & Hughes, 1978). Another important reason was that the social-cognitive perspective appeared to offer the benefits accruing to the rigour and formalism of the dominant view in psychology, yet within a framework which could and would address developmental social-interactional processes. In other words, the emergence of developmental social cognition as a distinct field of enquiry is interdependent with the widespread utilisation of the information processing metaphor. This is evidenced in the observation that many of the concerns of the field (as well as the underlying constructs) could be located in disparate areas of the behavioural sciences before definitions of social cognition and developmental social cognition began to appear (Cartwright & Zander, 1968; Forgas, 1981; Shantz, 1975; Stotland & Canon, 1972). The application of the cognitive approach to the study of a variety of social-developmental or at least socially oriented concerns, has proceeded rapidly and with some enthusiasm by researchers in child language, cognitive and moral development, educational psychology and learning impairment.

The argument I wish to develop is that the current theoretical frameworks have not fulfilled their earlier promise and by their nature (that is given their pre-theoretical constructs and implicit assumptions), are unlikely to provide adequate concepts and 'tools' necessary for our research purposes. The principal aim of what is to follow then, is to present an alternative framework for studying young children's social-cognitive skills. Towards this end, there are three subsidiary objectives. First, developmental social cognition research is critically reviewed (in Chapters 2 and 3), with particular reference to the principal theoretical positions and against a background of considerations and concerns which permit an evaluation of the current 'state of the field'. The specific misgivings outlined (initially in the remainder of this chapter) also underpin a critique of approaches which focus on the young child's social cognitive skills, or attempt to integrate social cognition research with developmental psycholinguistics (reviewed in Chapter 4).

A summary of this literature then serves as the springboard for the second subsidiary objective, outlining and developing an alternative conceptual framework for investigating and understanding young children's active engagement and participation with the social world (in Chapter 5). This approach takes up a number of ideas from within and beyond psychology, notably from conversational analysis, micro-sociology, pragmatics and from the ecological perspective, the notion of affordances. The concern is with understanding what might be required if we wish to formulate richer conceptual models of social-cognitive development.

The third objective is to consider lines of evidence which lend support to the proposed framework (Chapters 6 through 8). The focus is upon one way in which the framework can aid in our understanding one contributory aspect of the child's developing social-cognitive skills—the role of overhearing and its relation to the acquisition of conversation-participation abilities. Finally, the concluding chapter draws together the themes outlined, highlighting various implications of the framework advocated. The overarching goal is to provide a more adequate conceptual basis for developing appropriate models and methods to aid our investigations of social-cognitive development and particularly children's conversational-participation skills.

SOCIAL-COGNITIVE DEVELOPMENT: PROBLEMS AND PROSPECTS

I would like to distinguish between areas of research activity and primary theoretical orientations. Clearly there are a variety of subjects, applied issues and distinct domains of enquiry which now come under the rubric of developmental social cognition research and the range of topics is fairly broad. Consider one alignment in developmental social cognition which originates in ethologically inspired social interaction research (Bowlby, 1959; Hinde, 1979; Schaffer, 1984). This research holds to the information-processing perspective as one of its (normally implicit) central formulating constructs, combined with ideas from evolutionary biology and ethology. Historically this paradigm made a significant contribution to developmental psychology by showing that the infant was part of a symbiotic network (the 'mutuality' model, Schaffer, 1980) and should not be considered in isolation (Schaffer & Emerson, 1964; Stern, 1974). As long as the orientation here remained 'dyadic', that is, focused upon how the infant affects the parent and the parent the child, the approach was considerably successful. However, as attempts were made to extend the paradigm outwards to the study of 'triadic' and 'polyadic' interactions (the child interacting with three or more people—Liddell & Collis, 1988), the conceptual constraints deriving from an overtly 'meta-descriptive' evolutionary approach became more serious, particularly with reference to the relationship between theory and data (i.e. the proliferation and complexities of the latter which themselves helped clarify the theoretical limitations of the approach).

Another area of developmental social cognition research emerged from what was previously defined as moral development, where now themes, methods and specific topics are often subsumed under the category social-cognitive development. Examples of the 'transformation' of moral into social-cognitive development can be seen in Eisenberg's outline of prosocial reasoning (Eisenberg, 1986) and Hoffman's conception of the development of empathy (Hoffman, 1982). Whether this or that approach derives from innatist conceptions (Turiel, 1981) or maturational-Piagetian views (Kohlberg, 1966) their position or status as developmental social-cognition research is closely tied to the concentration upon performance and measurement criteria (Lefebvre-Pinard, 1982), that is, indices of developing social cognitions. What is interesting about much of this work is that by adopting a social-cognitive perspective the terms of reference appear to have moved away from precedents which were more directly related to pre-theoretical concerns of 'ethics', onto formulations which place the emphasis upon the child's developing understanding or cognitions of social behaviour.

A further important strand arose from the concerns of practitioners in educational and clinical settings. Although one result of the Piagetian influence upon educational policy was a move away from the rigours of disciplined rote-learning to more child-centred educational practice, arguably the Piagetian framework is directly applicable only to the more formal areas of the curriculum (science and mathematics). Those concerned with topics somewhat outside of cognitive-developmental domains derived only limited benefit from this approach. In contrast, part of the appeal of the social cognition approach is that here is a representational/constructivist framework with a generally applicable metaphor suitable for a range of educational concerns (e.g. from sociometric indices of peer relations in the classroom through to discourse-based approaches to reading development). It also remains grounded in the requisite formalisms of educational science policy.

Similarly, clinicians and practitioners in learning impairment, mental handicap and remedial language contexts envisage substantial advantages, particularly given that the social-cognitive view provides a terminology of attention deficits, information processing constraints and related terms as a consolidating language, a shared focus for research and homogeneous methodological constructs applicable to a wide variety of child subject groups. The learning-impaired and mental-handicap developmental literature looks towards social-cognitive developmental research for additional reasons. First, there is the pertinent need for contributory comparative (baseline) data to assist intervention or development programs. Second, there is the necessity to theoretically understand the relationship between models of development and models of impairment, particularly given that there are very few models of social-cognitive impairment as such (Shute & Paton, 1990). Third, there is an underlying problem with the uncritical adoption of models from 'normal' development paradigms into the study of impairment (e.g. the sometimes unwarranted assumption that by examining impairment and how it changes one necessarily gains insights into how 'normal' processing works). The social-cognitive perspective holds the promise of providing a unifying construct or at least the requisite point of origin for divergent approaches, each sensitive to the concerns of specialist target groups.

Given the pre-eminence of cognitive science in psychology, the benchmark or point of orientation for the majority of current formulations of developmental social cognition research is the information processing framework (in its symbol manipulating representational sense). Arguably while there might be debates between nuances of various positions (e.g. Piagetian vs. Vygotskian) the 'discourse-frame' remains firmly grounded upon the computational metaphor. Consider the way in which the more dominant meaning of the term social cognition has become equated with the application of the information processing metaphor (to the study of social phenomena and processes), noted by Forgas (1981). In his emphasis for a social cognition outlook he argues:

'Cognition, when taken as a domain concerned with all processes of knowing, is intrinsically, inevitably and profoundly social. Our knowledge is socially structured and transmitted from the first day of our life, is coloured by the values, motivations and norms of our social environment in adulthood, and ideas, knowledge and representations are created and recreated at the social as well as the individual level' (p.2).

Beyond the recognition that the use of the word 'transmitted' itself is predicated on a 'computational' discourse, there are a number of points which together might suggest that adherence to the information processing metaphor has led to theoretical impoverishment, that is as far as understanding developmental social cognition as a skill or ability is concerned.

The first reason derives from a commonly found distinction in psychology: some fields of enquiry are to be properly addressed as individualistic (attention and memory) while others (communication) are intrinsically social, and on few occasions is there any attempt to remind ourselves that this differentiation is based upon theoretical assumptions, which are themselves controversial and need to be substantiated. Given that memory and learning how to remember may itself be established in social-discursive practices (Edwards & Middleton, 1988), as well as the fairly extensive research highlighting the social nature of categorisation (Tajfel & Forgas, 1981; Zajonc, 1980), while there may not yet be sufficient grounds for abandoning such a distinction, there is an increasing requirement for theoretical justification.

The second is the inherent danger of arguing that all cognition is intrinsically social while at the same time maintaining that there remains an important and uniquely essential 'individual level'. It has been argued elsewhere that part of the reason why cognitive psychology is largely viewed as non-social is because language is not considered as a fundamentally social phenomena (Farr, 1981); that is, the emphasis has been on language as a formal symbol system. This of course is not surprising given that the birth of psycholinguistics can be traced to the publication of Chomsky's (1957) monograph on competence grammars. Some theoreticians in cognitive science have made serious attempts to highlight the limitations of abstract and formally complex models of language (e.g. Givon, 1984), pointing out the inherent dangers of strictly formal 'rationalistic' approaches to language understanding. However, a more serious problem revolves around a presupposed relationship between language and identity.

This issue arises with reference to the philosophical and conceptual basis for the scientific status of concepts, categories and those various hypothesis regarding the nature of language and thought (Chomsky, 1957; Rosch, 1975; Saussure, 1966; Whorf, 1956). If one holds to a cognitive/computational conception (Chomsky, 1988; Fodor, 1983) of language and cognition, then beyond the various debates on precisely how to model formal rules acting upon representations of information processing activities (Clark, 1987; Karmiloff-Smith, 1979; Pinker, 1984; Rumelhart & McClelland, 1986) the underlying agenda locates thought as being first and foremost 'inside the individual's head' and an inherent essential property of that individual. The point here is that whatever particular conception of cognition or language understanding that follows has placed the issue of 'identity' (of the cogito or logos) as *the* central question. All consequential attempts to adequately address 'interaction' dimensions are already compromised by the metaphysics of this position.

In contrast to such post-Kantian formulations (of cognition) other threads of continental philosophy (particularly Hegel, Merleu-Ponty, and Derrida) have sought to demonstrate that a number of philosophical arguments concerning identity (and representation), based upon *a priori* categorisation, contain a number of serious inherent contradictions. These serve to make them unworkable or at least severely constrained by outdated conceptions of 'grand truths' and the centrality of identity (Descombes, 1980). This is not the place to enter into the ramifications of recent philosophical developments for psychology—problematic though they may be—see Feldman and Bruner (1987) and Stitch (1983), only that with regard to language there are now serious grounds for arguing that not only are many models within cognitive psycholinguistics unhelpful but that there are alternative emerging theoretical frameworks which may be better placed to provide the basis for a *social* social cognition (e.g. Sinha, 1988).

A third reason for calling into question the appropriateness of the current theoretical orientation is the emphasis on one of the essential building blocks of the current framework supporting social-cognitive theories, the developmental dimension itself (Durkin, 1988; Flavell & Ross, 1981). For example, in this vein Forgas (1981) argues

'... the analysis and understanding of children's efforts to make sense of the world (is) a necessary stage in explaining adult social cognition ...' (p.264).

What is problematic here (as in other sub-fields of developmental psychology) is the theoretical 'circularity' which derives from employing a developmental perspective as an evidential tier in the supporting foundation of the perspective, without paying due regard to the fact that the adopted developmental view already presupposes the same pre-theoretical constructs. In that sense any significant contributions will largely be confined to the empirical and not theoretical level.

Why an overemphasis upon, or adherence to, the information processing metaphor is problematic can be summarised. There is often little attempt at theoretically justifying the 'individual/social' dichotomy prevalent in much of the research. The attention on the formal symbol-manipulating aspects of language has overshadowed the social nature of language use with respect to social cognition, and attempts at addressing the nature of interaction are constrained by the pre-theoretical philosophical underpinning of current conceptions of cognition. Sufficient attention is not given to the potentially comprised contribution of a distinctly 'developmental' perspective, and the issue of 'separability' tends to be ignored or simply not recognised as problematic. What I mean by separability is the recognition that our everyday experience is not of going around 'constructing' our representational worlds in order that we may act. The implications of this observation are not immediately clear; however, it is easy to detect a degree of conceptual coherence in this assertion, for how could we formulate an act independently of our already inhabiting a comprehensible world?

If social cognition research is to provide the requisite theoretical framework for our investigations into how young children begin to participate in (and make sense out of so as to take part) the social world then it must seek to engage in the necessary level of theory construction. Arguably this will require meta-theoretical (i.e. metaphysical) effort as well as conceptual and methodological ingenuity. In other words one of the prime restrictions upon the development of appropriate methods to guide our investigations, is the paucity of considered theoretical development, particularly the absence of work which critically considers the relationship between pre-theoretical assumptions and methodological practice (but see Williams, 1989).

Whether conceptions are broad-based or more locally oriented what is conspicuous by its absence is a critical evaluation of the various theoretical orientations in developmental social cognition research. This book is based around the argument that we are in need of a theoretical framework which does justice to the uniquely 'social' nature of the information the child is being exposed to as apprentice participant in the social world. The emphasis is very much on the child as participant and thus the focus upon skills and abilities. There are two reasons for this. One is the argument that the currently dominant theoretical frameworks either pay only lip service to the importance of dynamic and participatory aspects of social cognitive contexts or simply cannot accommodate the complexity of participation within their parameters. The second is more fundamental and relates to the ontological status of information processing social cognition as a heuristic. It will be argued that as far as understanding how it is that children come to successfully participate in the social world, the emphasis on individual cognition (that is, 'self', 'identity', 'categories', and 'concepts of knowing') has not proved particularly helpful. The suggestion is that we require a framework that will allow for the development of models, which move the focus as far as possible away from 'in the head' philosophies towards conceptions of social-cognitive interaction and participation which are not simply 'emergent' of social interaction processes but constitutive of social practices between humans.

CHAPTER TWO

Individualistic Social-cognitive Development

Various reasons provide the impetus for embarking on a commentary of contemporary research strategies in this area. Pre-eminently, identifying why currently dominant views of social-cognitive development are inappropriate for the study of children's participative social-cognitive skills, clears the ground for building the foundations of an alternative approach (brought into place in Chapter 5). In addition, identifying the primary theoretical constructs helps to bring together an increasingly disparate field, as well as allow for an evaluation of the current 'state of the art'. It is also an opportune moment for reviewing a burgeoning research field.

Developmental social cognition research can be considered as falling into three groupings: (a) constructivist and representational frameworks (Piagetian and information processing accounts); (b) social interaction approaches (the Genevan school, Vygotsky and Mead); and (c) discourse and linguistically oriented perspectives (developmental social cognition and language). In this chapter the Piagetian and information processing persuasions will be reviewed. The following chapter examines social interaction accounts and approaches, leaving for Chapter 4 approaches which consider the relationship between social-cognitive development and language, discussed there alongside research which addresses children's social-cognitive skills and abilities.

The review is specifically concerned with summarising and considering the currently dominant theoretical views underpinning studies of the development of social-cognitive skills. As the focus is on the child's participation in the conversational context, the review will be oriented towards work which either directly addresses relevant issues in this area or has important implications for the way such research is undertaken (theoretical frameworks, models and methods). That it to say, this is not intended to be a complete and comprehensive review of all developmental social cognition research, a considerable undertaking in itself given that it would include studies concerned with 'non-participatory' aspects of social-cognitive development, for example, attitude formation (Emler & Hogan, 1981) or developing social knowledge of economic systems (Jahoda, 1982). The intention is to critically evaluate a substantial proportion of the research work and examine the main conceptual constructs underlying the sub-themes of the field.

CONSTRUCTIVE AND REPRESENTATIONAL PERSPECTIVES

Within this broad theme the two most influential frameworks are reviewed, starting with the Piagetian approach which both historically and to some degree conceptually, anticipated the concerns, constructs and methods of the later computationally inspired information processing approach, the second framework evaluated.

THE PIAGETIAN APPROACH

Piaget's theory of intellectual development has provided the backbone for various theories of cognitive development (e.g. Flavell, 1977), moral development (Kohlberg, 1966), social-cognitive development (Doise & Mugny, 1985) and recent theories in language development (Howe, in press). The uptake of Piaget's ideas within education and educational psychology has been considerable, in large part because of the unambiguous nature of his outline of the emergence and development of children's knowledge.

Piaget was first and foremost a genetic epistemologist and was concerned with identifying the biological substrates of knowledge. He was critically concerned not with content (specific performance with regard to whether a child knows X) but with the underlying cognitive structures which make knowledge possible, and how these structures function in relation to the environment. Piaget's earlier ideas, although somewhat diffuse, emphasised the importance of representation and egocentrism. This contrasts with the more rigorous research on children's abilities to classify, make sense out of, and generally 'cognise' the world (carried out in the 1950s and 1960s). This later work was conceived with reference to a mathematical model of cognition (called the Grouping) and it is important to recognise that this framework was Piaget's way of attempting to capture the essence of the child's cognitive activities. It is not simply a kind of list (of what a child can and cannot do) but an abstraction which describes basic processes—from which one can infer the evolution of a comprehensive and integrated structure.

Contrary to some interpretations of Piaget's research he did not ignore the role of social interaction. It played an important role in at least two areas; his ideas on children's egocentrism and his formulation of cognitive-developmental change (particularly conflict). Piaget's early work was particularly concerned with the notion of egocentrism. This he said was a very basic quality of children's thinking. The young child has significant problems with the notion that other people have a point of view that is different from them. Gradually, throughout the pre-operational period (up to around age 6–7), although she knows that other people exist, she still cannot really manage to put herself in their place: cannot appreciate that others' points of view are different. The emergence of 'non-egocentric' thinking is brought about through interaction with other people who have different viewpoints, her recognition that differences of viewpoint are a matter for concern and more generally the realisation through social experience, that the way she thinks is not the only way to understand the world.

With regard to cognitive-developmental growth (movement from one stage to another) social interaction plays a pivotal role. A fundamental aspect of the mechanisms responsible for cognitive change was the conflict engendered through the social interaction context. Through the interaction with other people the child comes to recognise that something in the way she is thinking is not quite right, and she has to accommodate appropriately. This accommodation results in the transformation of one qualitatively distinct stage into another. Social interaction is the (indirect) trigger for development.

Shantz's (1983) review of the previous 15 years of social-cognitive research is illustrative for a number of reasons. The orientation is largely Piagetian (construed as broadly constructivist) although placed within a representational framework incorporating essential components of the information processing paradigm (e.g. schema theory). The child as both scientist and social psychologists are offered as metaphors, and her review considers research which moves through individual, dyadic and group contexts/levels of social-cognitive understanding. That is, the individual child's reasoning process is the starting point and from there we move upwards (and outwards) to increasing levels of complexity. Shantz (1983) relates various themes of social-cognitive developmental research to these levels (perspective taking or whatever), accomplished in a scholarly fashion where the topics range over a number of diverse areas (e.g. attribution of intention, authority relations and the relations between cognitive abilities and social behaviour).

However, beyond the application of a constructivist metaphor, there are in fact few well formulated models guiding the major themes. What is interesting are the areas of neglect Shantz (1983) identifies, and her predictions concerning future research questions. Regarding the former she suggests that the long-term goals of social-cognitive theory should be to understand the child's cognitions (about others), 'as the child both participates with them and observes them' (p.487). In addition she emphasises that there has been insufficient study of the social world of the child and this neglect has contributed to the impression that children are 'bootstrapping their way to social knowledge and adaptive social reasoning' (p.542). Her most serious criticism of the area is the acknowledgement that when it comes to the study of the relations between social behaviour and social-cognitive development there are few specifically detailed theoretical guidelines.

There are around half-a-dozen research or review papers which can be considered as distinctly Piagetian in outlook (note these are discussed separate from social interaction approaches to social-cognitive development which found inspiration from Piagetian ideas—see Chapter 3). Although Piaget's earlier research provides a rich source of ideas for developmental social cognition research, for methodological and historical reasons there has been an almost exclusive emphasis on the later work. As noted above, his later work starts from an internally coherent conception of formal operational thinking (i.e. the n-ary logico-mathematical model), where all stages of development leading to this ideal abstraction should be viewed as antecedent and requisite distinct formalisms, which the child constructs through her interactions with the environment. Change is brought about along equilibration principles and it is with reference to such constructs that debate regarding the development of social-cognitive abilities centres.

Given the pivotal role of the equilibration principle in Piaget's formalist conceptions, explanatory accounts of cognitive development have focused upon the facilitatory nature of conflict engendered by social interaction 'encounters' (see Bryant, 1982; Light, 1983). Disequilibrium engendered by conflict becomes the driving force for change. Much debate surrounds whether it is necessary (for the child) to experience 'cognitive conflict' through interaction with other people or whether as long as there is conflict of some kind (physical, i.e. derived from exposure to problem-solving scenarios as such), then change and development will take place. And such developmental changes are not simply quantitative but qualitative. In practice it can be argued that two research strategies have emerged. For those of an anti-Piagetian strain, a research discourse of surprise where children of increasingly younger years are seen as possessing sophisticated cognitive skills (e.g. role taking) because they can in fact engage successfully in context-sensitive versions of Piagetian tasks. In contrast, the neo-Piagetian perspective takes the position that social knowledge is no different from any other type of knowledge (e.g. notions of causality or spatio-temporal thinking) and social development is so closely tied to cognitive development that there is no sound argument for a distinctive social-cognitive approach.

Youniss's theoretical work (Youniss, 1978; Youniss & Volpe, 1978) serves as a good example of a Piagetian social-cognitive development view. He argues that the principle basis for social cognitions is the contrasting relations that the child might be exposed to across adult and peer interactions and in support of this position presents data on the differential effects of such contexts. Notwithstanding the emphasis upon outcome rather than process, Youniss recognises the importance of the dynamic nature of what is involved (in participation) in two senses. First, the child has to find herself in situations of engagement where her actions will be obstructed (i.e. in ongoing conversations) so as to recognise regularities and 'rule relations'. Second, the social-cognitive experience of self and other only emerges out of the sense of maintained order, identifiable through such series of interactions. This work is an interesting attempt at deriving the benefits accruing to the logical formalism of the Piagetian position while at the same time offering what Youniss calls a 'radical epistemology', which posits relations as the unit of analysis.

Where Youniss's (1978) approach fails however, is with the emphasis on the child's reflections on relations rather than on the possibility that the structure of the talk or conversations that the child is in (and part of) provides, in a much more direct sense, the information regarding relations. This is not to say that reflection is not important, only it overlooks the fact that the detection and specification of roles and relations is dynamically available as part of the presuppositional framework underpinning the very act of engaging in conversations[1] and using talk. It is time to examine in much more detail the nature of the discourse which makes up adult-child conversation. We can note in passing that Youniss's (1978) thesis has not been developed over the last 10 years possibly reflecting the disenchantment of the Piagetian approach (e.g. the extensive research which highlighted methodological limitations (Bryant & Trabasso, 1971; Donaldson, 1978).

One perspective within the Piagetian framework (Chapman, 1986) recognises the inappropriateness of operational logic approaches to social-cognitive development and instead concentrates upon Piaget's sociological work (Piaget, 1965/1977). What is interesting about Chapman's (1986) approach is his attempt to link Piaget's general theory of social exchange to other social-theoretic ideas (e.g. Goffman and Habermas) in a way which emphasises social value and mutual reciprocity as a framework for formulating a (social-psychological) account of development. By highlighting Piaget's social exchange formalism[2] Chapman's (1986) paper can be seen as a partial reply to critiques of Piagetian ethnocentrism (e.g. Buck-Morss, 1975). Further, Chapman (1986) re-formulates Youniss's (1980) social-cognitive model of parent-child and peer-peer reciprocity in an interesting way, suggesting that other related models could benefit from a similar re-analysis (e.g. Furth, 1978; and see Keller & Reuss, 1984).

Chapman's (1986) analysis assists in the articulation of reasons why a Piagetian approach, as expressed in such studies as Furth (1978), is unlikely to provide the conceptual framework for social-cognitive developmental research. First the principal reason why a logical-mathematical approach cannot accommodate socially related phenomena is because all such formalisms are structures motivated towards closure. In contrast social and biological phenomena are inherently open and unstable in the sense that explanatory accounts are construed with reference to elements external to the system. For example, where co-participants are mutually concerned with aiding each other's learning in a conversational context, ideally they would be oriented towards providing what they do not quite know they are going to need. Such predispositions would increase the likelihood that spontaneous and unanticipated leads in such talk might emerge. It is very hard to see how the Piagetian approach can accommodate phenomena of this kind.

Second, as Chapman (1986) recognises, the Piagetian approach is taken to be exclusively concerned with the development of operational ways of thinking. It is unlikely that this perspective is going to lead to the development of innovative methods for investigating social participation. Third, formulating an account of social-cognitive development, which integrates cognitive-development theory within a general theory of social exchange and reciprocity, although providing a coherent sociological model of individual development, remains inappropriate for investigating the child's emerging social-cognitive skills. Piaget's sociological theory cannot adequately address how it is that the child acquires such concepts as value, debt, satisfaction, and so on within the mechanics or medium where such acquisition is made possible (i.e. participation in discourse). This approach glosses over how participation as such bears upon the various social-cognitive constructs said to be developing within the child.

The role of symbolic and pretend play continues to command the attention of child linguists and cognitive developmentalists (Lloyd & Goodwin, 1990) particularly the relationship between engagement in such play and the development of representational abilities (Howe & Ogura, 1988). The relation between play and social cognition is considered by Stamback, Ballion, Breaute, and Rayna (1985) from a Piagetian perspective. Using an observational approach, they looked at pre-school children's knowledge of social rules and social conduct, reflected in the way the children presented short dramas involving puppets. They suggest that the dialogue demonstrates the child's 'on-line construction of new knowledge and new constructive processes' (p.146).

Stamback et al. (1985) make the claim that particular cognitive mechanisms (those of a logical nature) lead to the successful 'construction' of pretend play, which itself (because it utilises social interactive procedures) promotes social interaction skills. These in turn lead to enhanced social-cognitive development. The basis for successful social participation is to be located within cognitive processes, again questionable given evidence that children can participate competently in the social world well before they exhibit signs of 'logical' processing (Dunn, 1988). This study, although concluding with a re-emphasis on the importance of social-cognitive conflict, is more an argument concerning the use of naturalistic observational methods than a reasoned case for the Piagetian position.

Higgins (1981) also outlines a Piagetian perspective developing an account of role-taking and social-cognitive development. He emphasises the conceptual distinction between centration and egocentrism, through an analysis of the different abilities involved in 'controlling the self' versus being able to 'interrelate multiple factors' (altruism will be related to the former and conservation skills the latter). Higgins's reconceptualisation is more an attempt to separate out 'informational' from 'self/affective' aspects of role-taking for methodological purposes than a serious contribution to a theoretically complex issue. Finally, another paper that adheres to Piagetian formalisms is Selman's (1981) argument for an epistemic approach to the emergence of children's conceptions of friendship. Selman (1981) views social cognition as an expression of 'deeper meaning: the study of what is meant rather than what is said' (p.269) and he goes to considerable lengths to outline a structural developmental model. However, this is derived methodologically from a baseline of 'common-sense' questions, which ultimately conflates a descriptive taxonomy with a stage model outlook. The applicability of the model is evaluated only with reference to its usefulness as an assessment tool.

To summarise, the principal shortcomings of the Piagetian approach to social-cognitive development are the constraints arising from a logico-mathematical conception of human cognition, arguably appropriate only for particular kinds of representational processes and cognitions (e.g. problem-solving; inferential processing; number manipulation; solving physics problems). The emphasis is on particular forms of knowledge which a lay person might only consciously engage in at most 10% of the time, and children considerably less. There is understandably an undoubted reticence for many workers in developmental psychology to move away from a framework which is both conceptually sophisticated and has provided a range of important metaphors (and methods) for the study of cognitive development. However, attempts at utilising the Piagetian perspective for the study of social-cognitive development particularly where the emphasis is upon children's participation skills, are more likely to result in formulations akin to squeezing a quart into a pint pot. There is not enough evidence to suggest that such an approach would be useful, or that the theoretical framework provides an adequate basis for the study of dynamic interaction processes.

INFORMATION PROCESSING APPROACHES

The second individualistic theme subsumes a variety of approaches, which for one reason or another fall within the information processing framework. In a similar fashion to accounts of adult social-cognitive processes (e.g. Fiske & Taylor, 1984), developmental social cognition here, originates from notions of 'theories of mind' (Bretherton, McNew, & Beeghly-Smith, 1981), 'ontological mental entities' (John-Steiner, 1987), 'schema/script' representations (Nelson, 1981) and in large part established within the familiar terrain of processing constraints, representation, modularity, inference and problem-solving and so on (Bem, 1972; Forgas, 1981; Higgins, Ruble, & Hartup, 1983). Under one heading a number of exemplars will be considered leading onto an analysis of what has become known as the 'theory of mind' literature, concluding with a summary of the major conceptual and methodological limitations of this orientation. We can turn first to a number of exemplars of the approach.

(a) Exemplars of the Orientation
In a complementary development to the way in which the 'script' framework proposed by Schank and Abelson (1977) was taken up in cognitive psychology (Bower, Black, & Turner, 1979) variations of the same concept began to appear in developmental social cognition. Nelson (1981), for example, argues that children are provided with scripts (of

social events—i.e. through participation and observation) and what they have to do is learn how to play their part in this or that context. Within this metaphor, general event representations are derived from and applied to social settings, where the child's roles, rules, procedures and so on, fill in the 'slots'.

The interesting thing here is the application of a theoretical (dramaturgical) metaphor comprising plays, scripts, roles, and slots which possesses or at least warrants the status of a 'formal model' within the literature. Nelson (1981) attests to this when she attempts to draw the distinction between being a playwright and merely a 'bit player'. The child here is cast in the bit player role or more appropriately the apprentice bit player role where one assumes the social world is the stage. In particular following Schank and Abelson (1977) and then Nelson (1981), a vigorous research theme has emerged seeking to demonstrate the validity and applicability of this model (e.g. Furnam & Walden, 1990; Nelson & Gruendel, 1979; Nelson & Seidman, 1984).

Furnam and Walden (1990) carried out a series of experiments on the relationship between having script knowledge and being able to engage in communicative interactions. Children were first assessed for the kinds of scripted knowledge they appeared to possess (e.g. going to McDonalds), then separated into categories by ability, and subsequently studied during interactions with other children similarly assessed (allowing comparisons of degree of 'knowledge scripts'). Beyond suggesting that having more world knowledge does not necessarily lead to more sophisticated cognitive processing, Furman and Walden (1990) found that script knowledge only assisted conversational turn-taking for younger (5 year old) not older children. One difficulty in evaluating this study (and a problem common to many) is that the dependent measures of communication failure do not include indices of 'ongoing' interaction and conversational participation. This may reflect a more general orientation of this approach, that is, the sense of implied 'determinism' with respect to the role of developing social cognitions (as causal determining constructs). In other words what the child needs to do is simply learn the scripts and social skill success will follow.

An additional problem with the way the script metaphor is employed is the assumption that as actors know how a given story (script) evolves, takes shape, and ends, we simply have to identify the kinds of roles we are in and then 'run off' the appropriate script. This ignores or glosses over what is centrally important in ongoing participation contexts (conversational or otherwise) in the sense that engagement can, and more often than not, result in unforeseen possibilities (particularly for children who would have few rigorously developed scripts). In other words many of our interactions have a potentiating sense (to a greater or lesser degree). There is some recognition of this in Nelson's (1981) proposal that the ideal script will be sufficiently 'skeletal' for the inclusion of expected components, while still flexible enough to incorporate the unexpected.

The script scenario also fails to address the problematic status of the relation between language use, scripts and social cognition. Wittgenstein (1953) argues cogently that the presuppositional basis of linguistic items is 'swallowed whole' by the language learner and does not involve tuition in scripting knowledge. In other words there must be structural components surrounding the use of words in conversations, which provide the 'scripting' basis for ensuing interchanges, and thus there is no necessity to posit (or at least to emphasise) a separate system of scripting representations. This might help explain why Nelson and Gruendel's (1979) conception of true communication (turn-taking, joint conversation, elaboration and co-ordination) leaves out implicature[3], arguably the pre-eminent essential component for any communicative interaction to take place at all (Grice, 1981).

A small number of other studies attempt to incorporate other information processing ideas from cognitive psychology (Gelman & Spelke, 1981; Higgins & Wells, 1986; Shure, 1985; Stein & Goldman, 1981). For example, Shure's (1985) paper is a good example of the limitations of a strictly information processing intervention programme for social skills training. His programme might be summarised as adherence to the principle that if you can think before you can act, then you increase the likelihood that you will engage in those 'problem-solving' activities which result in successful social outcomes. As Selman (1985) comments, Shure's (1985) demonstration that thinking might help is a sufficient but not necessary condition for social cognition and the research cited by Shure (1985) remains at best exploratory.

Another influential notion has surrounded animate/inanimate differentiation. Gelman and Spelke (1981) give a good example of the importance attached to the distinction that children appear to make when they start to use language specific to animate or inanimate objects. Their argument is that very different 'kinds of thinking' accrue to both domains—that is children have to learn to 'think appropriately' about each domain.[4] The idea remains speculative, that is, how precisely this relates to a distinct social-cognitive domain is unclear, particularly given the little regard that is paid to the contexts within which such culturally determined distinctions are acquired. In contrast, Stein and Goldman (1981) conceive social cognition as the interaction between previously acquired knowledge systems and the 'information structure' of new events children experience. It is this which produces an internal representation of the events and one way of representing such events (and previous knowledge) is via 'story grammars'. Stein and Goldman (1981) set out to argue that children's knowledge about social situations is structured in such a fashion. One reason why this style of approach gained popularity in cognitive psychology (Kintsch & van Dijk, 1978) is that the formalism accruing to the syntactic approach, although somewhat discredited (Golinkoff, 1983a), could be re-written and the same principles and procedures employed in the analysis of story structure.

Utilising a social perception perspective to social-cognitive development, Higgins and Wells (1986) suggest that there are two important forms of memory information (related to social experience) and they argue that children's abilities to make social judgements are based on how such systems develop during specific life phases. However, the proposal regarding the 'distinctiveness' of such life phases and precisely why such life phases 'cause' the effects claimed remain undeveloped. Higgins and Wells (1986) do suggest that the overemphasis upon information processing theory encourages investigators to underestimate children's, and overestimate adult's, capacities.

There are one or two other computationally inspired accounts of social-cognitive development. Kosslyn and Kagan (1981) outline ways in which the methodology of the information processing approach can aid social cognitive developmental research. Ross (1981) attempts to incorporate attribution theory and models the child as 'intuitive scientist', arguing that a developmental account will help us understand why it is that adults exhibit inferential shortcomings. However, within developmental social cognition research these ideas have either not been developed or have emerged in complementary domains (social psychology). The child as 'intuitive scientist' is one identifiable theme in the 'theory of mind' research to which we can now turn.

(b) 'Theory of Mind' and Social Cognition
Arguably, one of the most influential expressions of the application of the information processing metaphor to social-cognitive developmental research is what has become known as 'theory of mind' literature (Astington, Harris, & Olson, 1988; Leslie, 1987; Wimmer & Perner, 1983). This area emerged out of early work by Premack and Woodruff (1978) and Premack (1983) who proposed that a person can be said to possess a 'theory of mind' where:

'he imputes mental states to himself and others ... [A system] of inferences of this kind is properly viewed as a theory because such states are not observable and second because the system can be used to make predictions about the behaviour of others' (Premack & Woodruff, 1983; p.515).

In the sense that the concern of an information processing approach is first and foremost with symbol-manipulating representational systems, then the 'theory of mind' approach is firmly placed within information processing cognitive science. Butterworth, Harris, Leslie, and Wellman (1991) make clear that what is being assumed in this area is that our 'theory of mind'

' "constitutes a basic human knowledge system", where "a mentalistic stance is a core feature of our everyday thinking" ' (p.1).

In a recent review of this emerging literature, Astington and Gopnick (1991) identify at least six distinct theoretical strands: constructivist; innatist-modular, linguistic-cultural, computational/recursive, simulation, and script-narrative. Of these only one (the linguistic-cultural) is not influenced in one form or another by the computational/ representational constructs central to the information processing approach. The above quote should also call our attention to the underlying assumptions of the theory of mind orientation (a *knowledge system* ... and a *mentalistic* stance), making the incorporation or consideration of social-semiotic and enculturation theories somewhat difficult.

Theory of mind crosses those boundaries that might separate cognitive and social-cognitive development, however in a fashion which gives precedence to the representation/computational role of the child's 'mental states'. Formal cognitive definitions of 'theory of mind' emphasise the link between intentional action, mental states and everyday reasoning about the behaviour of others. Astington (1988) alludes to a more socially oriented analysis in her examination of three principle components of the theory of mind. First, a theory of mind is a commonsense or folk psychology, and children's theory of mind underlies their ability to give commonsense explanations and predictions of behaviour by ascribing mental states to themselves and others. Second, mental states are expressed in speech acts, and third, social interaction is an interaction of minds mediated by language. Within this view it is argued that only older children (aged 5 or more) have metapragmatic understanding and can comprehend the role that language plays in social organisation.

Astington, Harris, and Olson (1988) suggest that the significance of the changes which take place around the third and fourth year, is that children begin to understand, predict, and explain their own and others' talk and actions, by recourse to the concepts expressed by mental terms (such as belief, know, pretending and so on). Olson (1988) asserts, 'a theory of mind is a set of explicit and interconnected concepts for representing those representational states' and Astington (1988) argues that during the pre-school years children will come to understand the distinction between seeming and being, and the recognition of the disguisability of intentional and emotional states. Within such a set of constructs then, a theory of mind is the ability to explain and predict events (discursive or otherwise) through an understanding of the theoretical concepts of beliefs, desire, knowing, promising, intention and feeling.

The paradigmatic example of what Astington and Gopnick (1991) call the 'innatist-modular' approach to the theory of mind is Leslie's work (1987, 1988). Leslie (1988) argues for the importance of 'de-coupling' cognitive processes in meta-representational cognition with particular reference to the child's understanding of pretence, where a child must learn how to represent a pretending act, its precise nature and how it might relate to other literal activities. The metaphor of 'de-coupling' is with reference to 'higher order' processes surrounding, for example, beliefs about beliefs, that is, maturational processes begin to come into play around 18 months to 2 years of age which aid the emergence of representational states now 'set free' or de-coupled from immediate 'sensori-motor' forms of cognition.

There are at least two problems with this type of model. First, the ontological status of representational opacity remains uncertain (Sinha, 1988), that is, there is considerable philosophical debate over the necessity for postulating *a priori* propositional attitudes, where the basic assumption is that intuition or experience follows from judgement/categorisation (Kant rather than Descartes). Second, Leslie's (1987) model rests upon a somewhat negative orientation of the childs' actions, her cognitions perceived as 'abuse' by reference (object substitution) or 'abuse' by existence' (use of imagery objects). In other words the way in which this model is conceived starts from a particular and, for some, already compromised set of criteria for the conditions upon representation (see Descombes, 1980), and then offers the suggestion that the only way the child's obvious difficulties (i.e. their lack of ability as implied by the model) can be overcome is by positing meta-cognitive 'de-coupling' mechanisms. The explanatory account is based on considerations of the acquisition, processing constraints and development of this theory of minds as it evolves to full adult representational ability.

Further, in this model, one specific accomplishment in the childs' gradual participation in personally accountable social interactions is that of pretence and pretending. Leslie (1988) recognises the particularly problematic nature of pretence when he comments:

'it is odd that pretense is not the sober culmination of intellectual development but makes its appearance playfully and precariously at the beginnings of childhood' (p.234).

The issue here is with the manner in which pretence is both defined and emphasised. In Leslie's (1987) playtime 'banana-telephone' example (the child playfully using a banana as a telephone) what is overlooked is the fact that for the child the banana only attains 'representational' status through the responses and reactions to her use of it as a telephone. For example when a young, 14-month-old child picks up the banana, puts it to her ear and then imitates the talking that goes on when observing others doing the same (putting objects— telephones—to the ear in a quite distinct and noticeable fashion), what is significant is the fact that others around the child point this out, that is laugh and so on, in a way which *socially produces* the status of banana as a justifiable representation of a telephone. Although this may be seen as leaving aside the problematic nature of the imitative action in the first place, it does emphasise the point that what is ignored in much of this literature is an analysis of those particular circumstances which justify (as far as the child is concerned) the use of the word 'telephone' for what is quite clearly not a telephone.

Thus rather than the question here being 'why does the child imitate?' our concern is why and in what way are imitative actions on the part of the child taken up as representational by those interacting with the child, while other equally and potentially powerful imitative actions are clearly not. It could be argued that what is needed is a 'theory of mind', which moves the emphasis away from the child possessing 'representational states' and towards an analysis of the practices, which surround the child beginning to employ language which presupposes the existence of others' 'mental states' (knowing, believing, desiring, and so on).

Wimmer, Hogrofe, and Sodian (1988) get somewhat closer to this position when they implicate the role of adult talk is assisting the conceptualisation of informational access for the child's developing theory of mind (through access to knowledge and beliefs). They ask what are the circumstances which lead the child to recognise that mental functioning may be causally related to an observed event. However, their resort to appeals of 'conceptual insight' reflects one of the most common constraints upon the application of the information processing metaphor—the failure to recognise the compromised nature of its individualistic orientation, hardly a conducive framework for investigating social cognition.

Remaining with the 'theory of mind' literature, Chandler, Fritz, and Hala (1989) are concerned with the significance of language use in their examination of false belief (the child's recognition that somebody else might believe something which she herself knows in fact not to be the case). Their suggestion is that by 2.5 years children are quite capable of employing a range of deceptive strategies that trade upon an awareness of the possibility of false belief and presuppose some already 'operative' theory of mind. Chandler et al. (1989) focus on the role of deception for evidence of a working knowledge of false belief, where unambiguous proof of the latter is taken to be 'all definite steps to disinform others by dishonestly supplying them with information known to be untrue' (p.1269). There may be an argument here for suggesting (from this and other related studies) that a child does not become a full member of the social world until they learn how to deceive.

It is clear, however, that in these kinds of studies (Wimmer & Perner, 1983) there is considerable ambiguity surrounding ideas of deception, pretence and false belief.[5] The notion of the child being able to impute false belief states to others is problematically related to the kinds of studies which are carried out in order to uncover the implicated representational processes. For example, the issue of any distinction between passive and active deception is not adequately addressed. That is, not responding so as to let somebody else believe whatever they wish (something false), is quite different from actively engaging in sets of actions which are designed so that others will carry out a series of intentional actions, these based upon their assumption that you are not only telling the truth, but also often providing (for children in these studies) a new and socially significant piece of information.

The precise role of the relationship between language, social cognition and 'theory of mind' is also rarely addressed in this literature. Perner (1988b) suggests that the ability to comprehend 'second-order' states rests fundamentally on recursion. The social significance of human interaction (for Perner) depends on the mental states of the interacting partners, with particular emphasis on the claim that higher-order mental states are made available through recursion, which then leads to 'richer social interactions'. He also takes issue with the Gricean analysis of intentionality (Grice, 1981) arguing that children do not have to carry out a complex analysis of intentional communication (see Levinson, 1983). However, this misses the point that children nevertheless do have to distinguish and recognise that an implicative act has occurred (is occurring more generally) before recognising the intended meaning. Further what is important about implicatures (or presuppositions) is that they may offer one approach to conceptualising the relationship between the dynamics of conversations as it is happening, and what is being communicated (Chapter 5, and see also note in Perner, 1988a, p.289).

Interestingly Olson (1988) does identify the locus for the 'ascription' of intentional and propositional states in the child's acquisition of language. He says:

> 'The beginnings of belief and the beginnings of an awareness of those beliefs are both tied to the acquisition of language. The former depends upon the acquisition of a language for formulating and expressing propositions, the latter depends on the acquisition of a metalanguage for talking about those propositions' (p.423).

This point is worth emphasising. Rather than formulating computationally complex (if internally consistent) theories of 'de-coupling' of meta-representational states (Leslie, 1987) what is important is when and in what ways does the child recognise that the use of meta-representational language terms (such as belief, know) are sanctioned and appropriate.

Finally, Beal (1988) takes the view that communication (translation of thoughts into messages) is a bridge between the 'mental worlds' of different people. What is problematic for children is that they don't understand that there exists a 'literal' level of the message which can be independent of the meaning any speaker intends and that the quality of the message has an influence on the success of the communication. Possessing such knowledge presupposes the existence of a theory of mind. However, the 'literal vs. non-literal' language distinction (Clark & Lucy, 1975) is itself somewhat controversial (Eco, 1979; Gibbs, 1986) evidenced in the observation that even 'literal' scientific texts follow socially prescribed conventions of rhetoric and discourse (Billig, 1987). Another issue which Beal (1988) ignores is the dynamic nature of any communicative context, that is, one of the most important determiners of understanding and misunderstanding is the 'display' of such by partners in any interchange, and the monitoring of such display. This point is developed by those conversational analysts utilising an ethnomethodological approach to the investigation of talk.

The principal shortcoming of the 'theory of mind' literature is that before one can adequately address issues surrounding what might reasonably be inferred from a child's use of mental state verbs or expressions, we need to examine the presuppositions and strategies of reasoning upon which cultural formulations of everyday life depend for their intelligibility, never mind effectiveness (see Kirkpatrick & White, 1985). We cannot simply assume that because children learn how to participate in social contexts, where the use of 'mental state' verbs is encouraged and ratified, that they then possess opaque representational 'theories of mind'. Despite a considerable and increasing amount of activity in this area (Butterworth et al., 1991; Hobson, 1991; Winner & Leekam, 1991) we not only await evidence that the possession of a 'theory of mind' will facilitate the young child's acquisition of social-cognitive skills, but also a more critically considered level of theorising.

More broadly and to summarise this section on representational and constructivist approaches, a number of issues require qualification and development. It is not difficult to identify one important limitation of the information processing view. As a rule, our experience is not that of going around 'constructing' our representational worlds in order. We appear to act upon and re-act to our environments in a much more 'direct' way; and the model developed in Chapter 5 takes up elements of an 'ecological' or 'direct perception' approach. Furthermore, adherence to the principle of 'methodological solipsism' (the commitment to a consideration of formal symbol systems abstracted from considerations of their relation to either 'input' stimuli or 'output' behaviour), beyond being questionable on philosophical grounds (Russell, 1987), works against attempts to specify relations between developmental social-cognitive theory and prescriptions regarding social skills or abilities. This might be cited as the main reason why much of the assessment and intervention research on children's social abilities remains behaviourist in outlook (Barton, 1986; Stokes & Osnes, 1986) that is, restricting the concerns to stimuli and behaviour.

There is also the issue of the appropriate 'level of analysis'. For example, for the study of the early stages of visual perception or the processing of lexical items in short-term memory, the micro-analytic information processing approach has proved to be of considerable use (Morton, 1979; Pomerantz, 1981). However, with respect to a more macro-level, what is centrally problematic is that the information processing metaphor, while apparently concerned with process and change and the flow of data through any system, rests in theory upon assumptions about stable sets of events. In practice it is methodologically 'static', unable to accommodate dynamic aspects of active participation in social-cognitive contexts (i.e. conversations). There is only the illusion of being concerned with change, and attempts to incorporate into the framework 'interaction'—that is where two or more participants 'act upon', and dynamically change, each other—are limited by the emphasis on the individual's possession of requisite 'representational' processes.[6]

A further reason for the questionable status of information processing conceptions (and other neo-Kantian constructivist/representational theories) is the 'logocentric' emphasis on identity and individuality. In philosophy of mind and philosophy of language there is considerable debate regarding computational/cognitive accounts of self, and subject-object relations (Descombes, 1980). At least four other major shortcomings of the information processing account of social cognition can be traced to certain ontological contradictions. First, the emphasis on identity/individuality leads to contemporary models of interactivity (Clark & Carlson, 1981; Trevarthen, 1977) which presuppose the centrality of subject/speaker to a degree which works against the creation of realisable social accounts of cognition. It might be argued that this is as true for currently conceived 'social-interactional' theories as for individualistic cognitive orientations. That is, social accounts within all 'logocentric' paradigms are always predicated on somewhat restrictive formulations of individuality and identity.

Second, any meta-theoretical stance based upon Cartesian or Kantian constructs of identity are forever doomed to 'static' formulations. Reason (1984) points out that any claim regarding 'self-subsistent' identity can only be understood (logically) on pains of our recognising such a position as an embodiment of contradictions (following Hegel and Wittgenstein), and at pains of becoming, in other words, dynamically and historically. There are both logical and empirical grounds for arguing that if we wish to understand social-cognitive developmental abilities as they are reflected and instantiated in conversational contexts, then our accounts may well have to be both 'internal' and dynamic (that is conceived and understood from the perspective of analyst as participant).

A third problem (and related to the previous point) arises from a failure to recognise that exploratory hypotheses are more often than not 'contaminated' by the dominant metaphor. For example, a growing body of literature concerned with children's communicative abilities in social contexts (Dunn & Shatz, 1989), attempts to identify social-cognitive correlates of conversational skills. The way in which 'conversation' in modelled is such studies is by appeal to naive notions of common ground, which are themselves compromised by debatable conceptions of communication (Clark & Carlson, 1981).[7] The subsequent results are then interpreted in a way which supports such 'mini-theories', that is failing to recognise that there may be contrasting models which could equally accommodate the same results while providing a richer basis for model development.

Finally, and more recently, there is an increasing interest in an alternative conception of human cognition, parallel distributed processing (PDP) or connectionist models (Hinton, 1981; Rumelhart & McClelland, 1986). Resting upon a neuro-psychophysiological metaphor, this framework claims to be more explicitly concerned with issues of internal representation. The orienting perspective here is that of a 'neurally inspired' model of cognitive processing. It is argued that any conception of cognitive processes must pay heed to the obvious facts of 'brain-style' processing. Rumelhart and McClelland (1986) suggest that macro-models such as production systems or schema-theoretic accounts (e.g. Schank & Abelson, 1977) emerge out of the interactions of the microstructure of connectionist models. The idea now is 'brain as representation'.

However, postulating mental states and then modelling procedures as differential functions upon neural network connections (those states), although possibly appropriate for language acquisition studies, which axiomatically view language as a cognitive object (e.g. Plunkett, 1990), hardly amounts to a realisable model for understanding how young children begin to make sense out of the social world. There remains the underlying suspicion (my own) that beyond saying that younger children will have limited information processing capacities (in comparison to adults or older children), there may be little to be gained from applying the information processing metaphor to social-cognitive developmental domains.

A final argument of this part of the review is that the information processing account overemphasises the information processing 'metaphor' to a degree that does not readily facilitate conceptualisations of social interaction processes and skills. Part of the reason for this is that the information processing approach (and the computational perspective generally) has a tendency to conflate theory and data. Feldman and Bruner (1987) point out that when computational cognition was a model of the mind and thinking, predictive adequacy and epistemological promise were assured. However, when the mind became a computer, the issues changed to metaphysical problems and questions of the 'real'. This has led to an identifiable tendency to juxtapose theory and data in cognitive science and to claims that all cognitive phenomena which cannot be incorporated within the computational framework are simply not worth consideration (Stitch, 1983). The next question one can ask is whether accounts which favour a distinctly social interaction approach have provided more appropriate theories, models and methods for social-cognitive developmental research, the topic of the following chapter.

NOTES

1. Self-monitored reflection is likely to be a developmentally later and a much less important, and particular, form of rational activity.

2. Which specifies value, exchange, debt, satisfaction and so on in a way which defines 'disequilibrium' predictions as a function of the model/matrix outlined.

3. Before communication can ensue I need not only to recognise your intention to communicate, but also need to display my recognition of your intention (displayed as a 'to be read' sign).

4. Carey (1985) and other research which focuses upon early conceptual thinking in the child, attach considerable importance to the possibility that the very earliest (and most important) cognitive distinction which needs to be made derives from the child being innately possessed with at least two distinct cognitive structures: a naive physics and a naive psychology.

5. See Leekam (1991) for comment on this point. Note, one reason can be traced to the conceptual complexities involved in philosophical concerns with truth and deception, and how these might relate to social practice.

6. Williams (1989) comments on Vygotsky's analysis of the relation between methodology and psychological theory which is very pertinent here. As he puts it 'The formation of a theory is a twofold process: The theory begins with some object of study, or unit of analysis; for example a reflex, an introspectible subjective state, a behaviour, a cognitive capacity. It then develops a general explanatory principle; for example, appeal to conditioning, introspection, flow chart model, and so defines itself from the perspective of the logic of this philosophical tradition. This view of the relation between psychological theories and philosophical perspectives underscores the importance of developing a critical awareness of the presuppositions that support the content of a particular theory' (p.111).

7. Although Clark and Carlson's (1981) model of discourse/conversational interaction and their conception of 'common ground' has been influential within cognitive psychology (Sperber & Wilson, 1986) there are at least two reasons for suggesting it remains a misguided or inappropriate model of discourse comprehension. First, their perspective simply begs the question of conversation and communication, that is, it simply addresses the process by structuring the outcome as successful or unsuccessful conversation. Second, what they mean by 'mutual knowledge' is tantamount to 'justified true belief' but they employ the term in such a way that it avoids examining the process of justification. One indication of the currently disparate nature of this area is reflected in the fact that while Clark and Carlson's (1981) account remains unconvincing it has found other adherents within social-cognitive developmental research. Newman (1986), for example, while restricting his definition of social cognition to 'the special problem of learning what others would think and learning how to make use of that information', attempts to bring together a model of perspective-taking as recursion, with Clark and Marshall's (1981) co-presence heuristics. The suggestion is that inferential problem-solving social cognitions are only brought into play when misunderstandings take place and we are told that common ground 'co-ordinated' activities of collaborational social acts provide 'concrete' representations of knowledge 'held in common'.

CHAPTER THREE

Interactionist
Social-cognitive
Development

The preceding comments have, I hope, succeeded in identifying reasons why we might wish to be more circumspect regarding the potential of individualistic (constructivist/representational) approaches as guiding theories for our investigations of children's developing social-cognitive skills. This is only the first part of the story, however. As discussed in Chapter 1, within psychology there has long existed a tradition of considering some topics as intrinsically individualistic (memory)[1] while others as essentially social (altruism, attitude formation and so on). In this chapter I wish to consider developmental social cognition research which maintains or is at least emergent from social interaction constructs. As before the aim is to strike a balance between reviewing the major studies, identifying the underlying theories and approaches, and evaluating what has emerged with reference to understanding children's participative social-cognitive skills.

Over the last 15–20 years there has been a growth in developmental social cognition research which adopts or emphasises the importance of the child's social interactions. There are three principle themes in this research; the Genevan school which Durkin (1986) has coined social social cognition (in contrast to *cognitive* social cognition—the themes outlined in the previous chapter); work inspired by Vygotskian perspectives on development; and one or two studies which can be traced to Mead and the symbolic interactionist school. These different research traditions have been brought together precisely because each in their own way emphasises the importance of the social world (and social interaction processes) for the child's developing social cognitions.

THE GENEVAN SCHOOL

This social interactionist perspective (Doise & Mugny, 1984) argues that social interaction itself establishes the fabric within which children's social understanding develops. Thus the confrontational aspects endemic to everyday social interaction (i.e. differing perspectives coming together through social interaction) gives rise to the formation of new social-cognitive structures within the individual. It is argued that via the facilitative and constraining aspects of social interaction contexts, social cognition is achieved. However, although there is a wealth of data with regard to effects arising from interpersonal relations and group processes (particularly in social psychology, e.g. Brown, 1988), there is considerably less detail on process. Furthermore, although the focus in now upon the social interaction context, explanations for the mechanisms of socio-cognitive change remain largely neo-Piagetian, that is, an emphasis on conflict and confrontation as the 'triggering' process, whereby one stage of socio-cognitive development might evolve to the qualitatively distinct next stage.

The prediction here is that children who engage in social interactions will develop (perform) faster than those children who are either working on their own or who rarely interact; and children who are nearer transitional boundaries between cognitive stages (concrete operational and so on) will benefit from social interactions to a greater degree than those in the middle of a stage. The principal and crucially important element which facilitates social-cognitive development in such interactions is cognitive conflict. Through the interaction with other people the child comes to recognise that something in and about the way she is thinking, is not quite correct and she thus has to go through an accommodation process. Social interaction is the trigger for development given that the equilibratory nature of the cognitive system will always seek to maintain balance (Piaget, 1954).

Cognitive conflict is the catalyst for developmental change engendered by the social-cognitive disjunctures experienced in social interactions, and studies by Doise and Mugny (1979, 1984) and Mugny and Doise (1983), looking at the relationship between social interaction and performance in various cognitive domains (spatial transformation tasks, mathematical problems and so on) lend support to this assertion.

There are, however, a number of problems which together suggest that this view again would not serve as an appropriate model for investigating children's social-cognitive abilities. First, there is the question of what conflict is. Does it mean to say that the child (through conflict) recognises that her interpretative schemas cannot incorporate (assimilate) a new and distinctly divergent information event? At what level are we to categorise this 'meta-cognitive' ability, given that the possession of such implies that she must surely already have evolved into the next qualitatively distinct stage (which the social interaction is said to be facilitating)? Or does the conflict simply engender a sense of frustration, the resolution of which demands she engage in new forms of participation which she knows about principally through watching and listening to others interacting? It is also argued that only towards the end of a specific stage will she begin to recognise the divergencies, which, of course, has been shown to be logically incompatible with the existence of décalage phenomena (Ginsburg & Opper, 1983).

Light (1983) comments that the young child is restructuring her mental states by symbolically manipulating the world and making inferences on the basis of these symbolic manipulations. He points out that what is important is the claim that it is not simply about imitating somebody else, but that 'learning acquired in social interaction, arises from fundamental cognitive re-structuring' (Mugny et al., 1981, p.32). The provision of cognitive models, 'suggest to the child some relevant dimensions for a progressive elaboration of a cognitive mechanism new to him' (Light, 1983, p.326). Arguably the sense in which they warrant our attention as social-cognitive models, is that whatever is involved in the acquisition of social cognitions, they can only be located in conversational contexts, that is, discourse or actions related to its presuppositional accomplishment (e.g. what can be inferred from the use of this or that particular word, what is to be understood as relevant here, why it is that you are not getting the point and so on).

Second, there is the question of how conflict is actually related to social interaction. Not all interactions lead to conflict and/or progress. Some interaction contexts simply lead to compliance (Russell, 1983), or where there is considerable asymmetry (parent-child) it has been suggested that little will be gained, a point Piaget emphasised with his comment that, 'Criticism is born of discussion and discussion is only possible amongst equals' (1932, p.450). The debates, however, have centred around the assertion that conflict is necessary. One question is whether the conflict has to be derived from interaction with others or whether intra-cognitive conflict will suffice (see Light, 1983). Bryant (1982), for example, demonstrates that where strict controls are employed in these experiments, then if anything it is not conflict which leads to enhanced cognitive performance but agreement. Cross-cultural comparisons have also cast doubt upon the relative importance of inter as against intra-psychological social-cognitive conflict facilitating cognitive development, with considerable variability with respect to cultural context (Mackie, 1980). Further, results in the predicted fashion only emerge where the child already possesses a partial grasp of the required task activities (Russell, 1981). Only some degree of asymmetry should be present, but not necessarily in the sense that one child (in the typically socio-cognitive conflict context) has the correct model and the other experiences conflict, thus facilitating change. This would appear to place the emphasis on participation *per se*, and again implicate the important role of developmental social-cognitive conversational skills.

Third, the way in which dialogue and discourse has been considered is questionable. Doise and Mugny (1985) have argued, for example, that the cognitive progress of a child is enhanced where the social-cognitive conflict is intensified. The experiments here involved comparing situations where either one or two 'disagreers' were interacting with a child in a spatial transformation task. The results indicated that children who found that they had to argue with two (rather than one) person subsequently performed better during post-tests, implicating the role of perspective taking. However, children often find the demands of three-party conversations (Garvey & Berninger, 1981) quite unique and will need to develop a more complex set of strategies to deal with such situations. The authors overlook the possibility that the 'intensification' engendered was principally a result of engaging in three-party rather than two-party conversations, and the subsequent good performance of the children cannot be separated from considerations of the participation demands inherent to multi-party conversations. The conversational coherence which has to be maintained is much more complex (Craig & Washington, 1986) and experience in such contexts will enhance later performance (on related representational/perspective taking tasks) because the more a child needs to defend her position, the more well-defined her *socially-produced representations* would become.[2] Quite simply, through any increased amount of discursive behaviour one is forced to engage in, the more articulate one's 'representational account' becomes, itself made available through the very act of participation.

Some support for this line of reasoning emerges from a study by Bearison, Magzannen, and Filardo (1984) who sought to identify the conditions which influence peer collaborative learning. Observing children on a spatial reasoning task (following Doise, Mugny, & Perret-Clermont, 1975) they found that either 'not enough' or the 'wrong kind' of talk or debate would hinder the potential for learning. That is, children who debated with each other either excessively or not enough, showed no gains compared with children who had carried out the tasks on their own. Where children expressed extended justifications for their actions (during social interaction sessions) and pointed out why they disagreed, post-test gains were more substantial.

Other research in this area addresses the issue of conversation and discourse more directly—see Light (1983) for a review. Russell (1981, 1982) suggests that often children are lacking a suitably appropriate 'propositional attitude' and what they require is exposure to those contexts which will lead them to constructing the 'shared meanings' of adult culture (i.e. what adults define as important). Heber (1971, 1981) talks of the facilitative nature of instructional conversational contexts, arguing that the important factor in the enhancement of cognitive development through social interaction is the 'guiding of the child towards the right considerations' (adult cultural norms and values). Dickson, Hess, Miyake, and Azuma (1979) refer to this as the 'cognitive socialization' which occurs in adult-child dialogue and Walkerdine (1988) outlines various arguments around the notion that reasoning emerges from, and through, the social processes of discourse.

At issue here is what is presupposed by terms such as *co-constructed discourse*, the *negotiation of shared meanings*, and the *co-ordinations of understandings*. For example, the latter assumes: (a) ones' understandings are quite properly to be located 'in one's head' as private languages and; (b) one wishes to co-ordinate them with others. But the problem is how can you possibly know you have got such understandings (and misunderstandings) unless you participate in dialogue (at some level), and when you do, how, why and through what process do you clearly distinguish between your own, as distinct from other's, discursive representations—given that they are both irretrievably interlocked with the dynamics of the talk?

Notwithstanding such reservations, the social approach to social-cognitive developmental research at least recognises that it is somewhat limited in what it can tell us. For example, in response to a challenge regarding the methodological limitations of some of this work, Doise (1985) comments:

'several dozen experimental observations show that apparently nothing occurs during a situation of socio-cognitive conflict: effects only appear when systematic comparisons are made between the post-tests of different experimental conditions' (p.250).

More recently, Doise (1990) favours what he calls a socio-constructivist view where the child has to be seen as mastering schemas, behavioural repertoires and so on, which 'enable' participation in social interaction. He talks of a 'spiral of causality' beginning with the mental state of the child which itself makes possible engagement in social interactions. These interaction scenarios in turn qualitatively enrich the emergent new individual states and thus (under certain circumstances) facilitate progress. Doise (1990), for example, argues that we need to understand social role 'scripts' which govern the social interactions in which the child may participate. This attempt to integrate the script formulation within a neo-Piagetian based social interaction account is, however, open to the criticisms highlighted in Chapter 2.

In summary, the Genevan approach, while making a valiant attempt at adapting and applying a neo-Piagetian explanatory account of social-cognitive development, again does not appear to offer a conducive theoretical framework for investigating developmental social-cognitive skills. Theoretically it is constrained by the overemphasis upon the role that conflict must play. Methodologically, it has yet to move beyond demonstrations of effect (change has occurred) to concerns of process and structure. And, finally, although the importance of engaging in talk is emphasised, conversation itself has not been studied in sufficient depth.

'SOCIAL-INTERACTIONIST' SOCIAL-COGNITIVE DEVELOPMENT

I can now move to other attempts at outlining uniquely 'social' social-cognitive perspectives in this area, work inspired by Mead's (1934) symbolic interactionist argument regarding the development of the self, and approaches derived from Vygotsky's (1934) social-semiotic view of cognitive development. An adequate understanding of these perspectives requires a fairly detailed and careful reading of the philosophical background of which they form a part (e.g. Dewey and James for Mead; Marx and Saussure for Vygotsky). Research within these strands often uncritically assumes one or other general metaphor or orientation, simply outlining general positions rather than attempting to develop a more detailed analysis of the relation between the pre-theoretical constructs and the particular models (Forgas, 1981; Leahy, 1985). This may be part of the reason why, despite the high citation frequency of Mead and Vygotsky, few clearly specified models of social-cognitive development have been developed. There is a clear difference between the originating positions and the ways in which the views have been taken up.

Although we can align both Mead and Vygotsky within distinctly social approaches to social-cognitive development we must be conscious of where they might differ in addition to their complementarity. First, both views locate the transformational 'inter-psychological to intra-psychological' process or medium of social-cognitive change in the use of language. Second, both views implicitly question the ontological status of 'self' and identity, that is, where fashioned upon a definitive notion of a private 'individualistic' subject. Third, they give priority to the role of *action* and the *sign / gesture* in development, for Mead the source of the self-reflective 'I'; for Vygotksy the employment of words, or signs, as tools.

However, while Mead emphasised the role of language, it was more in relation to the way in which language use would 'arouse' the appropriate response (or attitude) in both listener and speaker, leading to a particular and context-specific delimiter of self, and to a notion of the generalised *other*. It was the tripartite relation between employment of gesture, attitudinal response of the other, and subsequent following through of gesture inspired action, which formed the 'matrix' for self-representation in everyday life. In contrast, Vygotsky's view of language was interlinked with his dialectical materialist conception of human development which emphasised the use of *signs* and *signification systems* by participants. Sinha (1988) reminds us:

> 'Whereas Mead took communication and interaction to be constitutive of social process, for Vygotksy the historical process rather determined the available repertoire of signifying and other psychological activities, and thus, ultimately, the actual course of development' (p.96).

(a) The Vygotskian Approach

Vygotsky's (1934) views can be considered as a particularly unique combination of Marxist, Darwinian/evolutionary and structuralist/ semiotic ideas, as various researchers have noted (Sinha, 1988; Wertsch, 1985; Wood, 1988). The social interaction context is the starting point, and social-cognitive development consists of a progression from the social to the individual, from the inter-psychological to the intra-psychological. Thus, through a child's interactions with other people, initially spontaneous behaviour comes under increasing control (self-regulated). For Vygotsky what was important was to identify the initial conditions for, and the development of, self-regulatory behaviour, particularly given that becoming aware of one's own behaviour is the first step towards attaining the status of an independent individual.

The increasing interest in Vygotsky (Garton, 1984) is paralleled by the earlier dissatisfaction with Piagetian accounts of cognitive development (Donaldson, 1978) and the gradual rise of English translations of his early works. Wertsch (1985) argues that contrasting cultural ideologies gain expression through the Western educationalists' emphasis upon stage centred 'performance-measure' accounts of development (e.g. Piagetian—that is concentrating on what the child can do at point X), contrasted with Soviet 'potentiating' continuity based models (e.g. Vygotsky—where the focus is on what the child might be capable of in the near future). Certainly Vygotsky's outline of the zone of proximal development lends support to such a contrast.

There are at least three levels in Vygotsky's framework. Again, Wertsch (1985) stresses the interdependence of each level where a complete understanding of any one is not possible outwith the larger framework. At one level there is a developmental or 'genetic' method where it is argued that if we wish to comprehend mental processes then this will entail incorporating various genetic domains (phylogenesis, sociocultural history, ontogenesis and so on), such that quite distinct explanatory principles may be at work at different developmental stages, interacting in quite particular ways. At another level there is considerable emphasis on the mediational processes facilitating the emergence and development of higher mental processes ('tool' and sign use and related semiotic processes). Finally, there is the principle axiom taken up by social-cognitive researchers, the argument that all individual mental processes emerge from social interaction processes. Unfortunately, this last theme is often considered in isolation from the other two.

While this is not the place for a detailed explanatory account of Vygotsky's theoretical views, there are at least two reasons why we should be cautious in viewing this perspective as a welcome riposte to either Piagetian or information processing accounts of social-cognitive development. First, the genetic method while a considered and sophisticated philosophical outlook, does not lend itself particularly to the development of an appropriate theoretical framework (for our purposes). Second, although the importance of mediational processes is emphasised, there is a certain inconsistency in the logic. Note on the one hand there is considerable emphasis on mediational 'copying' phenomena, such that:

'any function in the child's cultural development appears twice or on two planes. First it appears on the social plane, and then on the psychological plane ... First it appears between people as an interpsychological category and then within the child as an intra-psychological category' (Vygotsky, 1934, p.163).

and

'The very mechanism underlying higher mental functions is a copy from social interaction: all higher mental functions are internalized social relationships' (p.164).

At the same time the genetic or developmental method proposes that such internalisation transforms the process itself and changes its structure and function. In other words, the translation of 'outside' social interaction scenarios into 'inside' internal cognitive structures, can itself change the nature of that structure and the way it functions. The problem is that it remains unclear whether it is the 'structural mechanisms' which are being internalised, or the structural mechanisms and their contents, or whether the internalisation is giving rise to associated 'generalisation' abilities. Also, who precisely is 'carrying' out the transformational process (from the inter- to the intra-psychological). To have any logical coherence this argument must be able to posit a 'biologically pure' originating epistemic subject. As Sinha (1988) notes this simply evades the issue of whether social-cognitive development should be conceived as the transformation of the social to the individual, or the individual to the social.

Leaving aside conceptual problems for the moment, one of the central constructs in Vygotsky's theory is the idea of a zone of proximal development. This is typically defined as the distance between a child's present developmental level where determined by independent problem solving and the level of potential development as determined through problem solving under adult assistance/guidance, or in collaboration with adequate (usually older) peers. It is this idea which underlies much of the research, focusing on the strategies shown by a more competent dyad member and how these are eventually taken over by a less competent participant in order to regulate and monitor her own behaviour.

For example, Rogoff, Ellis, and Gardner (1981) studied the interactions of mother-child dyads (aged 6 and 8 years) and argue that the mothers of the younger children 'stretched' their corresponding zones of proximal development by giving much more intense instruction (so as to compensate for the child's lack of skill). In a similar fashion Pratt, Kerig, Cowan, and Cowan (1988) carried out a study with 3-year-old children and their mothers, arguing that one definition of a good tutor is somebody who will 'seek out' the zone of proximal development, 'gradually reducing support (within it) as the child becomes capable of more independent task performance' (p.837).

Other work has adapted Vygotsky's approach to social-cognitive development for more pragmatic reasons. In a study concerned with some of the methodological shortcomings of early infancy research, Heckhausen (1987) cautions against the traditional emphasis upon age as a useful predictor of developmental change. In a longitudinal design investigating mother-infant interactions (aged 14–22 months) she found that infant age had significantly less influence than infant performance on both rate and kind of maternal instructions and strategies. She comments:

'Mothers can rely on a shared history of experiences with their children when making inferences about the significance of performance currently exhibited by the child for estimating his or her current competence level, and thus the *boundaries of the zone of proximal development* (p.213—my italics).'

Beyond assertions that such a zone does in fact exist and that its parameters can be measured and defined, we need to consider how emergence into the 'zone' takes place and how 'travel' across it is accomplished (the implication being that the border forever recedes in the potentially unlimited nature of facilitative adult-child interactions). In a study of computer assisted teaching, Emihovich and Miller (1988) argue that in order to assist in the crossing, children must be provided with the appropriate levels of adult initiated discursive 'scaffolding', a construct employed by Bruner (1983) in language learning and reading research.

In an attempt to address the issue of facilitative adult-child interaction, Wertsch, McNamee, McLane and Budwig, (1980) examined problem solving strategies in a jigsaw-puzzle game. Looking at children across three age groups (between 2 and 5 years) during interactions with their mothers in this 'copy the model' task, they report that with the increasing age of the child, there is a corresponding decrease in the eye-gaze 'regulatory' behaviour of the mother (instructional procedures by the mother). This, Wertsch et al. (1980) argue, reflects the fact that as the children get older they begin to take over the regulation of the visual checking of the model (previously done by the mother). It is in this kind of way that interpsychological strategies (interaction sequences) become intra- psychological strategies.

Leaving aside the problematic nature of the design of this study[3], what is not addressed is the role of conversational participation and the discourse surrounding the looking behaviour on the part of the mother. An essential element of Wertsch et al.'s (1985) argument is that:

'the younger ones (children) apparently did not interpret the adults communicative moves as being about strategic actions appropriate for a particular goal, whereas the older one's did' (p.1220).

This position is based on the unwarranted assumption that the mothers would have been instructing the younger and older children in an equivalent fashion, overlooking the fact that caregivers are particularly sensitive to their own perceptions of their child's abilities, and adapt their communicative strategies along such metapragmatic principles (McGillicuddy-DeLise, 1982; Miller & Sperry, 1988).

Nonetheless, Cavanaugh and Perlmutter (1982) propose that the Vygotskian approach epitomised by the Wertsch et al.'s (1980) 'microgenetic' method serves as a useful example of ways to study how knowledge of memory might be acquired—see also Edwards and Middleton (1989) and their research into learning how to remember. Wertsch and Sammarco (1985) argue that one of the advantages of a Vygotskian based account of development is methodological; a single unit of analysis (tool mediated action) can serve as a unitary construct for social-interactional and individual levels of functioning. Again there is the commitment or at least an orientation towards development as 'potential', for example:

> 'In this view signs are not considered to be auxiliary means whose use merely facilitates already existing social or psychological processes. Rather they are viewed as playing a fundamental role in determining what these processes *can* be' (p.278—my emphasis).

One major problem with the way in which the emphasis on sign use has been developed in this area is the gap between concept formation and the use of language. In other words while there may appear to be significant mileage in conceptualising representational processes with respect to the emergence of word meaning—or what used to be called semantic development, Clark and Clark (1977)—this is in sharp contrast to the way words (as units speech acts or moves) in conversation are actually employed. That is, part of the problem may be located in the manner in which cognitive development has traditionally emphasised the importance of concepts and categories (i.e. in ways which are in many respects incompatible with discussions of mediational processes emergent from socio-semiotic practices).

Vygotsky's analysis of concept development is based in part upon the capacity of words to enter into decontextualised relationships with other words. He traced the origins of concept development to contextualised signs as indicative functions of speech, and argued for ways in which semiotic functioning evolves to the stage where decontextualised sign-sign relationships provide the basis for regulating the child's activity. However, the precise role of mediational processes remains problematic. Wertsch (1985) argues that Vygotsky wished to emphasise two *opposing* (my italics) tendencies of language; the employing of language as an abstract, decontextualised symbol system and the use of language in everyday (contextualised) communicative settings. The claim is that both operate simultaneously in determining the structure and interpretation of speech and thus, 'genuine social interaction depends on generalisation' (p.96). It remains unclear as to what distinguishes one language tendency from the other, as it is arguable that what is taken as 'abstract' sign-system usage is itself rooted in particular conversational social-discursive practice (Bloor, 1983; Pimm, 1987; Walkerdine, 1982), while the ability to engage in conversation successfully, implies a no less sophisticated understanding of social practices and discourses which serve as the material presuppositional basis for participation as such.

A reading of the available literature also shows, that in sharp contrast to Piagetian social-cognitive accounts, the Vygotskian approach gives rise to a common interpretation that there is less to be gained for the child through interaction with peers. In contrast to adult-child interaction, in peer-peer interaction children cannot adequately expose each other to the appropriate forms of 'stretching' strategies. On this point one or two studies have examined the strategies shown by the more competent member dyad member, and how these are eventually taken over by the less competent participant to regulate and monitor his/her own behaviour. Radziszewska and Rogoff (1988) attempted to tease out the relative importance of adult-child versus child-child collaboration, studying interaction during a planning task (with 9–10 year old children). Adult-child guidance was found to be considerably more effective, with 'talking aloud' strategies implicated as being the most important strategy predicting success. Similarly, Zukow (1986) using a cross-sectional approach examining adult-child interaction and play, argued that the influence of the caregivers' interactions with the child (during play) is considerably stronger than anything the child might do on her own. The caregivers, Zukow (1986) suggests, provide the child with 'demonstrations of culturally recognizable activities, guiding the child's participation in them, and interpreting the on-going activities as such' (p.229).

To summarise here briefly, part of the reason why there has been a steady increase in Vygotskian perspectives on social-cognitive development arises from the theoretical commitment to the social interaction context married to accompanying metaphors emphasising the (unlimited) cognitive potential of children (that is within appropriate instructional interactions). While this has helped initiate a move away from the formal limitations and pragmatic constraints of Piagetian based views, there are a number of conceptual and methodological problems which suggest that again, it would not serve our purposes. First, social-cognitive developmentalists have so far restricted their concerns to only one theme of Vygotsky's theory, in part because the complexities of his social-semiotic formulations are difficult to transform into realisable models and hypothesis. Second, there are a number of seriously unresolved conceptual issues (e.g. does the 'epistemic' subject transform, or copy, strategies enacted in the social world?), and third, the somewhat vague formulation of the zone of proximal development is not helped by the paucity of supportive evidence. There is little doubt that there are a host of important ideas in Vygotsky's work; however, this has not yet engendered the appropriate level of theoretical activity necessary for formalising hypotheses for investigating social-cognitive skills. It remains unclear whether it can. The final theme in this chapter considers the symbolic interactionist approach and the work of Mead (1934).

(b) G.H. Mead

Despite the frequent citing of G.H. Mead in both adult social cognition and social psychology research, very few studies have built directly on his ideas, in the sense of specific model building, predictive adequacy, formal development and so on. Farr (1981) argues that researchers in social cognition have tended to either ignore or misconstrue Mead's position. As he puts it, 'Mead was actually advocating a more advanced form of behaviourism than Watson had been propounding. Mead was arguing that Watson had not gone far enough' (p.255). Certainly the significance of Mead's ideas on communication with reference to notions of mind and the self, cannot be adequately understood without a consideration of the philosophical school of pragmatism and their emphasis upon action. It cannot be overlooked that the central thesis for Mead was the proposal that what determined the relation between any individual and her environment was acting within and upon that world.

Part of what is problematic in Mead's outline for researchers in social-cognitive development is that although he suggests that the location where the 'emergence' of mind and self occurs is language use, the level of description and argument is philosophical and analytical, rather than psychological. His emphasis on the role of gesture was paramount, 'the meaning of a gesture by one organism is found in the response of another organism to what would be the completion of the act of the first organism which that gesture initiates and indicates' (Mead, 1934, p.210). Thinking as the 'internalisation' of gestures was an important idea resting on the argument that the gestures so internalised, gain the status of significant symbols precisely because they mean the same for all members of a community using them. Or as Mead puts it, 'they respectively arouse the same attitudes in the individuals making them that they arouse in the individuals responding to them' (p.195).

There is, however, a problem in Mead's proposal that through the use of language, speakers and listeners endorse and subscribe to the same attitude 'induced' by the use of this or that word(s):

'the conscious or significant conversation of gestures is a much more adequate and effective mechanism of mutual adjustment within the social act—involving as it does, the taking, by each of the individuals carrying it on, of the attitudes of the others towards himself—than is the unconscious or non-significant conversation of gestures' (p.192).

Beyond the problem of the empirical inaccessibility of speech act intentionality (I cannot gain access to what somebody else intends when they say something), attitude is being defined as a particular stance 'called up' by the speech act (what some linguists call its perlocutionary effect—the effect an utterance has on its intended audience). This, however, presupposes that there is a one-to-one relation between utterances and attitudinal stances, a somewhat unwarranted assumption. The main problem is with the level of detail (e.g. precisely how and in what way is language use linked to particular 'attitudinal stances'), which raises the possibility that the use of the term 'attitude' gets in between and obfuscates the relations between conversation as action and participant's particular use of this or that sign-system (language).

For these reasons it may be that while Mead's ideas provide a range of important ideas for students of social cognition only one study has attempted to utilise this framework directly. Fine (1981) has adopted Mead's (1934) perspective in a study of pre-adolescence impression management in 9–11 year old boys. Given the limitations of a strictly descriptive approach, this account does offer a coherent interpretation of the ways in which children appear to devise methods for 'constructing social meanings consensually'. The emphasis is very much on the ways in which children approaching adolescence acquire skills and techniques of social negotiation in cultural institutions (peer friendships) which provide 'didactic training'. It is interesting here to note Fine's (1981) comment on the development of the self:

'the developmental issue is not one of unitary development of the self, but the interactional issue of acquiring behavioural flexibility to cope with situations and of seeing behaviours involved in this coping as part of one's repertoire of behaviour' (p.48),

which concurs in an important way with Ignjatovic-Savic's (1985) interpretation of Vygotskian development:

'But Vygotsky's view on the influence of socio-cultural factors upon development does not allow any notion of the universalism of cognitive structures nor of the invariable sequence of developmental steps. It follows from Vygotsky's theory that there is no one unique direction of development but more divergent lines instead.' (p.293).

Fine (1981) argues that such social skills (self-presentation skills in pre-adolescence) differ from many others that the child is acquiring in that they do not consist of a core of knowledge, behaviour patterns or social norms; rather they consist of techniques for negotiating social reality. This negotiation is a process that requires an understanding of the social dynamics of peer interaction. One other study in the area touches on the symbolic interactionist position. Leahy and Shirk (1985) develop an interpretation of the differentiating processes arising from self-monitoring in the different social situations children are exposed to. Their outlook, however, is incorporated within a constructivist Piagetian framework, and in effect much of their supporting evidence is better suited to an analysis along information processing lines. It can be viewed as a more recent example of the gap between Mead's ideas and the ways in which these find expression in social and developmental psychology.

Finally, there is a problem with the notion of mutual adjustment and co-operative negotiation outlined by Mead (1934). This should be seen as part of the moral ethics inherent and central to Mead's position, and not to be viewed as an outline programme of psychological investigation. There is clearly an overemphasis in Mead (1934) on the beginning of an act, which is difficult to incorporate in subsequent research frameworks which share his concerns (e.g. conversational analysts). There is also a blurring of the distinction between verbal and non-verbal behaviour in that both are subsumed under the category of gesture:

'Language is a process of indicating certain stimuli and changing the response to them in the system of behaviour ... the actual gesture (voice, eye gaze or whatever) is indifferent as long as it does call out the response to that thing which is indicated' (p.218).

INDIVIDUALISTIC AND INTERACTIONIST SOCIAL-COGNITIVE DEVELOPMENT: A SUMMARY

A wide range of material has been covered in this and in the previous chapter. The discussion so far has touched on a number of conceptual, methodological, and empirical issues ranging from the conceptual constraints arising from applying a logico-mathematical approach (Piaget), through the difficulties accruing to the overemphasis upon the information processing metaphor and onto problems and misnomers arising from social interactional perspectives.

Arguably the major problem with the social interaction perspectives in social-cognitive developmental research is that they fail in their attempt to incorporate social theoretic approaches to the individualistic orientations of contemporary cognitive psychology. One reason for this is that they are not sufficiently adept at recognising the compromised nature of the 'social' positions being advocated, for example, the *social* social cognitive view of Doise and Mugny (1985). In other words, the favoured models of social interaction presuppose and emphasise individual cognition as *the* central construct. This in itself works against adequate conceptions of 'dynamic' social interaction.

Further, there may be a more general failure to recognise that when one or other theory/model/method is advocated then a particular metaphor or set of constructs is being assumed. In order to be in a position to critically evaluate the advantages and disadvantages of an approach it is necessary to clarify the assumptions underlying the adopted view. We also need to ascertain under what conditions *this* and *not that* metaphor can be fruitfully employed (its scope and adequacy) for the phenomenon under scrutiny. This is not to be read, however, as an endorsement for 'grand scale' meta-theoretical or global model of social-cognitive development. Earlier attempts within cognitive psychology serve as useful reminders of perspectives which encompass all and explain little (Anderson & Bower, 1973). What is required is an examination of why it is that while one or other metaphor for human development might suffice for the study of children's mathematical understanding, it clearly fails when we wish to examine how children learn to participate in group contexts. We need to pay much more attention to the criteria we are adopting when employing models to aid our investigations.

NOTES

1. Notwithstanding group remembering research (e.g. Clark, Stephenson, & Rutter, 1986).
2. It should be noted that in these particular experiments the context was such that the child could see clearly that the position she was taking was in fact the correct one (Doise & Mugny, 1985).
3. The claims that are made would under more rigorous conditions require a longitudinal design.

CHAPTER FOUR

Conversational Contexts: The Site for Emerging Social-cognitive Skills

INTRODUCTION

In the previous chapters I have spent some time isolating general orientations within the emerging literature on children's social-cognitive development (individual or social) and examining the various theoretical approaches underlying the research strategies adopted. The importance of this has been twofold: the necessity to make sense out of a burgeoning and increasingly disparate literature, and as a device for bringing into play the foundation stones of an alternative framework for studying children's social-cognitive participation skills.

I wish now to consider research closer to my own concerns. This interest subsumes studies on the role of language and social-cognitive development, and work, which seeks to address directly the development of children's social-cognitive skills. Although these distinct sub-themes in the literature are rarely considered together, the emphasis in this book is upon understanding how infants and young children begin to participate in and make sense of the social world. The focal concerns are with the theoretical, methodological, and empirical issues surrounding the development of communicative abilities or 'social-discursive' practices as well as identifying criteria for understanding and evaluating social interaction skills, that is with reference to the dynamics of conversational contexts. The proposal is that wherever else developmental social-cognitive processes might be located, the site for their 'uncovering' is the conversational context.

Substantiating such a proposition is not difficult. Consider, for example, the importance of interaction for cognitive-developmental theory, in particular the whole question of developmental change, whether of a co-operative (Bryant, 1982) or conflictive nature (Light, 1983). The conversational context is *the* medium for interaction. Again, there is the pre-eminent position given to conversational contexts (i.e. presupposed by use of the phrase 'social interaction') in the *social* social cognitive theories outlined in the previous chapter. Some theoretical accounts (e.g. Vygotsky, 1934) would argue that all forms of cognition must at some level be social phenomena (Wertsch, 1985) and conveyed principally through dialogue (this being the primary medium for the transformation of inter- to intra-psychological functional processes).

At a more pragmatic level the most commonly used criteria for lack of, or unsuccessful, social-cognitive skills are based upon evaluations of the child's participation in conversational contexts (Guralnick, 1990; Roberts, 1986). For example, one of the problems identified with autistic children (Jordan, 1992), is that the skills involved in being able to recognise and monitor ongoing participation are simply not utilised. The early difficulties such children experience with confrontational aspects of interaction may prevent them from recognising and displaying appropriate conversational participation skills.

There are also studies which equate communicative competence with participation in conversation (Garvey, 1984; Golinkoff, 1983b; Ochs & Schiefflein, 1979). This point is highlighted by the observation that from the first year children participate in conversations about the social rules of their world (Dunn & Munn, 1985) including rules about how to engage in conversations, what is to be expected and what it is to be held accountable (Becker, 1988b). More generally, there are few theoretical accounts of social-cognitive development which do not place considerable importance on either interaction (between organism and environment—broadly conceived) or participation (parent-child synchronicity, peer-peer interaction and so on). This again implicates the conversational context as *the* locus or site for acquiring the necessary skills for exploring, and subsequently learning to take part as a full participant in, conversations. Before considering ways in which social-cognitive skills have been defined, however, we can first begin our analysis of the conversational context at a more general level by examining research work on the relations between language and social-cognitive development.

LANGUAGE AND SOCIAL-COGNITIVE DEVELOPMENT

The gradual intersection of overlapping topics in child language and developmental psychology has contributed to the emergence of a distinct 'sub-field' of research examining the relationship between language and social cognition (Durkin, 1987). It has been argued (see Ryan, 1974) that the process of acquiring a language in itself constitutes a form of social cognition, although this view is not shared by those who prefer to address the acquisition of language as 'formal object' (Atkinson, 1986). A social-cognitive perspective of language acquisition also runs counter to much of developmental psycholinguistic research, for example, Snow and Galbraith (1983).

Golinkoff (1983b), casting a historical glance over language acquisition research, points out that the early, largely syntax based, research themes (McNeill, 1969) came to be replaced by semantic and pragmatic orientations (Snow & Ferguson, 1977). The latter though are seen as having failed to live up to their earlier expectations, in part because they tended towards description rather than explanation. This itself contributed to a divergence between the study of *language acquisition* and *child language* research commented on by Atkinson (1986).

The recent emergence of a social-cognitive approach to child language recapitulates an earlier phase of research (Halliday, 1973) which recognised that synactically inspired models, which focused on language as a 'cognitive' object, were limited. Instead the emphasis was upon functionalist conceptions and what children do with language (i.e. communicate and interact). However, the form in which these ideas were expressed in developmental psychology (Bruner, 1975a; Schaffer, 1977) were predicated upon rather restricted communication models (closely aligned to information processing models), ones which mitigated against the requisite level of theory construction. Subsequently there was a return to syntactically based interests (e.g. Pinker, 1984; Wexler & Cullicover, 1984), however, now accompanied by a more clearly defined separation of research interests.

The more recent wave of research into social cognition and language can be viewed not so much as an attempt to bring together what have become divergent approaches, but rather a programme of shared links or points of contact. In a similar fashion to the way that different theoretical orientations address topics in developmental social cognition, there are at least three themes in the recent literature examining the role of language and social cognition.

First, there is work which takes as axiomatic the formalistic/rationalist accounts of language acquisition (language as object) where the approach simply does not warrant detailed consideration of socio-cultural mappings on innate specifications, and where it does, a Piagetian account is often favoured (Edmundson, 1990; Howe & Ogura, 1988; Karmiloff-Smith, 1979). There has been a marginalisation of social-cognitive topics (Ingram, 1989), accompanied at the same time by the recognition that their import has not been adequately addressed (Messer & Turner, 1992). While it remains to be seen whether the 'connectionist' inspired programme (Plunkett, 1990) can answer and surmount Habermas's critique of 'monologic' communication models, much of this literature is clearly committed to a fundamental distinction between cognitive/representational and social-semiotic processes.[1]

A second theme considers various issues bearing on the relationship between language and social cognition from developmental and pragmatic concerns. These range from Piagetian inspired studies of social deixis (e.g. Hollos, 1977), through issues of intentionality and implicature (Dore, 1983; Ryan, 1974), and onto 'theory of mind' considerations which recognise but do not fully address the role of language and social cognition (Astington, 1988). It is instructive to note the way in which this recent development is considered. Durkin (1988) asserts that:

'the social world is fundamentally a linguistic one and contact with, indeed evidence of, other minds is mediated principally through language ... and ... as social cognition researchers advance the study of children's understanding of mental processes, social relations, emotions and personality characteristics, they raise issues for child language researchers of how to describe and explain vocabulary development in these domains and how this relates to current theories of semantic development' (p.92).

What requires emphasis here is that we cannot simply assume that the bringing together of various subject topics under the umbrella of 'language and social cognition' will necessarily aid either child linguists or developmental psychologists. We need to recognise the constraints which arise with attempts at integrating research themes which are themselves predicated on incompatible meta-theoretical assumptions (e.g. compare connectionist inspired language acquisition theories with developmental perspectives on children's knowledge of social honorifics). Arguments which simply assert that the social world is a linguistic one contribute to a glossing over of significant and problematic issues presupposed by such a position. For example, there is considerable debate over claims regarding the innate specificity of categories and concepts versus the role of their 'social production' in and through discourse (Sinha, 1988). The social world is not fundamentally a linguistic one, but a participative one where participation and communication involve using language as one particular sign-system. The third approach boundaries socio-linguistic and socio-semiotic approaches to language acquisition (Halliday, 1973; Sinha, 1988; Walkerdine, 1988). Sinha (1988), for example, argues for a socio-naturalistic approach to language and representation, one which he recognises is, 'directly orthogonal to the main stream of cognitive science'. He questions the validity of formal theoretic accounts of language where he says:

'is it possible or useful to attempt a theorization of individual mental representations and processes without reference to the interpretation and evaluation of social actions by sign-using communities' (p.3).

The emphasis here is upon the pragmatic negotiation of meaning (signification) within episodes of social exchange. Much of this research seeks to examine the ways in which social-discursive contexts bear upon language, broadly conceived as a social-semiotic process (Walkerdine & Sinha, 1978). However, it may be the case that although this third line of research draws attention to some of the limitations of formalistic accounts of language and representation, its scope may be somewhat limited given that it continues to share a number of the same pre-theoretical assumptions of those it criticises (Sinha, 1988).[2] It is too early to evaluate the influence of this third theme of research on language and developmental social cognition.

Other identifiable research strategies in this area also exhibit difficulties in their attempts either to apply information processing constructs, or maintain a general orientation towards the ethological approach. Consider, for example, the research on children's early conversational abilities. Here, work has examined what children say in their earliest conversations (Dunn & Kendrick, 1982a; McTear, 1985), what is said to them (Snow & Ferguson, 1977) and the ways in which different contexts can have an important influence on the procedures and strategies children appear to employ (Ervin-Tripp, 1979; Garvey & Berninger, 1981).

There is a sense in which underlying assumptions (i.e. observations of interactivity 'from the outside' and often in line with an 'ethological' orientation) can provide only a limited account of what it is to participate in conversational contexts. That is, although we have in place various accounts of participation and interactivity (Messer, 1983; Stern, 1974), these tend to hold to one version of 'objectivity' such that their pre-theoretical constructs are hampered by an overconcern with maintaining or holding to an 'outsiders' perspective. The levels of complexity which are described (e.g. Trevarthen & Hubley, 1978) then fail to map onto realisable and accountable models of social-cognitive development. There is considerable difficulty in accommodating dynamic and participative aspects of the young infant's early social world. It can be noted that where there are attempts to incorporate ethological/behavioural models of 'dynamic' interactivity, this results not only in a data 'explosion', but a theoretical cul-de-sac.[3]

We lack a sufficiently developed psychological theory or model of what it is to be in 'a conversational context' (as participants) and know very little about how children learn to participate as conversationalists. It can be noted that the precise and subtle mechanisms identifiable in everyday talk (Sacks, Schegloff & Jefferson, 1974) presuppose a relationship between participation (skill) in conversation, and the motivating characteristic of talk itself, which could benefit considerably from analysis based upon 'internalist' conceptions. However, before considering what is implied in such an account, we need first to examine the current research on developmental social-cognitive skills.

Defining and Measuring Developmental Social-cognitive Skills

It would be useful to make a number of comments regarding the emphasis being placed on conversational participation and how this relates to definitions of social-cognitive skills or abilities. There may be some advantage in differentiating the words *ability* and *skill* placing each at end points on a nature/nurture dimension. Ability is commonly considered as something that one just has or possesses innately or at least 'naturally' (and so the semantic relatedness to such words as *forte, capacity, calibre, talent, art, capability, potentiality* and so on). Skill on the other hand is taken to be much more about learning and action upon the environment (i.e. *dexterity, strength, smooth procedure, workmanship*). The word '*competence*' lies somewhere in between the points on such a construct, however we need also to note the difference between the possession of a *skill* and the verb *to be skilled*. Dictionary and thesaurus definitions certainly juxtapose all such terms, however, in light of the socially oriented emphasis of my developing argument, and the focus upon the child's active and successful participation in social contexts, my preference for employing the word 'skill' and setting the discussion around the development of social-cognitive skills, serves to emphasise the concern with understanding the child's sense of 'engagement' with the social world. It may also remind the reader that part of the intention is to change the emphasis of our orienting assumptions away from 'inside the head' predications onto more detailed considerations of the 'social-discursive' underpinnings of language use. Use of the term 'ability' tends to encourage an 'essentialist' and 'innatist' form of discussion, which mitigates against certain socially focused theoretical accounts.

Developmental social cognition research has not exhibited much concern over the ways in which definitions of social-cognitive abilities or skills are employed, reflecting the fact that definitions have in large part been tied to fulfilling pragmatic goals (e.g. assessment procedures). As the concern here is with theory construction and the provision of a richer conceptual framework for our investigations, a more detailed case needs to be made for the definition of skill adopted. This is developed through an examination of examples from contemporary literature.

It is not surprising to find definitions of social-cognitive skill reflecting a concern with external validation of behaviour. Thus, for example, Combs and Slaby (1977) define such skills as:

> 'the ability to interact with others in a given social context in specific ways that are *societally acceptable or valued* and at the same time are personally beneficial, mutually beneficial or beneficial primarily for others' (p.162) (my emphasis).

Likewise, Ladd's (1981) and Rogosch and Newcomb's (1989) criteria for the outcome of social-cognitive skills is established with reference to sociometric status (how peers regard a child's behaviour). Gresham (1986) and McFall (1982) define social skill as competencies, that is evaluations based on judgements by significant others. It is also interesting to see that by far the majority of social skills training and intervention programmes remain influenced by behaviourist theory and operant conditioning constructs (Barton, 1986; Hake & Olvera, 1978; Stokes & Osnes; 1986), consanguineous with a performance orientation.

It is clear, moreover, that measurement and assessment criteria have contributed to the definition and scope of developmental social cognition research. In the applied branch of this research (e.g. Oppenheimer & Rempt, 1986; Slaby & Guerra, 1988) the phrase 'social-cognitive skills' involves the juxtaposition of numerous (often conceptually unrelated) items, thrown together because they appear to be tapping some or other 'social' dimension. The result is an inconsistent 'pot-pourri' of measures, which may or may not be related to the skills children have to acquire in order to participate in social contexts. Strain, Guralnick, and Walker's (1986) review of assessment and development regarding social competence and social behaviours, serves as a useful indicator of the malaise   surrounding   the   theoretical   coherence   of   applied social-cognitive developmental research. They argue for an integrative theoretical model, which in practice amounts to no more than a taxonomy of views and opinions about how best to proceed (along a familiar listing of biological, cognitive, social learning and ecological themes). The metaphor is one of the child's adaptiveness, however it equally attests to the authors' resourcefulness at paying homage to the dominant themes of the preceding decade, that is, without questioning whether the various theories and approaches have in fact proved beneficial.

Where concerns are not so closely tied to measurement and assessment, conceptions of social-cognitive skills are anticipated by the theoretical views driving the particular research question. For example, Lefebvre-Pinard (1982) wished to specify in more detail the link between social cognition and social behaviour. Using a standard role-taking tasks (after Kurdek & Rodgon, 1975) it is argued that no predictive relation can be found between a child's ability to take the perspective of another and how they behave socially. Subsequently, when Lefebvre-Pinard (1982) looked at the children's skills in naturalistic contexts, they appear 'surprisingly' sophisticated (this is for pre-school aged children). Beyond the obvious limitations of this study (e.g. particularly their a-theoretical notions of communicative adequacy), there is a failure to recognise the inappropriate nature of the implicit (Piagetian/ information processing) theoretical framework and the manner in which this drove the design of the study. Having found that (a) children are very adept at a range of interactive conversational abilities and (b) that these skills bear no apparent relation to standard measures of social- cognitive skills, Lefebvre-Pinard (1982) suggests that we should look to older children to find evidence for the proposed relationship. Alternatively, they suggest that the earlier skills the children exhibit are not 'real' (i.e. conscious) skills, merely automated behaviour related to social cues, and instead what we should examine in more detail are meta-cognitive skills. Unfortunately, this appears very much to be a case of finding a set of results, which do not fit the particular relationship hypothesised and then questioning their validity by undermining their 'reality status'.

Likewise, the definitions advanced by researchers inspired by the ethological metaphor need to be viewed with caution (Eckerman & Stein, 1982; Mueller & Lucas, 1975; Schaffer, 1977). In this descriptive/'functional' approach to social-cognitive and particularly interactive skills, the emphasis or at least the orientation is with a fine-grained or 'molecular' analysis of social interaction sequences and a related discourse of competence, social skill outcome, delayed social skills development and so on. Eckerman and Stein (1982) argue:

'interactive skills are behaviourally and functionally defined. They do not presuppose knowledge about the young child's intentions or social understandings, but rather provide us with a 'window' to the infant's growing understanding of others and the processes of social interaction' (p.47).

Although there are some (largely empirical) advantages, as well as considerable interest, in this fusion of ethological, social-functional and cognitive-developmental themes (Hinde, Perret-Clermont, & Stevenson-Hinde, 1985) there are also significant shortcomings which together cast doubt on the theoretical potential of this perspective. First, it too often 'submerges' or obfuscates the constraints of its pre-theoretical underlying assumptions, leading to a certain seduction with description (which although beneficial for empirical requirements, only provides us with a very general metaphor). Second, a concentration on description facilitates the false impression of how skilled children appear to be, especially with communicative and conversational skills. Third, the methodological legacy of mainstream cognitive development leads to studies which emphasise only certain task-related aspects of social contexts (e.g. objects and play—Eckerman & Whatley, 1977; Ross, 1982) and interaction scenarios often drawn along lines of peer-peer versus child-adult social-cognitive skills. Given that we remain ignorant of many of the complexities of conversational contexts *per se*, we must question the grounds for the prevalence of such distinctions. This is not to say that such comparisons will not prove to be valuable, only that more often than not, considered theoretical reasons for their importance are not forthcoming.

THE ESSENTIAL SOCIAL-COGNITIVE SKILL: PARTICIPATING IN CONVERSATION

The central proposition then is that participation in dynamic and 'on-line' conversational contexts is the most important social-cognitive skill that a child needs to acquire. The whole range of abilities, skills, attributes and characteristics of child behaviour, whether conceived as central constructs in cognitive or social-cognitive domains, are related to, and emergent from, participation, communication and engaging in dialogue with others. Within the research on young children's social-cognitive skills there are one or two studies which recognise the importance of the conversational context and the child's participative abilities within it. Putallaz and Gottman (1981) examined the strategies used by a child when joining another two children (already playing with one another). Their criteria for distinguishing 'unpopular' and 'popular' children and success in such contexts was determined by their conversational abilities. Unpopular children act like 'newcomers' attempting to control the situation and drawing attention to themselves, whereas popular, skilful children entry via appropriate utilisation of the conversational context (by referring to ongoing actions of the game, for example). More generally Guralnick (1990), in recognising the shortcoming of current assessment criteria regarding social-cognitive abilities (particularly learning-impaired children), calls for the incorporation of 'critical social tasks' into the assessment of peer-related social competence. The primary examples given are skills such as gaining entry into groups of already interacting children, and repair of self-talk in ongoing conversation.

Given the discussion earlier it is clear that the term 'skills' is a problematic concept. It can be used to indicate repetitive learned practice or highly crafted artistic ability. The sense in which the definition of skill (and social-cognitive skill) is developed in this book focuses upon the young child's ability to recognise and comprehend events within conversations in ways which facilitate her ongoing and subsequent participation. Employed in this way, skill encompasses what has traditionally been separated into non-verbal and linguistic aspects of any participation context. Other commentators have noted that the functional distinctiveness attributed to non-verbal communication channels (for example, by Argyle, 1969), is unwarranted on both theoretical and empirical grounds (Beattie, 1983; Graddoc, Cheshire, & Swann, 1987). Non-verbal/verbal distinctions all too often reflect methodological convention rather than theoretical rationale. This can lead to somewhat odd propositions that language behaviour should be classified as 'adaptive' behaviour, whereas interpersonal and 'task-related' behaviours are social-cognitive skills proper (Reschley & Gresham, 1981).

The precise and subtle mechanisms identifiable in everyday talk (Sacks et al., 1974) presuppose a relationship between participation (skill) in conversation, and the motivating characteristic of talk itself, which could benefit considerably from analysis based upon 'internalist' conceptions. The tendency to examining talk as if 'through a passing window' leads to some rather unwarranted assumptions. For example, it has been argued by Sacks et al. (1974) that taking turns in a conversation should be conceived as a local management system based upon assumptions of economy (gaining and sharing the 'floor') and equality (see Taylor & Cameron, 1987). Likewise, it is claimed that the very finely tuned cross-party timing of turn-taking (measured in a few micro-seconds) itself motivates participants to pay very careful attention to the ongoing flow and 'predictability' of talk. This, of course, begs the question with respect to the skills involved in learning how to avoid 'taking the floor', or how to participate by 'active' silence.

There are a number of social-cognitive conversational skills which require explanation. For example, what are the skills used to monitor and self-regulate participation and 'engagement' in conversations; what skills are associated with being able to recognise and distinguish between 'important' structural elements of conversational patterns; can we identify the skills which make it possible for the child to provide (and facilitate) opportunities for a partner's contribution to the ongoing talk; are there distinct skills for a variety of conversational contexts (dyads; group conversation; classroom participation and so on) or do they arise from a more general set of core social-cognitive conversational skills?

There are, then, reasons for seriously considering the proposition that through an examination of conversation (e.g. the coherence, narrativity and followability of talk), we may be able to uncover how it is that the young child begins to use language in a fashion which allows us to infer that she is utilising a range of 'discursive concepts'. The ability to use words in a way which warrants other's justifiable attributions of intentionality is what allows her to learn the parameters for participation/conversation itself.

One aim of this book is to provide a framework which will change the orientation of our understanding (and our investigative tools—empirical and theoretical) away from looking (and presupposing 'mind' as existing) 'inside people's heads' and onto a consideration of 'social practices'. The starting point is the theoretical commitment to conversation or more technically the production of 'social-discursive' practices, as the framework within which we can study the emergence of social-cognitive developmental skills (particularly those expressed in talk). Two important issues arise from asking how it is that the young infant moves from being a non-ratified (overhearing) participant in conversational contexts to a fully fledged 'engaged' and 'engaging' conversational partner. First, we will need an 'internal' account of conversational skill development, that is, as if from the infant's/child's viewpoint and second, we will need to ascertain whether an explanation of this development amounts to an account of the primary mechanism of social-cognitive development. A theoretically coherent account of such a model could provide us with a richer conceptual framework for investigating precisely how various conversational contexts have a bearing on language development. Participation in dynamic and 'on-line' conversational contexts is arguably the most important social-cognitive skill that a child needs to acquire.

NOTES

1. Models which assert that communication is possible and successful on the assumption that speakers and listeners possess the same pre-established code, which as Ryan (1974) points out does not explain the 'structure of intersubjectivity' that makes the application of such codes possible.
2. For example, the commitment to mentalistic accounts of propositional attitudes.
3. Where animal ethologists have attempted to outline the complexities of interaction along dyadic-triadic-polyadic lines, this has led to very large data sets which are both cumbersome and contribute little theoretically.

CHAPTER FIVE

A Framework for Investigating Social-cognitive Skills

INTRODUCTION:
THE 'ECO-STRUCTURAL' FRAMEWORK

In the previous chapter I summarised why contemporary theoretical views of developmental social cognition are unlikely to provide us with fertile theoretical frameworks for investigating the development of children's participative social-cognitive skills. I wish to define the development of social-cognitive skills as first and foremost emergent from conversational participation abilities. The intention is to bring into place a number of ideas which have a bearing upon the development of social-cognitive skills, given the argument that the central starting point is the child's participation in conversational contexts (broadly conceived). An alternative framework is now sketched out, one which draws together or at least borrows from various areas often conceived as being somewhat divergent. The eco-structural framework is not an attempt to integrate a variety of perspectives in an 'all-encompassing' theory. Rather, it is better considered as an orienting framework or conceptual matrix, which while providing outline points of reference for developing this or that specific model of social-cognitive development, maintains and seeks to articulate the diversity of some of its central constructs. The use of the phrase 'eco-structural' is employed so as to emphasise the ecological perspective, as well as highlighting the commitment to examining the structural components of conversational contexts.

A sufficiently rich theoretical framework for studying children's participation in conversation is what is required, and the requirements for the necessary level of theory development need to be fulfilled at various points, theoretical, conceptual and methodological. The five areas outlined in Figure 5.1, not only provide points of reference but also in their interrelatedness, diversity and on occasion very contrastiveness, attempt to draw a boundary frame around the essential components involved in the study of children's early developing social-cognitive skills. This is a framework which emphasises the dynamic nature of participation. Following an outline of the principal elements of the framework in this chapter, the remainder of this book examines a model of overhearing which serves as a 'test-case' of the potential of the framework.

It is also important to note that Figure 5.1 is not an attempt to represent linearly predictive or causal relations between elements, rather the aim is to identify, describe and examine various theoretical ideas which have a bearing upon the study of conversational dynamics. Recognising why particular elements do not coalesce or partially converge is to be seen as important as identifying occasions where ideas from divergent traditions appear complementary. Unless we begin to consider less formally constrained 'meta-theoretical' frameworks we will not furnish ourselves with the requisite tools for investigating children's developing social-cognitive skills. Part of the richness and vitality of such a framework derives from having to examine some of the contradictions implicit in its formulation.

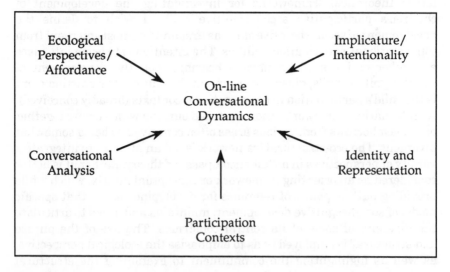

FIG. 5.1. An eco-structural framework

Ecological Perspectives and the
'Affordance' Metaphor

Starting with the 'ecological approach', in contrast to information-processing 'constructivist' accounts of perception, Gibson (1966, 1979) argued for an ecological perspective which emphasises the 'couplings' of organism and environment. The focus is upon the symbiotic relationship between animal and environment and to consider one without regard to the other is both misguided and ecologically invalid. In this view, one does not have to construct a picture of the world based upon impoverished perceptual information: rather the visual system (and Gibson's original argument is with respect to perception) and the structured information available in the visual field available to an orienting person, specifies the perceptual world in a much more direct fashion. The environment, perception of it and action within it, are all directly tied up with, in fact coupled to, an organism. One resonates with the environment and the environment 'affords' the sets of actions and events which a moving perceiver will engage in. Through the detection of the 'style of change' in a stimulus, one is provided with the specification of the characteristics of events, and learning involves detecting the 'invariant' and 'transformational' aspects of events (and perception of them).

One important aspect of this perspective which is often overlooked or misconceived, is the relationship between the perception or recognition of objects, events and so on, and what such objects 'afford' in terms of activities or sets of actions. Aspects or attributes of situations, events or objects, permit or sustain certain forms of activities for the perceiving organism. So, a square solid object of sufficient strength and durability will afford sitting on, trees afford climbing, and so on. However, square solid objects will only afford sitting on for an adult if they happen to be about knee high, otherwise (if smaller) they might afford being stood on, used as a ladder, or whatever. The point here is that 'affordances' *offer*, or have the *potential* for, sets of actions; they do not cause or require them. This is not a stimulus-response kind of approach, cloaked in the language of the 'ecological niche' and animal-environment synchrony; rather it is a framework which allows or, more importantly, stresses, the dynamic qualities of organism-environment contexts.

Gibson's (1966) early work in perception emerged out of his concerns as a trainer of air-force pilots during the 1950s in the U.S.A. and over time the orienting constructs of his research changed from stimulus-response psychophysics into what he termed an 'ecological approach' to perception and action. This is based upon a radical reformulation of Euclidean geometry termed ecological optics. This work has existed since the mid 1970s as a parallel contrastive theme to the dominant paradigm in visual perception research (i.e. information processing accounts). Numerous papers chart the various controversies (Johannson, 1973; Neisser, 1976; Ullman, 1980) regarding these divergent perspectives and there have been partially successful attempts at introducing the ecological approach into other areas of psychology, for example, environmental psychology (Landwehr, 1988); developmental psychology (Pick, 1987) and social psychology (McArthur & Baron, 1983).

One of the oft-cited advantages of this approach is that dynamic aspects of organism-environment interactions can be considered, that is, while maintaining a commitment to the requisite degree of formalism (Michaels & Carello, 1981). For example, Lee and his colleagues (Lee, Lishman, & Thomson, 1982; Lee & Reddish, 1981; Lee, Young, Reddish, Lough, & Clayton, 1983) have developed ecological-optic formal descriptions of various perception-action domains (e.g. bird flight, ball-hitting and gait during jumping). Likewise, Abernethy (1990) has examined squash playing, arguing that novice players fail to extract the relevant affordances (available to expert and novice alike), while Berthenthal and Bai (1989) and Stoffergen, Schnuckler, and Gibson (1987) have carried out an analysis of the optical information utilised by young infants learning to sit and walk. Within social psychology Schmidt, Carello, and Turvey (1990) attempt a description of the affordances made available during interactions between people. Adopting an ecological approach to social perception McArthur and Baron (1983) goes as far as to make the claim that:

> 'research within the ecological perspective will reveal the meaning that is communicated by social events. More specifically, such research will reveal what it is in a person's movements, gestures, voice and facial appearance that communicates to us that person's momentary intentions, emotional state ... and what it is in the interactions between two people that communicates to us the nature of their relationship even when we cannot hear the words' (p.217).

While recognising that there is clearly a considerable gap between the formal predictions and modelling of the 'affordances' detected by a flying gannet (Lee & Reddish, 1981) and McArthur and Baron's (1983) claims regarding the 'intentionality' given off by people during their interactions, the possibilities inherent in the idea of 'affordances' and 'affordance structures' warrant our consideration.

Gibson (1979) asserts that, 'The affordances of the environment are what it *offers* animals, what it *provides* or *furnishes*, either for good or ill' (my emphasis). There is an intrinsic relation between perception of an environment and action within it. It is the affordance that is perceived, defined, that is, as those behaviours which can be entered into with respect to the environment. To detect affordances is to detect meaning, based here upon a concept of information where information is interlinked with both perception and action (by an organism). Information is 'revealed' in objective physical events: that is, it is dynamic, changing, multi-modal stimulus information. The ecological approach holds not only to a metaphor of 'dynamic revelation' accompanying movement in and through an environment, but also to 'electro-computational' notions of 'resonance' and 'modulation' and the 'tuning-in' of perception.

Baron (1980) likewise, places considerable emphasis upon exploratory activity in the world rather than constructive activity in the head. That is, the actions of the perceiver as organizing and structuring inputs from the environment, and the complementary and reciprocal nature of action and perception. Leaving aside for the present the problematic nature of the 'epistemic' subject who must (in theory), nonetheless choose between sets of potentially available affordances, the emphasis on an affordance as a 'dynamic potential' revealed through participatory action could contribute significantly to a framework aimed at understanding children's engagement in conversational contexts. Two points of note here. First, the sense in which Gibson developed the idea of affordances and behavioural 'niches' is somewhat different from forms of 'ecological-genetic' determinism (Wilson, 1975). Gibson (1979) again:

'the concept of affordance is derived from (these) concepts of valence, invitation and demand but with a crucial difference. The affordance of something does not change (disappear, cease to exist) as the need of the observer changes. The observer may or may not perceive or attend to the affordance, but the affordance, being invariant is always there to be perceived' (p.138).

and,

'for all we know there may be many offerings of the environment that have not been taken advantage of, that is, niches not yet occupied. An affordance cuts across the dichotomy of subjective/objective and helps us to understand its inadequacy. It is equally a fact of environment and a fact of behaviour' (p.129).

Second, and more important, the way in which the idea of an affordance and affordance structures has been employed, pre-eminently addresses both the centrality of dynamic participation, and the importance of interaction as 'potential' (that is, both as *realised* and *to be realised* in the future).

I wish to argue that the predominant orientation of sensory-cognitive processes (that is, arising from, but not exclusively, visual perception), leads to our engaging in constructivist conversational practices which build upon our skills, or predispositions, to detect and extract affordances. Following certain constructs of the 'mutualist' position and the evolutionary importance (dominance) of the perceptual senses, the structuration endemic and intrinsic to human cognition (linguistic, behavioural and systems theoretic) is produced through interaction so as to serve our propensity for recognising 'perceptual'/sensory forms.

In other words, part of the result of the dominance of visual and perceptual systems is our possessing a range of particular types of cognitive/biological recognition and display behaviours which provide, and form the basis for, cognitive 'recognisability'. Von Hofstein (1983) has suggested, for example, that the infants' earliest actions when attempting to catch a moving object are interdependent with the visual/kinesthetic information made available as affordance structure. It may very well be the case that when we are actively engaged in a conversational context, we produce those structures which allow our predisposed 'perceptually biased' cognitions to operate. In conversations, and in the construction of them, we make available and use patterns and structures (of talk/language) so as to signal and identify those aspects of the ongoing talk which have to be picked up, ignored, made recognisable, or whatever.[1] As social beings we build upon our own dispositions to respond to *invariant* and *transformational* affordances by constructing them, and making them available so as others' dispositions can be utilised. This process can be termed the 'structuration' of conversation. The child has to learn how to provide conversational affordances for those she is interacting with.

However, before moving on to other lines of argument which might lend support to the above, there are two particularly problematic issues for the ecological perspective. The first is the issue of representation and the second the claims regarding 'affordances' as evolutionary/natural structures. It is clear that the ecological approach largely sidesteps the issue of 'higher cognitive' and representational processes, on occasion by arguing that before we can ask the 'how' of perception (and associated problems of representation—Marr, 1982) we need first to analyse the nature of the information available (Michaels & Carello, 1981). At other times proponents argue that representational and inferential processes themselves can be viewed as special 'indirect' forms of generic 'ecological' affordance processes (e.g. Gibson, 1979; Johnson, 1988), hardly a tenable proposition given that this simply side-steps the issue by reconstituting or redefining contemporary definitions of cognition. McArthur and Baron (1983) argue that the past history of one's interaction with the environment consistently 'retunes' the perceptual apparatus on an online basis:

'the ecological view is that most, if not all adaptively relevant properties [of representational structures] are extensionally projected' (p.235).

Gibson (1979) alludes to the intensionally representational 'results' of perceptual activity where he asserts:

'perceiving precedes predicating ... in the course of development the young child first hears talk about what she is perceiving. Then she begins to talk about what she perceives. Then she begins to talk to herself about what she learns (alone in her cot for example) ... and finally her verbal system probably begins to verbalize silently in much the same way that the visual system begins to visualize, without the constraints of stimulation or muscular action, but within the limits of the invariants to which the system is attuned' (p. 260).

There is clearly a failure to address the complexities involved with the issue of representation, and Sinha (1988) points out that Gibsonian representational constructs are 'mnemonically stored 'abstractions' of affordances' (p.133), predicated upon the notion of a memory store. This he says, can only lead proponents back to where they were trying to get away from, towards neo-rationalist mentalistic accounts of cognition. It needs to be emphasised that while the framework being proposed here adopts some of the constructs of the ecological approach, these must be considered in a way which is distinct from other meta-theoretical assumption of the 'direct' perception view. The intention is to utilise central elements of the affordance metaphor, particularly with respect to its ability in providing a sufficiently detailed formalism for investigating dynamic processes. Part of this will involve an examination of the value of a social-dialogic notion of representation, that is one which focuses upon the 'productive' nature of representations instantiated or emergent in conversation. In other words the affordances of concern here are socially constructed representational constructs—directly recognisable as structurally invariant (and transformational) components of conversations (i.e. utilised and made available by participants). That is, predicated upon a conception of representation as *socially produced* aspects of conversations.

Representations are both recognised and provided by participants as affordance structures in and through talk.

The second problematic issue within the Gibsonian or ecological view is the emphasis on the recognition or importance of 'natural' affordances. In other words, there is an implicitly privileged status accruing to concepts, ideas and metaphors derived from an evolutionary perspective (Michaels & Carello, 1981; Turvey & Kugler, 1984) and a corresponding underplay of the role of 'cultural' affordances. This not only begs the theoretical question of whether all affordances are more properly conceived as cultural constructs (that is all those beyond the immediacy of pain, danger and biological recognition mechanisms), it also contributes to the difficulties surrounding conceptions of learning within this perspective. Learning or what is sometimes referred here to as 'the education of attention' is, it is said, intrinsically tied to the one's history of resonation with the environment or more specifically:

> 'the stimulus information to which perceivers are attuned may vary as a function of their perceptual learning, goals, expectations and actions' (McArthur & Baron, 1983, p.237).

In a similar fashion Michaels and Carello (1981) assert that there are a range of potential purposeful behaviours, constrained by instinct, learning, or culture called effectivities. They assert that:

> 'whether an organism does X or Y 'determines' the affordance it can detect. Because information specifies behaviours that are afforded and because different animals have different sets of effectivities, affordances belong to animal-environment systems and nothing else' (p.42).

In a more considered attempt at addressing the issue of learning and the role of intention, Turvey and Kugler (1984) outline the ecological approach in a proposal not dissimilar to Grice's distinction between 'natural' and 'non-natural' meaning (Grice, 1982). They suggest that there are two forms of information: one which is 'indicational' in the sense that it has a role which is indicative for a set of actions to be carried out and tied to the concept of 'rule', convention or practice, and a second 'specificational' form which is more akin to 'natural meaning'. We must, however, guard against an implicit 'elementism' favoured by supporters of the ecological position (e.g. Baron, 1980).[2] There is an argument for proposing that affordances are social-cultural constructions, which have a bearing upon representational and conversation processes only as an indirect result of evolutionary processes (for example, as predispositions to recognise affordance structures).

What does this imply for a view of developmental social cognition which seeks to emphasise participation in conversation? The young child needs to learn to detect invariant and changing aspects of the social world, and to recognise those circumstances where novel events are likely to occur (i.e. potentially significant contexts). What is being suggested, is that perceiving or participating in social interaction contexts as an overseeing or overhearing young infant, affords those very skills (as potential sets of appropriate actions) necessary for social-cognitive development. It is time to consider in more detail the source and form of the social information which exists or is available in the child's social world: in other words, to examine what this information is, how it might be structured, and how young children might begin to detect and use socially significant information in order to successfully engage in the world.

Consider what is implicated in the notion of the extraction and detection of structured social information (and change in such structure). We have only a very limited notion of what form invariant and transformational *social structure* information might take. However, as a starting point a primary factor contributing to the acquisition of early social-cognitive skills is the young child's ability to identify the important cues and sources of social information, in other words, to learn what social interaction contexts afford (both 'directly'—as chairs afford sitting on—and their potential—chairs can be used as ladders, and social interaction contexts can be used for trying out social interaction skills).

The primary vehicle for this process is likely to be through watching, listening and then participating in social interaction. The child's entry into the social world is intrinsically tied to the affordances of that world. Observing and overhearing contributes directly to the acquisition of the skills necessary for participation and can, theoretically, be distinguished from overhearing and overseeing, as self-monitoring. The notion of 'affordance' and the detection and extraction of information can be reformulated with respect to the young child's ability to detect socially significant information.

CONVERSATIONAL ANALYSIS: THE INDUCTIVE APPROACH TO THE STUDY OF TALK

The second topic or dimension in the framework which has a bearing upon the dynamics of conversational contexts is conversational analysis, which derives from the ethnomethodological approach (see Figure 5. 1). This tradition places centre stage the investigation of participants' own methods, techniques and forms of rationale for interpreting and producing their social worlds. Following the ideas of Garfinkel (1967) and others (e.g. Turner, 1972) a number of research studies began to apply 'inductive' methods to the study of talk. In this paradigm numerous studies have described many structural elements of conversation ranging from turn-taking procedures, local-management practices, use of intonation patterns, interruption strategies and so on (Goodwin, 1981; Levinson, 1983; Sacks et al., 1974).

Likewise, during the 1970s, a number of studies concerned with children's conversation began to adopt a similar approach (Ervin-Tripp & Mitchell-Kernan, 1977) although, more often than not, such studies were reported alongside work which holds to the quite distinct methods and approaches of discourse analysis (e.g. Sinclair & Coulthard, 1975). Levinson (1983) highlights the different theoretical underpinnings of discourse and conversational analysis, that is, largely syntactically formulated and descriptive linguistic approach of discourse analysis contrasted with the largely 'inductive' ethnomethodological approach of conversation analysis and their commitment to avoiding premature theory construction—although see Cameron (1989).

The emphasis here is very much on the dynamic participatory processes involved in conversations. The framework outlined in Figure 5.1 seeks not only to highlight contributory factors, which have a bearing upon the dynamics of conversations, but in addition aims to provide impetus for the development of richer conceptual models. There is clearly a case for seriously considering models of conversation which are axiomatically 'internal' accounts, sufficiently sophisticated models of what it might mean psychologically to be 'inside' a conversational context.

There are a number of issues I wish to consider concerning conversational analysis. The first is the hypothesis that many of the structural patterns identified by the conversational analysts could be considered from an ecological viewpoint (i.e. as affordances and affordance structures). The second is the idea of structuration developed above, and the suggestion that participants themselves utilise the affordance structures in talk such that they both recognise their occurrence, produce them and employ an orientation to their occurrence and ongoing development during participation in conversation. Third, I wish to touch on the problematic nature of power relations in talk and more recent views which assert that while the conversational analysts have made significant contributions to our understanding of talk, their explanatory accounts require a more considered analysis, particularly with reference to assumptions of shared resources in conversation. Finally, a re-consideration of why an 'internalist' account of conversation can usefully employ aspects of the affordance metaphor is outlined.

Consider first the structures identifiable in talk. Schegloff and Sacks (1973), in a paper outlining the patterns observable within 'closing' and 'opening' sections in conversations, demonstrated that it is the presupposed nature of their very recognisability, which had a direct bearing on the evolving pattern and coherence of talk. What is interesting from the point of view of 'affordance structures' in conversations is that the participants oriented the production of their discourse to their ongoing perceptions of the talk as not only the 'unit of reference', but also as the act to be accomplished.

Adjacency pairs—expressions which co-occur as pairs often distributed across a number of utterances—(Coulthard, 1977), transition relevant pauses (gaps of a particular duration denoting that now is an opportunity to change turns in the talk), summons-answer sequences, opening and closing sections of talk and so on, for example, see Levinson (1983) and Taylor and Cameron (1987) for reviews, are all recognisable structural patterns of talk, realisable as conversational affordances. Sacks et al. (1974) argue that such patterns are manipulated, used and produced by participants as part of a local managements system and there are a number of studies testifying to the split-second timing, and 'on-line' perceptual abilities of participants orienting themselves to such mechanisms (Goodwin, 1981; Rutter, 1987). Sacks, Schegloff, and Jefferson (1974) propose that turn-taking rules in conversation derive from the operation of a local management system based upon principles of 'economy' and the sharing of that favoured resource 'taking the floor'. Studies of conversation make it clear that the overall coherence and managability of talk (as an accomplishment between participants) is a highly conventionalised and socially instituted form of interaction. In addition, the synchronistic interaction abilities of young infants in pre-linguistic proto-conversations (Stern, 1974; Trevarthen & Hubley, 1979) and the sophistication of young children's timing in their early conversations (Garvey & Berninger, 1981) lend support to the 'directly' perceptible affordance nature of conversational contexts. It is quite clear that the invariant and transformational elements of such phenomena could be considered as affordances, particularly where this would help to highlight the sense of potential, and the immediacy, of conversations.

Moving to the second issue and the idea of 'structuration', i.e. the production of affordance like conversational structures by participants for co-participants, it is necessary to look in more detail at particular structures in conversation to envisage how this might operate. The Schegloff and Sacks' (1973) study of closing section in talk serves as a useful example. They pose the problem of how it is that two people manage to succeed at closing a conversation, that is, given the observation that the continuation of speaking turns could go on indefinitely (without a precise mechanism for solving the closing problem). As they put it:

> 'Our analysis has sought to explicate the ways in which the materials (units and exchanges) are produced by members in orderly ways that exhibit their orderliness, have their orderliness appreciated and used, and have that appreciation displayed and treated as the basis for subsequent action ... simply it is the closing as the problem for the participants which is our interest' (p.290).

Given that it is the production of recognisable 'affordance structures' in conversations which is our concern, the participants must somehow organize their co-convergence at a point in the conversation where one speaker's turn completion will not occasion another speaker's talk, and will at the same time not be heard as the other's silence. What is needed are techniques or methods for providing ways to introduce previously unmentioned mentionables (such as 'oh, by the way, one of the reasons why I came by to see you to-day was ... ') which makes recognisable the structural properties of a closing section, itself then permitting appropriate 'terminal exchange' adjacency pair inclusion. One important technique then is the use of the adjacency pair format. This derives from the fact that the adjacency pair provides

> 'a deterministic 'when' for it (the closing section) to happen (i.e. 'next') ... a means for handling the close order problem, where that problem has its import through its control of the assurance that some relevant event will be made to occur' (Schegloff & Sacks, 1973, p.299).

The specific way in which adjacency pair sequences are used as a technique by participants as 'affordances' requires that the first utterance of such a pair is recognised as having a particular 'first pair part' status. So, if a participant wished to methodically provide for 'closing section implicativeness', that is, indicate quite clearly that she is concerned to move towards providing the opportunities for initiating those distinct patterns identifiable as closing sections of conversation, then there are highly conventional and immediately recognisable procedures for doing this. Schegloff and Sacks (1973) point out that because of the organisation of turn-taking, 'unless close ordering is attempted there can be no methodic assurance that a more or less eventually aimed-for successive utterance or utterance type will be produced' (p.301). It is in this sense that we can consider the relationship between the recognition of 'structural affordances' in talk and procedures and processes produced by participants in order that they can accomplish necessary moves in conversation. The term 'structuration' is employed so as to help articulate how this operates, and highlight the fact that the participants are oriented towards the accomplishment of talk and themselves provide and produce 'structuration' strategies.

It is also worth noting that in the example referred to above, the reason why two utterances are needed is that a current speaker can display that she understood what a prior first pair part was aimed at, and subsequently whether she is willing to go along with it. In addition, whoever used the first pair part can see whether what she intended is understood and has been (or will not be) accepted for its 'closing section' implicativeness. Recognition and display of conversational patterns can not only be considered for their 'structural regularities' but as dynamic potential 'on-line' affordances oriented to by participants.

This brings us on to a consideration of some of the more problematic assumptions underlying conversational analysis. While emphasising that there are many advantages in adopting the conversational analysis approach, Cameron (1989) and Taylor and Cameron (1987) point out that the explanatory accounts are in danger of simply being circular. There is simply an appeal to examples of the phenomena as explanations for their expression and furthermore analysts uncritically assume underlying principles of negotiation and agreement. Sacks, Schegloff, and Jefferson's (1974) proposal that turn-taking rules in conversation are based upon principles of 'economy' and the sharing of that favoured resource 'taking the floor' is questionable given that often participants are not oriented towards equality and a fair distribution of resources (Zimmerman & West, 1975).

We can note that the way in which turn-taking resources are provided is likely to be critical for defining power relations in ongoing conversations suggesting that such role-relations also are amenable to an affordance analysis. For example, invitations to contribute might be offered by speakers in a very offhand way indicating a certain attitude or example of power, towards other participants. Fisher (1976) describes how power relations are expressed through a very sophisticated form of conversational insults by Barbadian speakers.[3]

Again, and with reference to the use of the first pair part as a pre-closing initiation attempt by a first speaker, a second speaker might assert or indicate power by displaying her failure to understand (before we can go on to the closing section, please be much more specific about X), or simply pretend she misunderstood so as to carry on the conversation (this being somewhat more insidious of course). Further, the 'pretence' can be either displayed (so as to exert power over the first) or disguised (simply to exert power but not to let A know that this power is being employed). Such considerations lead Cameron (1989) to call for an analysis of the institutional nature of talk. Certainly we need to investigate the presuppositional basis of conversational procedures, that is, that range of social-cultural practices which provide and establish the parameters of our communications. Any consideration of children's conversational skills (particularly in their talk with adults, teachers and other figures of authority) should include the study of how children acquire the necessary abilities to recognise the 'social-discursive' expression of power-relations, and in addition consider how children then reproduce such role-relations themselves (e.g. Shatz & Gelman, 1973; Wells, 1979).

Over and above such caveats, one crucial contribution that the conversational analysis approach makes is the focal concern with the ongoing dynamics of conversational contexts. The numerous devices described should help us understand and examine the way in which participants themselves are oriented towards the ongoing conversation as the 'single unit' to be accomplished. Schegloff and Sacks (1973) place considerable emphasis on this point, describing the participants orientation to the ongoing conversation and:

' ... and to THIS single conversation, as an instance, in which ITS development to some point may be employed as a resource in accomplishing its further development as a specific, particularized occurrence' (p.311).

The important point here is that the basic features of conversations (affordances) have a particular importance not only as analyst's constructs, but more significantly as processes, procedures and strategies utilised by participants conducting the business of talk. As Schegloff and Sacks put it, 'conversationalists construct conversations in their course, and in doing so they are oriented to achieving the co-occurrence of said features, to do so' (p.293).

PARTICIPATION CONTEXTS: GOFFMAN'S MICRO-SOCIOLOGICAL ANALYSIS

Another theme in the eco-structural framework involves a consideration of participation contexts, and ways in which ideas of interactivity and engagement have been developed within the social sciences. Over the last 15–20 years of research in developmental psychology there have been a considerable number of studies of a 'dyadic' orientation (mother-child; father-child and child-child). However, and partly in response to Bronfenbrenner's (1979) call for ecologically valid studies beyond the dyadic relationship, there has been some move towards studies of 'triadic' and 'polyadic' relations, that is, towards understanding the myriad forms of relationship the child experiences in the multi-person world (Liddell & Collis, 1988; Schaffer, 1984). Topics of concern range from second-order effects (Corter et al., 1981), social referencing (Campos & Spendberg, 1981), sibling studies and twin studies (Dunn & Kendrick, 1982b; Savic, 1980) and from an ethological perspective, expressions of dominance relations in peer group settings (Chase, 1980; Strayer & Strayer, 1980).

As attention has turned to more complex relationships and interactions, there has been a corresponding development of requisite research techniques and methods (e.g. Markov chain modelling, distributed network models and sociometric techniques). While there has been a willingness to adopt and adapt methods and techniques from other disciplines (e.g. ethnographic methods from social anthropology and observational methods from ethology), there has been more resistance towards incorporating conceptual frameworks outside mainstream developmental psychology.

Consider, for example, the emergence of the study of polyadic relationships (Datta, 1983; Forrester, 1986; Hinde, 1979; Liddell & Collis, 1988; Schaffer, 1984). The guiding metaphors here derive from those of evolutionary theory and information processing psychology and while these have proved useful as 'meta-theoretical' reference points for the study of the individual and the dyad, where one is concerned to look in detail at participation in multi-person contexts, only general guidelines emerge. For example, it might be argued that much of this literature holds to an implicit assumption that there is a developmental progression from dyadic through triadic and onto polyadic interaction abilities, which, of course, glosses over the fact that most children are exposed to multi-person interactions from birth. Schaffer (1984), for example, suggests that polyadic skills are likely to be linked to both age and attentional capacity. However, given that it is not clear precisely what a polyadic skill or ability might be (beyond the suggestion that they are unique to polyadic contexts and are likely to be more complex than 'dyadic' skills), and that to date the requisite level of theoretical development has not emerged, such proposals reflect the somewhat constrained and 'over-descriptive' ethological orientation. Participation contexts are of sufficient complexity and importance that more considered and also more imaginative attempts at providing appropriate theoretical frameworks are required. In part, this monograph can be viewed as a suggestion of how this might be accomplished.

This brings me on to a consideration of Goffman, whose work has a direct bearing upon our interest in the dynamic conversational context, and can be linked to a number of ideas in the ecological approach. It is interesting to note the somewhat marginalised status Goffman's work has within the disciplines of psychology and sociology, possibly because psychologists consider his writings to be too sociological (rarely amenable to quantitative analysis), while sociologists view his approach as over-individualistic. Schegloff (1988) points out that Goffman's psychology was one of the relations between an individual and 'ritual' interaction, and Collins (1988) argues that his micro-sociology should be seen as an attempt to tread a middle course between 'relativity and objectivity'. Drew and Wootton (1988) suggest that Goffman's concern was to:

'investigate the procedures and practices through which people organized and brought into life, their face-to-face dealing with other people. To investigate this domain required finding means of access to these procedures and initially ways of conceptualizing these resemblances between different occasions' (p.6).

There are at least three elements of Goffman's work which warrant out attention. First, was his concern with the 'display' of behaviour and what he called the doctrine of natural expression. This has important implications for the study of conversational dynamics and the idea of affordances outlined earlier. Second, there is his conceptualisation of the various participant roles identifiable in interaction contexts. The taxonomy of participant roles offers a fruitful way of categorising the nuances of 'polyadic' contexts, and one that is based on firmer theoretical grounds (Giddens, 1988). Third, his ideas concerning the nature of talk itself, in particular the role of participation dynamics.

(a) Goffman and the 'Doctrine of Natural Expression'
Goffman (1979) outlines what he calls the 'doctrine of natural expression':

'we assume that among humans a very wide range of attributes are expressible: intent, feeling, relationship, information state, health, social class and so on. Lore and advice concerning these signs, including how to fake them and how to see behind fakeries, constitute a kind of folk science' (p.7).

He proposes that we routinely seek information about properties of objects (animate and inanimate) that are perduring, that is enduring and in some way read as naturally basic, some information about the characteristic or 'essential nature' of people and objects. The fact that such information as 'signs' both exists and is displayed, is a central tenet of Goffman's perspective. In an essay on the recognition and display of that essential characteristic 'gender' Goffman (1979) points out that although this most cherished distinction is taken as the prototype of expression, 'something that can be conveyed fleetingly in any social situation and yet something that strikes at the most basic characterization of the individual,' it is nevertheless complicated. Goffman (1979) points out:

> 'The human objects themselves employ the term 'expression,' and conduct themselves to fit their own conceptions of expressivity; iconicity especially abounds, doing so because it has been made to. Instead of our merely obtaining expressions of the object, the object obligingly gives them to us, conveying them through ritualizations and communicating them through symbols' (p.7).

There are at least three interesting aspects of the 'doctrine' which we might note. First, given that there must potentially be an unlimited number of properties of an object or person which could be selected out for attention, it cannot be the overall structure of an entity which gets expressed but rather quite specific situationally bound contextual elements. 'Structural' and affordance-display aspects of individual expression are interdependent with the dynamics of any ongoing participation context.

Second, this process of expression is intrinsically 'social' and not to be explained by appeal to notions of instinct:

> '(it) ... is a socially defined category which employs a particular expression, and a socially established schedule which determines when these expressions will occur. They (people) are learning to be objects that have a character, and for whom this characterological expressing is only natural' (p.7).

What is important here is that these configurations of what we take to be natural expression are not simply elements passively processed in an everyday fashion, but are an integral part of what we produce or what can be generated in social situations.

Third, the distinction between 'biological elementism' and human display in accordance with the doctrine of natural expression needs to be emphasised. As others have noted biological sex determination must be distinguished from gender display. Goffman (1979) puts it:

'These acts and appearances are likely to be anything but natural indexical signs, except insofar as they provide indications of the actor's interest in conducting himself effectively under conditions of being treated in accordance with the doctrine of natural expression. And insofar as natural expression of gender are—in the sense here employed—natural and expressive, what they naturally express is the capacity and inclination of individuals to portray a version of themselves and their relationships at strategic moments—a working agreement to present each other with, and facilitate the other's presentation of, gestural pictures of the claimed reality of their relationship and the claimed character of their human nature' (p.7).

The parallels between this line of argument and the notion of affordance should be emphasised, that is affordances as those participatory and conversational display structures produced by participants in specific social-cultural settings. While they are available as directly cognisable phenomena, they are not necessarily 'simplistic' or obvious. Giddens (1988) hints at this where he highlights some important distinctions within what we might call Goffman's dramaturgical metaphor:

'individuals who act out roles cannot be just like individuals who act at roles ... Role distance can be a way of demonstrating supreme confidence in the performance of tasks involved in a particular role. By demonstrating to others that he or she does not fully 'embrace' the expectations involved in a role, the individual might actually validate rather than cast doubt upon its authenticity' (p.260).

Thus, precisely because roles are not displayed and carried out in stereotypical ways, then this very 'spontaneity' or flexibility becomes an important element in their recognition (by others) as displays of authenticity.

What is also interesting about Goffman's work is the utilisation of a 'dramaturgical' metaphor within an orientation of evolutionism. Collins (1988) asserts that Goffman did not support any simplistic 'processualism' or reality constructionism, arguing that his contribution was the application of a kind of social determinism constrained by the structural realities operating at the micro-behavioural level. Again, we can consider his notion of 'frames' and framing along affordance lines. Working on three levels (the physical, social ecological and institutional), frames are not cognitive objects or mental rules but rather behavioural scenarios tied to the dynamics of unfolding conversational contexts. These are alignments to situations such that there is a compulsion to behave in some and not other specific ways, and, where the constraints at one level of a 'frame' are breached or extended, there remain in place others which allow for change only in predictable and recognisable ways. Goffman defended the 'realist' view that the physical world exists and has a primary reality, 'situations ... are something that participants arrive at, rather than merely construct'. The mental realm, he points out, is not 'a free-floating realm but a derived realm' and it is out of the basic physical frame that the mental emerges, always anchored to it.

The second, the social-ecological frame, emphasises Goffman's evolutionary position where the importance of 'display' is paramount and so:

> 'When nothing eventful is occurring persons in one another's presence are still nonetheless tracking one another and acting so as to make themselves trackable' (Goffman, 1983, p.103).

The third, institutional frame, exemplifies the 'institutional' nature of talk, in a way, however which again does not imply a causal dependency. Collins (1988) again:

> 'The rituals of social life should not be regarded as an 'expression' of the properties of institutions; it is a form of activity established 'in regard' of those institutions. There is only a loose coupling to the qualities of the institutions themselves' (p.53),

leading to the argument that each participant can be in several complex layers of frames at the same time. We might note that the suggestion that these layers have a structure in relation to one another is for Goffman support for the argument that they are not simply created by the observer. This point is too often ignored by those who favour the idea of the mutual construction of worlds of 'intersubjectivity'.

(b) Participant Roles and the Micro-sociological Order

A second important way in which some of Goffman's ideas can contribute to our framework is through the distinctions he outlined with respect to interaction roles. For example, he distinguishes between overhearers and participants, the latter again sub-divided into non-ratified and ratified participants. McGregor (1983) has extended this kind of distinction for overhearers and 'eavesdroppers' and Levinson (1983) emphasises that such distinctions can contribute significantly towards the analysis of person deixis. If we wish to conceptualise and study distinctions between dyadic, triadic and polyadic contexts, Goffman's taxonomy of participant roles can serve as a useful theoretical starting point. Such an outline provides an illustrative taxonomy of player-parts and does so with reference to the dynamics of conversational contexts. We can, for example, use the categories, speaker, addressee and third party, not only as constructs to aid in our understanding of the ongoing dynamics of speaker moves, but as methods for guarding against the tendency towards 'speaker-centrism' which pragmatics and conversational analysis exhibits (e.g. see Humphrey-Jones, 1986).

(c) Dynamics of Interaction and Participation Immediacy
A third and final important element of Goffman's analysis, is his emphasis upon the dynamic conversational context, and in particular its sense of immediacy.

> 'Talk creates for the participants a world and a reality that has other participants in it. Joining spontaneous involvement is a unio-mystico, a socialized trance. We must also see that a conversation has a life of its own and makes demands on its own behalf. It is a little social system with its own boundary maintaining devices' (Goffman, 1967, p.113).

Giddens (1988) comments that participation itself 'presumes and calls forth a monitoring of each individual of the other's responses in relation to the context' (p.258). And so, on occasions where someone does something odd, this is recognised in an 'immediate' sense by those around precisely because such events or behaviours are taken as a display or sign that they are not quite under control. Again, Goffman (1963, p.16):

> 'We are clearly seen as agents of our acts—there being very little chance of disavowing having committed them; neither having given nor received messages can be easily denied, at least among those immediately involved ... in the presence of another ... every case of interaction thus has a confrontational nature, but it is one typically balanced and managed by the resources individuals mutually apply to ensure respect and consideration for one another' (p.16).

Suggestions of this kind help to highlight the conceptual distance between the notions of interactivity proposed in developmental psychology (e.g. McTear, 1985; Messer & Vietze, 1988) and the emphasis on dynamic participation suggested above. If nothing else it is somewhat difficult to argue that we simply decide to 'hold' off or claim 'time out' of participation while we engage in fairly complex sets of computational activities and inferences (i.e. necessitated by information processing models of interactivity). One final important way in which Goffman stressed the 'immediacy' and confrontational character of conversational contexts was through his suggestion that individuals are compelled to 'chronically display' agency to one another. Giddens (1988) argues this point on the strength of what happens in situations where an individual experiences a lapse of control and the concomitant display of 'response cries' which 'has the consequence of demonstrating to others awareness of the lapse, and that it is only a lapse, not a sign of generalized incompetence of bodily management' (Goffman, 1981, pp.101-103). The suggestion is that for the study of participation and social-cognitive development, a number of Goffman's ideas could be fruitfully adapted and considered alongside aspects of the ecological view. The notion of the doctrine of natural expression, the emphasis on role participation and role dynamics, and the outline of interdependent frames of interaction are all worthwhile candidates for consideration.

IDENTITY AND REPRESENTATION

In this section I wish to draw upon alternative philosophical/social theoretic accounts which might help contribute towards the 'eco-structural' framework, a framework aimed at better accommodating dynamic aspects of participation and 'internal' models of conversational activity. There is an important sense in which exposure to talk and speech/sound provides circumstances where the potential for conversation opens up. What is important about exposure to a social life within the conversational context, is the invitation (by virtue of one's humanness) to participate in its production. Exposure to and participation in talk both provides the young child with lessons in how conversational structures are parameterised and tutors her in the appropriate code/language for that cultural niche. Hacker (1972) points out that where learning language is concerned what is critical for the child is 'learning to recognize the circumstances justifying the use of an expression' (p.292).

Much of what has been argued thus far calls into question the formalistic and computationally inspired accounts of representation. As a response then to the limitations inherent to 'mentalistic' accounts there are two senses in which the account of representation suggested here has a bearing upon the dynamics of the conversational context. First representational processes are inherently *dynamic*. They find expression in, and are produced through, conversation or as Sinha (1988) puts it, *social-discursive processes*. Second, an account of representation, which accords with the occasion of conversation, could more fruitfully be based around notions of narrativity. This in turn has particular implications for contemporary ideas of identity.

In line with the argument that much of what is traditionally conceived as 'in the head' concept/category representational schemata being considerably more amorphous than we might wish to believe, serious consideration needs to be given to the relationship between the construction of 'representational processes and products' and engaging in talk i.e. dialogue. Wherever, and whatever else representational processes are (or whatever provides the basis for our inferences regarding the existence of representational states), they are instantiated and produced in and through the medium of conversation. There is a growing body of work which attends to assumptions of this nature, and examines the role that 'social-discursive' processes play in the construction of semiotic processes generally (e.g. Edwards & Mercer, 1986; Sinha, 1988; Walkerdine, 1987).

This is not meant to imply that we engage in talk so as to reinforce those representational beliefs we appear to possess, in the sense that these necessarily exist as forms of cognitive objects. Rather, it is precisely through the re-represention and production of dialogue and conversation that we construct for ourselves similar (or only slightly varying) stories/narratives such that their justifiable and warrantable status as cognitive objects is assured. In other words, our representations are always expressed along appropriate formulations given the social-cultural status accruing to the possession of representational categories (i.e. what we infer we must cognise as representations where we listen/monitor our own talk and internal dialogue).

Certainly for adults, one important proviso here is the ability to engage in productive dialogue with oneself (i.e. thinking). One can note with somewhat amusing curiosity that even when one is on one's own there are numerous instances of verbally rehearsing what it is you are thinking about (or 'conversing' with oneself). And it is striking that only by asking yourself a particular kind of question do you realise that you possess the answer and in fact must have 'known' it all along. In order then to see something or learn that in fact you know about it, you must at some level engage in what looks like a 'dialogic' process. Representational activity, where this is to be considered as cognitive activity has simply got a lot more to do with conversational/dialogic processes than has previously been recognised. The emphasis upon the production of representational processes and the role of the dynamic participation (that is, particularly in the 'unfolding' sense inherent to ongoing conversations) may be better understood with reference to ideas of narrativity and identity, ideas which have yet to find much favour within mainstream cognitive science.

We might note further that in the latter half of the twentieth century, philosophy has been particularly concerned with the problematic status surrounding notions of truth and identity (particularly European philosophy), which is beginning to exert some influence upon contemporary psychology (e.g. Feldman & Bruner, 1987). The conceptualist tradition (e.g. Quine, Shoemaker) develops accounts of identity which Reason (1984) asserts 'dwells upon a conception of identity which has its place in a world of substitutes, counterfeits and imposters':

> 'The paradigm here is that of personal deception: I claim that I am Mickey Mouse—but is that my true identity, or is the claimant actually someone else? In this tradition, there is less concern with the contents of identity—with what it means to have a genuine or authentic identity—and more concern with the conditions which must obtain for us to be satisfied that the question of genuine identity properly arises' (pp.10-11).

Narrativity may play an important role here, that is, it is only through the narrative construction of those material presuppositions which support conversations (and which are themselves derived from a matrix of everyday social practice) that any account of representational activity is justifiable. As an example of the importance and permeating nature of such material presuppositions, Reason (1984) cites Sacks's (1980) exegetical example, 'The baby cried. The mummy picked it up', where although we are told nothing about whether the baby and the mother were related, whether it actually stopped crying, whether it was lying in a cot and so on, all such 'material presuppositions'[4] come into play and provide for an understanding of the unfolding text (even in such a simple example). He points out:

> 'Narratives for which I can invent no material presuppositions are narratives grounded in systems of social practice with which I am radically unfamiliar, either directly in participation, or indirectly in knowledge. Such narratives are (for me) not followable, they are incoherent, unintelligible, unutterably alien' (p.15).

What is important is that the dynamics of conversation and the concomitant notions of identity and representation can only be understood historically (that is, in their following). Reason (1984) suggests that the understanding of any given text requires the comprehension of a series of inter-nested co-texts and in the same way:

> ' ... narratives require the co-text of an available social life; context is the representation of a co-text that can serve as a basis for material

presupposition within discourse which will also provide for a narrative understanding ... and ... Given the commitment to narrativity, narratives can be taken to generate material presuppositions in the course of their following' (p.12).

Particularly noteworthy here is that such narrative representations are predicated on notions of identity far removed from discussion of an idealised epistemic subject, thus calling into question realist notions of subjectivity/objectivity. Reason (1984) comments:

'It is this sense of identity as chronically open to challenge that also informs the vertiginous [dizzying] and skilful vision of the ethnomethodologists (and particularly the conversational analysts such as Sacks [1980].) All social identities are, for them, so vulnerable that we lose sight of any substantial, content-full identity in the obsession with making provision for and displaying a rational social world—one person's incisive 'doing' is another's potential reaction' (p.21, note 10).

It is conceivable then to argue for a view of identity and representation which, while drawing upon the institutional basis of social practices and everyday procedures (material presuppositions), at the same time provides a link with the importance of participation in conversation. And specifically, those conversational scenarios which make possible and support coherence and narrativity. It also highlights a link between notions of identity and notions of 'self'. It has been argued that the underlying 'self' has no enduring description, but is simply the human capacity for negotiating various performances and transformations (Collins, 1988). Goffman might have claimed that the self is much more akin to a subset of pre-dispositions or expectations of particular role scenarios. Collins (1988) comments:

'We are compelled to have an individual self, not because we actually have one but because social interaction requires us to act as if we do ... The self is only real as a symbol, a linguistic concept that we use to account for what we and other people do. It is an ideology of everyday life, used to attribute causality and moral responsibility in our society, just as in societies with a denser (e.g. tribal) structure, moral responsibility is not placed within the individual but attributed to spirits or gods' (p.50).

Understandably, those who persevere with the dominant theoretical orientations in developmental social cognition are unlikely to embrace many of the criticisms voiced in the earlier chapters unless alternative options are made available. Not only must more effort be made in making alternatives more readily understood, but additionally they need show how they could provide richer conceptual tools for the work in hand. A first and important step is to recognise that there are now sufficiently developed theoretical formulations of representation available, which can begin to accommodate dynamic and 'participative' aspects of interaction.

IMPLICATURE AND INTENTIONALITY

One of the primary questions arising out of our consideration of the dynamics of conversations and the recognition of affordances in such contexts, is how the infant and young child learn to utilise the predictability and projectibility of talk (conversational contexts). There are two conspicuous routes for this kind of learning: learning as participant and learning as a non-participant (but ratified observer). As a participant one can learn, through the self-monitoring of the range of successful and unsuccessful responses to communicative overtures, to provide the 'affordance' structures of talk—the structuration of talk. As a non-participant one can learn to recognise and utilise the information available in overheard and overseen contexts. Both elements are crucial components of what must be needed in order to learn what has been termed 'conversational implicature' (Grice, 1957). The argument here is that it is this nexus (between participation and overhearing) which lies at the heart of the emergence of social-cognitive skills. Understanding the processes involved requires some consideration of the role of intentionality and implicature.

In this fifth and final area of this proposed framework, the central ideas emerge from Grice's work (Grice, 1981), and in particular the notion of implicature. Conversational implicature at a general level can be defined as the force associated with the recognition (by the listener) of the intention (the speaker's) to communicate (see Levinson, 1983). While a detailed and complete outline of Grice's work has not been published, Grice and a number of other writers have outlined the principles in detail (Brown & Levinson, 1978; Grice, 1981; Taylor & Cameron, 1987), a consideration of which is beyond the scope of this volume. It is noteworthy that there have been few explicitly rationalist accounts of conversational behaviour within pragmatics and Grice's work has inspired a range of developments within linguistics, sociology and psychology (Brown & Levinson, 1978; Gazdar, 1979; Sperber & Wilson, 1986). Grice argues that interactional purposes are fulfilled through an orientation participants have to a fundamental conversational principle, outlined along such maxims as:

'make your conversational contribution such as is required, at the stage at which it occurs, by the accepted purpose or direction of the talk exchange in which you are engaged' (Grice, 1981, p.45).

Grice outlines various maxims and sub-maxims to which speakers and listeners orient their understanding (be relevant and so on), such that they are particularly sensitive to whether such maxims are being flouted or not and will employ conversational strategies with reference to this recognition. The somewhat complex picture proposed nonetheless provides a logically coherent account of the orderliness of everyday conversation. The Gricean account is, if nothing else, a principled defence of the 'rationalist' position regarding social behaviour, that is, the argument that conversation and related interactional rules are not merely derivable from accounts of social convention but are based on *a priori* rational principles.[5]

While Grice's work addresses a range of issues, the theme which is of concern to us here is implicature and intentionality. That is, whatever else communication might be, its purpose is achieved in part through being recognised as such (as an attempt to communicate) and the very recognition of intention is a central part of any theory of speaker meaning. From this view it is clear that we need to be aware of a particular distinction between speaking and communication, in that although speaking (and being exposed to speech) can be conceived of as a process whereby opportunities for 'conversation' are made available (to both speakers and listeners), communication (at least verbal) must combine speech with clear indications of intention (i.e. the display of intentional signals). Speaking is not conversation, and recognising the communicative affordances inherent in talk may be linked to a distinction between hearing the sounds of speech, and listening to and recognising talk.

The recognition of intentionality and how it relates to conversational implicature, has a particular bearing upon the dynamics of conversational contexts, in part because such an analysis will assist in crossing the divide between positions taken by conversational analysts (those who have sought to uncover the regularities of talk) and research in intentionality which has concentrated more on utterance interpretation. Of specific importance to our concerns is how the study of intentionality and implicature has been taken up in child language or developmental pragmatics. We can note in particular the research of Dore (1983) and Ryan (1974).

Dore's (1979, 1983) theoretical framework is based in part upon Garfinkel (1967) and Schutz (1962). Garfinkel's ethnomethodological approach outlines principles of accountability which form the background for the production and comprehension of our everyday conversations, such as background relevancies, mutual display, sequencing, and procedural interpretation—see Garfinkel (1967). Aligned to this and based upon the behavioural descriptions (see Stern, 1974) emphasising imitation and complementarity Dore (1983) argues that a parent's interventions in, and interpretation of affect expressions transform the child's affect displays from what can be viewed as 'intending-in' forms, to 'intending-to' expressions. Snow and Galbraith (1983) comment that Dore's work is a much too infrequent explanatory account of how it is that a young infant moves from expressions of affect to first word use.

The origins of words he says, occurs in the immediate context of affective conflict, 'arising as solutions to maintain and negotiate relations through dialogue—the affective inputs to intentionality and reference'. Dore (1983) argues that the first words should be construed as the acquisition of accountable objects, 'the word acquired is not merely the symbolic consequence of intentional development—it is the consequence of interpreted intentions particularly, B's (the child's) intending expressions are interpreted accountable by A (the parent)' (p.178).

Dore (1983) argues that over time the mother's interpretations move from making inferences about what the child is doing (e.g. manipulating objects) as intention-to-act to the interpretation of actions as intention-to-convey. An important phase in the transition from pre-linguistic to linguistic communication concerns a move from 'intending-in' expressions to 'intending-to' expressions. Dore (1983) glosses over problematic distinction regarding 'individualistic' or 'social' theories of mind by focusing on the affective relations between adult and child. Although this succeeds to some degree, there is a major shortcoming in that he starts from the position of the child's separability from the mother and then seeks to address the issue of how the child strives to maintain contact. It is equally logical to argue that as far as the child is concerned she has no notion of 'separability' in the first place, and in contrast may be considerably surprised when she gradually realises that she is a separate entity from her mother/father.

In other words, there is a problem here in that Dore begins from the position that the child's earliest cognitions are of being separate, and subsequently her motivations are to overcome the stress of individuation. Uncertainty, ambiguity and anxiety are reduced by being able to express states, needs, etc. by unequivocal symbols, Dore argues, and to do so the child is motivated to learning first words. Dore (1983) draws out the distinction between affect indexicals (early crying and delight sounds, e.g. squeals of glee and so on, normally dominated by gesture and tones of associated affect) and formal indexicals (i.e. early words) and asks 'what occurs between infant and parent that transforms the indexical into a word?'. We might also ask, what is it about parent-child actions and practices which allow some sounds to become words (and other sounds not)? And so the question is not how A communicates to her separate child B, so much as how AB become differentiated such that B (the child) becomes a distinct language-using ego entity. In Dore's theory the status of the epistemic subject is assured from the beginning.

Three questions are posed by Dore (1983). First, what is the influence of the parent's culture on the child's mind? Second, what is the influence of parents' socialised actions on the child's motivated actions and third, what is the influence of child's needs on the parent's responses? Before we can ask the first we need to ask, what practices and procedures lead the parent to interpreting the child's actions 'as if' she possesses motivated intentions and from which, others infer that she now possesses a 'mind of her own'? Before asking the second we need to examine how the young child acquires those skills necessary to display her recognition of the mother's intentionality, as well as how she then herself manages to display the intention to communicate (why does the mother accept some potentially implicative displays as intentional and not others?). We have yet to adequately answer the question of how the young child communicates to the parent that action X is to be read as intentional (recognised accordingly, within the appropriate normative conventions of accountability and so on), and contrastingly, how she learns when actions will not be deemed as intentional.

Finally, in an earlier study aimed at raising the issue of intentionality, Ryan (1974) provides a framework for the analysis and description of communicative skills that the child acquires in the first two years of life. She stressed that monologic models of communication did not explain the 'structure of intersubjectivity' that makes the application of 'linguistic codes' possible. Ryan argues that before 'true' language emerges two themes are important (a) the change from predominantly expressive or emotional use of words to their factual or descriptive use and (b) the change from pre-symbolic (words as attributes of objects) to full symbolic use. However, she points out (as Dore, 1983) that accounts of language neglect the affective environment in which the child develops. We fail to pay enough attention to the context of utterances, that is with particular reference to the adult's motivations to understand the child's utterances. Infants are provided with numerous examples where parents comment, interpret, misinterpret and extend their attempted utterances (Feagans, Robinson, & Anderson, 1988). Ryan

(1974) argues that 'it is the active interpretative process which is critical' and that the role of intentionality remains barely understood. In her analysis of the child's earliest gropings at word meaning she suggests:

> 'Grices's analysis of acts of communication as crucially dependent on the recognition of various complex intentions, makes it intelligible how in various limiting cases the standard meaning of words etc, is a dispensable element. The major problem then arises of identifying and describing the kinds of intentions involved, and how the necessary mutual recognition develops' (p.210).

In support of this argument Ryan (1974) points out that one important issue in language acquisition is the child's making noises such that adults interpret these as attempts to speak, with three related elements (a) key aspects of the utterance, such that adults make available examples of what is to be taken as 'conventional usage' through systematic interpretation of child's intonational use; (b) key elements accompanying the utterance, pointing, gesture, searching (e.g. Collis & Schaffer, 1975) and (c) the particular circumstances of the utterance. One example of the way in which interpretation must be related to such features of language use is the observation that non-standard sounds are often identified as the 'child's word for something':

> 'Even when they are uninterpretable, the grounds for giving an uninterpretable but persistent sound the 'status' of a 'word' for the child appear to lie in other features of the utterance, ... the existence of 'non-standard' words which cannot be explained as deviant imitations, implies that the child has learnt something about speech, independent of specific forms learnt from adult speech. She appears to have learnt something general about the notion of a word, as regards its circumstance and manner of usage, that is not tied to any particular actual instance' (p.202).

What is interesting about this position is Ryan's (1974) recognition that as far as the child is concerned, what matters is not so much whether she has used the correct word (i.e. been correctly interpreted), but that she is interpreted at all. Ryan reminds us that the 'context of rich interpretation' made available by parents, when viewed in combination with the considerable variability and ambiguity of one-word utterances, 'provides an extremely informative situation for the child as regards what she is taken to be meaning'.

This concluding theme in the framework highlights the problematic nature of intentionality, and in particular how it is that the young infant begins to recognise attempts to communicate (implicature) and subsequently learns how to display to others these intentions. One of the most important elements will be the opportunities that children have to watch and listen how others exhibit such intentions in their ongoing interactions. Critical also will be the child's ability to recognise under what circumstances utterances will be read as justifiably intentional or not.

OUTLINING THE ECO-STRUCTURAL FRAMEWORK

One important goal in setting out the various themes above was to articulate a way in which we can begin to consider less formally constrained 'meta-theoretical' frameworks. As a conceptual matrix the intention is to provide a series of reference points both to highlight complementarity between themes and to articulate points of contrastiveness and potential contradiction. A point which was emphasised in Chapter 1 was that we are too often unaware of the implicit criteria we employ when selecting this or that model or metaphor for our investigations. Arguing for a move away from contemporary approaches in social-cognitive developmental research involves questioning assumptions at a various number of levels, and while this outline has not attempted to present a 'formal case' it has sought to draw out what might be the more important issues.

By way of introducing and emphasising the focus on children's participation skills, this chapter began with a consideration of some of the current concerns of social cognition and language research. This provided a way into arguing for an 'internal' account of conversational skill, linked to a number of meta-theoretical, conceptual and methodological issues and the eco-structural framework outlined in Figure 5.1. Discussion of this then began with a look at the ecological approach, where possibly the most important issues to arise is the concept of an affordance and what this might contribute to the study of conversation. Considerable emphasis was placed on the sense of potential and the dynamics inherent to conversations.

In turn, the idea of the recognition of structural affordances in talk helped introduce the potential contribution of the ethnomethodologically inspired conversational analysts. Here a number of themes were developed, in particular a consideration of the very orderliness of talk and how participants themselves appear to be oriented towards providing and recognising regularity and related 'affordance' phenomena. Again, this helped establish a number of points of reference for the third section where the advantages of certain aspects of Goffman's micro-sociological approach were highlighted. Goffman's views may not only contribute significantly to the theoretical impoverishment of certain ethological approaches in developmental psychology but in addition provide (by way of the three levels of frame analysis) an additional complementary theme to the notion of affordance structure, and the very recognisability of role relations during participation.

The fourth and fifth themes addressed problematic issues concerning identity, representation and intentionality. There is clearly some difficulty in outlining alternative conceptions of these constructs, that is where there is a requirement to move away from a number of the more established positions in developmental psychology. With reference to identity and representation the aim here is to outline ways in which we might construct representational accounts which provide a theoretically coherent basis for developing models which focus upon the dynamic and participatory aspects of conversation (i.e. narrativity and the monitoring of coherence in talk). Likewise, while rationalist accounts might contribute towards our understanding of intentionality and implicature, what is required are more considered accounts of how young infants begin to recognise and then display intention. The eco-structural framework is one formulation of how these various factors might be considered.

NOTES

1. One example of this is described by Schegloff and Sacks (1973) in their examination of the use of the 'adjacency pair' in conversation. The specific way in which the adjacency pair sequence is employed requires that the first utterance of such a pair is recognised as having a particular 'first pair part' status. So if a participant wished to methodically provide for 'closing section implicativeness', that is indicate quite clearly that she is concerned to move towards providing the opportunities for initiating those distinct patterns identifiable as closing sections of conversation, then there are highly conventional and immediately recognisable procedures for doing this. Participants themselves then are sensitive to the existence and provision of such 'affordance' structures in conversations.

2. Baron (1980) appeals to unconscious or 'instinctual' aspects of affordance recognition, arguing that 'even in contexts where recognition of degraded perceptual information (of person through walking gait)'—the most accurate observers were—'unable to specify the type of informational invariant they were using to make their judgements ... it may be argued that judgements about causality or impression formation which emerge spontaneously in the course of online interactions may well occur at a tacit level rather than involve a conscious decision-making process' (p.597).

3. In Barbadian a popular way to insult somebody is to speak with somebody (while clearly in earshot of your intended target) in a very ironic and sarcastic way about the third person.

4. Reason (1984) comments that in order to establish a firm basis for any rational consideration of a given topic, we should orient our reading or interpretation of (said) topic towards those 'material presuppositions' necessitated by our species specific requirements (evolutionary narratives). The very existence of humankind grounds such presuppositions as 'real' premises.

5. Grice while adhering to rational principles nevertheless seems to recognise the normative basis of implicature 'the notion of value is absolutely critical to the idea of rationality or of a rational being. A rational creature is one who evaluates ... and all naturalistic attempts at the characterization of rationality are doomed to failure' (Grice, 1982, p.237).

CHAPTER SIX

Illustrating the Framework: Overhearing and the Development of Social-cognitive Skills

INTRODUCTION

The previous chapter outlined a framework which could assist in the development of more appropriate models of children's social-cognitive skills. The principal reason why this supporting conceptual framework might provide more realisable models, compared to those I discussed earlier (Chapters 2–4), is the pre-eminent concern with understanding the nature of dynamic participation. One way to ascertain the scope, salience and adequacy of the eco-structural framework is with reference to a specific model. In the next three chapters I consider a model of overhearing, in particular how overhearing and (more generally), exposure to 'overhearing contexts', bears upon the young child's developing social-cognitive skills.

Consider the suggestion that the young child's social-cognitive participation skills are related to the affordances of talk. That is, participation skills are dependent upon (and emergent within) the social-cognitive information provided in various overhearing contexts. There are a number of different levels in which this notion of conversational affordance can be developed, for example, the information available about the social status and influence of participants, information about the orientation of conversationalists to the ongoing development of the talk, the degree to which engaging in certain kinds of dialogue styles will make available some and not other possibilities in talk (e.g. for learning or affective dimensions), the recognition of intentionality and so on. Not least is the question of the processes and circumstances surrounding participation *per se*, that is, the role of overhearing for the children's social-cognitive skills: whether, for example, the child is engaged in talk as a participant or as a non-participant. There is clearly a difference between participants and bystanders, and this distinction warrants closer attention. Goffman (1976) asks us to pay more attention to the specific role of speaker/listener and participant, where he distinguishes different listener roles:

' ... those who overhear whether or not their unratified participation is inadvertent and whether or not it has been encouraged; those who are ratified participants but (in the case of more than two-person talk) are not specifically addressed by the speaker; and those ratified participants who are addressed that is, oriented to by the speaker in a manner to suggest that his words are particularly for them, and that some answer is therefore anticipated from them, more so than for other ratified participants' (p.260).

Developing Goffman's (1976) distinction between non-ratified and ratified overhearing bystanders, McGregor (1983) suggests that 'eavesdroppers' comprehend their own roles as listeners depending on whether they know neither, one or more than one of the participants in exchanges they overhear. The skills of the hearer, McGregor (1983) argues is 'fundamental to our understanding of conversational activity' (p.302) and only recently has this become a major concern in linguistics and conversational analysts (e.g. Humphrey-Jones, 1986). Others have pointed out that as analysts we are overconcerned with the speaker utterance to a degree which mitigates against our understanding communication:

'Ours is a speakers' civilization and our linguistics has accordingly concerned itself almost solely with the speaker's problems. This accounts for the rise of generative grammar and the prestige attached to this particular facet of the speech process. The skilful speaker wins praise; the skilful listener despite the mystery of this achievement is ignored' (Parker-Rhodes, 1978, p.XIII).

There are a few studies within cognitive and developmental psychology which address issues surrounding overhearing. Schober and Clark (1989) and Clark and Schaefer (1987) discuss the role of meaning and discourse, with reference to the roles of overhearer or addressee, suggesting that the process of understanding is dependent upon participant roles in such contexts. Oshima-Takane (1988) considers the child's understanding of deictic terms by considering what they learn from speech not addressed to them directly (i.e. what they overhear) and Farr, Braines, Aquirre-Hauchbaum, and Salvador (1986) argue that overhearing parental disparagement has a deleterious effect upon children's subsequent aggressive behaviour. Given that the listener and overhearer account for at least half of any 'interaction equation' there may be an object lesson in looking at what might be involved.

Speaking is not conversation, and recognising the communicative affordances inherent in talk may be linked to a distinction between hearing the sounds of speech and listening to talk. Talk provides opportunities for conversation and successful participation implies a social-cognitive skill which may be better explained, or at least investigated, from principles of detection and recognition rather than construction. The mechanisms described within conversational analysis (such as gaining the floor or conceiving talk as turn constructional units) help to highlight its dynamic projectability. In other words, participants are particularly adept at knowing when turns at talk change, or when a topic is foregrounded or presupposed, how to maintain topical coherence (and recognise when coherence is not being maintained), and so on, all to a degree which defies explanations based on information processing accounts. For example, according to Clark and Haviland (1977), in order to establish 'common ground', hearers must be able to listen, decode and interpret communication attempts against a cognitive model. However, this cannot accommodate findings which document the sophisticated nature of children's communicative skills at an early age (e.g. Craig & Washington, 1986; Dunn & Shatz, 1989). It is more likely that the structural formalities of talk convey or provide directly available 'affordances' such that the recognition of communicative intention is cognised in a much more immediate sense.

Thus, the child's entry into the social world is intrinsically tied to the affordances of that world. Observing and overhearing contributes directly to the acquisition of the skills necessary for participation and can theoretically, be distinguished from overhearing and overseeing, as self-monitoring. The notion of 'affordance' and the detection and extraction of information is re-formulated here with reference to the young child's ability to detect socially significant information.

It was suggested in the previous chapter that the precise and subtle mechanisms identifiable in everyday talk presuppose a relationship between participation (skill) in conversation, and the motivating characteristic of talk itself. In an important sense, the very immediacy of conversation both provides for, and demands, a level of social interaction which is both highly predictable (demonstrated by people's ability to recognise the next turn of talk in very subtle ways), yet offering or indicating the potential for unforeseen, and yet to be realised, new forms of social interaction. In a similar sense to the argument that perception of any environment is intimately linked to both movement within it, and the affordances it offers, perception of and participation in, conversational interaction is related both to the taking part, and to what such contexts afford. The very predictability and projectability of conversation implicates the presence of 'affordances'.

What then are the 'affordances' of talk? Can we identify invariant and transformational structures within conversation ? How do we learn to extract or recognise the socially derived 'meaning' of their appearance or absence (change, consistency and pervasiveness within contexts)? By focusing on overhearing contexts it may be possible to highlight structural aspects of social-cognitive information which in turn, could allow us to examine the relationship between overhearing and the detection of socially significant information. As non-participating overhearers and observers (and for young infants, in large part, this precedes any sense of participation) I would like to consider three distinguishing characteristics of overhearing: overhearing as happenstance, chance or opportunity; overhearing as attention focusing and overhearing as conversation monitoring or tracking. I will examine each in some detail, both analytically and in light of evidence which lends support to such a characterisation of overhearing and its relation to developmental social-cognitive skills. The remainder of this chapter considers the characteristics of overhearing as 'happenstance', chance and exposure to opportunity.

OVERHEARING AS 'HAPPENSTANCE', CHANCE OR OPPORTUNITY

There are a number of situations where simply by chance, one happens to be in the vicinity of people such that their talk is overheard. Goffman's (1981) mapping of the distinctions between ratified, non-ratified and 'eavesdropping' participants can serve as one useful starting point and one that is employed in Barbadian contexts to fulfil quite specific purposes (Fisher, 1976). McGregor's (1983) extension of the notion of eavesdropping along dimensions of listener familiarity highlighted a number of important issues, not least the observation that the comments his 'eavesdropping' subjects made 'demonstrated something of the enormous variety of variables and their interdependencies which everyday talk must involve' (p.302). With infants and young children, there are two senses in which I wish to consider overhearing as happenstance that is in line with the notion of exposure to social-cognitive conversational affordances: (a) exposure to participation, that is, overhearing as opportunity for the detection and extraction of social cues and conventions and (b) the relationship between social information and overhearing—as structural/sociometric information available in the child's linguistic environment.

(a) Exposure to Participation

With the former, when one is overhearing a conversation between two others (whether known or unknown), one is being given impromptu lessons in what is possible (in terms of social interaction) between people. It is not simply a case of hearing the forms of language or learning about turn-taking, or whatever. In addition, the parameters of social interaction (as far as the infant is concerned) are both being demonstrated and defined, through being acted out. There is clearly a historical precedence with certain aspects of this suggestion, in what was traditionally known as *incidental* and *vicarious* learning. A series of experiments during the 1960s by Bandura and colleagues (Bandura & Barab, 1969; Bandura, Grusec, & Menlove, 1966; Bandura, Ross, & Ross, 1961) suggested that simple exposure to examples of behaviour subsequently led to an increased amount of similar imitative behaviour by children (that is compared to contexts where there was no exposure). This remains one of the most frequently cited research paradigms where the concern with the deleterious effects of 'passive observation' and overhearing (e.g. studies into the effects of television). However a combination of unease with representational explanatory accounts[1] and the problematic status of incidental learning itself, resulted in this line of research becoming somewhat marginal to mainstream psychology, particularly given the upcoming prominence of cognitive/representational psychology in the early 1970s.

Overhearing and overseeing as examples of, and lessons in, what is likely to take between humans, is important in the sense of gaining exposure to contexts necessary for learning or detecting the affordances of social interaction. By watching what others are doing, one gains experience then, not only of those linguistic forms specific to the interface of social interaction and language (and it is hard to imagine how one learns deictic terms such as 'I/You' shifts except by watching and hearing others—Oshima-Takane, 1988), but also lessons in the negotiation of topic, power, status, beliefs, and so on. The parameters of social practice are provided for the overheard/overseeing child in the sense that others' conversations/social interactions provide the 'structural affordance' matrix, within which the child's recognition and display skills will later become established. Dunn and Kendrick (1982) and Dunn (1988) report on a number of longitudinal observational studies which looked in detail at the circumstances surrounding early adult-child interactions where siblings are introduced into families (what occurs after the birth of a second child). One of the most consistent findings of these studies was the fact that both younger and older siblings are particularly sensitive to observing and overhearing the interactions of others. Dunn (1988) comments:

> 'They monitor with interest the relations between others, comment and intervene in the interactions of others, co-operate with others in conflict against a third, and are able to use one family member against another. They understand something of the shared nature of family rules and of the distinctions by which such rules can be employed in different situations' (p.72).

The role of overhearing as exposure to social convention and practice is also implicated with reference to linguistic form. Romaine (1989) considers the social functions achieved through code-switching in bilingual contexts (e.g. Scotton & Ury, 1977). She points out that in Norway at the post-office or bank although the local dialect would be employed for everyday chit-chat, when it comes to the business at hand, then the official 'formal' use of Norwegian is required. Within sociolinguistics and social anthropology studies document such code-switching which follows quite specific social-functional and pragmatic goals. Romaine (1989) notes there are clear parallels between code-switching and forms of interaction in monolingual communities, citing Goffman's (1981) notion of changes in 'footing' during participation. Furthermore, and notwithstanding the cognitive/linguistic implications of code-switching in bilingual contexts for language acquisition, the infant and young child is learning a lot more than simple exposure to the sound of language form. Overhearing of such events and procedures demonstrates to a young child, not just what is possible, but what is probable, that is what is likely to take place given the particular context. In time, the young child recognises the opportunities accruing to specific forms of social interaction and the social conventions and norms achieved through the employment of distinct patterns of talk. This aspect of early exposure to participation and interaction contexts remains unexplored, and there are a number of ways in which methods could be employed to uncover how and and in what ways children utilise the range of 'impromptu lessons' provided for them (e.g. one approach would be to consider the different ways in which hearing and deaf children learn from watching and listening to others, i.e. using alternative sign-systems).

(b) Overhearing Contexts and the Social Information: A Study

Moving to the second form of 'happenstance' and overhearing, overhearing in group contexts (over time) exposes an individual to patterns of speech which contain information regarding the relationships between the people who make up such groups. One form of speech which is intimately tied to the social-pragmatic and role relations between people is deixis. The most critical element for the comprehension of deictic terms is understanding the use of such language forms within specific utterance contexts. Without directly cognising central features of the discourse/temporal context, possible ambiguities surrounding deictic expressions such as 'I/you'; 'here/there'; 'his/hers' cannot be resolved. The study of the young child's acquisition of deictic terms continues to engage considerable research effort, in part because such language forms offer one way to examine the relationship between language acquisition and socio-cognitive abilities (Brener, 1983; Collis, 1990; Oshima-Takane, 1988; Tanz, 1980; Wales, 1979). With reference to overhearing and the detection of social information, one interesting form of deixis for our purposes is third party (or person) reference, where one person addresses another about a third party (and our concerns here exclude the use of the third person pronoun in dyadic contexts).

Consider the situation where a speaker addresses a listener and refers to a third party who is present and, in Goffman's (1981) terms, a ratified participant. Adequate comprehension of third party reference at the very least entails the simultaneous cognisance between the speaker and listener of the existence of the third party being referred-to. Further, in order to argue that this comprehension is a 'beyond the dyad' or 'triadic' social-cognitive skill (involving participation strategies unique to the interactions between three people), it is necessary to draw the distinction between the actual presence or absence of the third party. The use of third party reference during an exclusively 'dyadic' encounter is akin to object reference and, therefore, there is nothing intrinsically 'triadic' about the interchange. However, reference in the presence of the third party (and ignoring those rare occasions where the third party is present but at a great distance—arguably equivalent to absence) may involve social interaction routines (such as alternating eye-gaze, intonational cues, or body postures and so on) distinct to the ongoing triadic interaction. More generally, other intrinsically triadic forms of speech, such as 'digs', are very familiar to us. The very nature of understanding a 'dig' from a recipient's perspective entails knowing that a speaker's supposed normal comment to another addressee in her presence is, in fact, directed at the recipient. The 'dig' achieves a good deal of its normative force precisely from the recognition of all concerned that the overhearer is 'formally' a non-ratified participant. What is important here, as well as being one route into examining the relation between overhearing and social structure information, is a consideration of the fact that from the young child's perspective, overhearing her own and other children's names being referred to in specific ways within particular contexts (e.g. association of friendliness between peers), could be significant in some way. This is especially the case in the pre-school setting (examined below), given that this is most likely to be the child's first introduction to a large-group context.

Studies have borrowed ideas and methods from ethology and sociometry in order to examine forms of social structure in play-group and classroom contexts (Chase, 1984; Smith & Connolly, 1980). Abromvitch (1980), for example, has identified both dominance hierarchies (based on frequencies of dyadic interactions between children) and 'attention structures' (indices of who pays most attention to whom) in the pre-school playgroup, arguing that such attention indices provide the most accurate picture of the children's interactions. Vaughen and Waters (1980) emphasise hierarchical structures in the pre-school playgroup, hierarchies of dominance in terms of who is attended to by other members of the group. By carefully assessing the amount of attention one would expect for each child, compared to the frequencies that were observed, Vaughen and Williams (1980) found that each child's interest seemed drawn towards those children to whom her peers paid the most attention to. In other words there was a consensus of attention, or an attention structure.

In multi-party or 'polyadic' situations then, naming is 'attention orienting' and can have particular significance for overhearing children. Piaget (1929) was one of the first to draw attention to the significance of naming (especially proper name usage) for young children, which from their perspective almost had a magical dimension. What is of interest to me here, is the role of overhearing and naming, particularly in that it is not simply the fact of overhearing your name which might be important (to the child), but also the way in which your name is used. Being addressed and at the same time being paired with (through the act of reference) another particular child, encompasses an 'information' dimension concerning the roles and relationships individuals have with one another.

For example, compare the social information implicated where a child overhears an adult addressing another child with 'Johnny, leave Peter alone, he's being a naughty boy today ... ', and 'Johnny, is Peter your best friend?' Beyond the observation that while such talk might serve for the adult the purpose of changing, or calling attention to, the behaviour of a third party, for other 'non-ratified' participant overhearers such talk makes available an important source of information. Through overhearing particular patterns of third party reference utterances, the child is being exposed to a verbal environment which 'ties' children together in particular ways and therefore could enhance their awareness of the social structure of the pre-school and their positions within it. Given that we know little of the selectivity of the children's attention to the social environment, the suggestion here is that overhearing names (especially your own in relation to somebody else) will be particularly significant for the young child. It is possible that via exposure to third party reference utterances, in particular 'addressee-referred-to child' associative patterns, over a period of time and across various contexts, could very well provide an 'attention structure' for the members of the playgroup as a whole. Patterns of name association may provide the requisite social information upon which certain 'social-structure' affordances of group contexts could be based.

Given my emphasis on the nature of overhearing and the possible relationship to the young child's comprehension of third party reference speech, the remainder of this chapter reports an observational study looking at the frequency, form and function of adult-to-child forms. The study took place in two nursery school settings in Glasgow, one a pre-school playgroup, the other a day nursery. Throughout the study, among the questions addressed were; what is the amount, form and content of adult-to-child third party reference speech in the pre-school nursery; what are the speech-act functions of adult-to-child third party reference speech; what are the adults doing with these forms of speech, and do the tasks performed relate in any way to the child's actions (what are the children doing when they overhear these forms)? The primary aim, however, was to consider whether a young child could 'build up' a picture of the social structure she is part of through overhearing particular patterns of third party reference spoken by the adults, that is, can a social network or sociometric picture be identified in overheard talk?

Method

Setting
Over a 10 month period, an observational study was carried out in two pre-school nurseries in Glasgow. One was attached to the University of Strathclyde, the other run by the local authority as a day nursery. Over 2000 examples of adult-to-child third person reference and group

addressing speech (used for the analysis described in Chapter 7) were collected and analysed. The particular pre-school nurseries were chosen because of their very similar environments. Both consisted of one very large room where approximately 15–20 children would be present, attended by at least 2 adults at any one time. While the nursery regimes were somewhat different overall, where the local authority nursery had a more restricted regime, the observational hours sampled ensured cross comparisons of periods where the activities in each nursery were the same. The speech of 6 adults was recorded (2 in the first nursery and 4 in the second) over 106 observational hours which ensured a representative picture of the everyday talk in the pre-schools.

Subjects
The subjects were 6 adult females (2 in one setting and 4 from the other), whose ages ranged from 19–34. As for the children, in the university nursery their ages ranged from 3 to 5.5, and in the local authority from 2 to 4.9. Roughly equal numbers of boys and girls were present in each nursery. No children appeared to have particular language comprehension difficulties, although there were a small number of bilingual children in the university nursery.

Observational Methods
A pilot study established that the average number of instances of adult-to-child third party reference was between 18 and 20 occurrences per hour. The loudness of the adult's speech and the pitch of the voice used, meant that the speech could be easily recorded in the form of field notes at the time of occurrence. A 'focal-animal' observational method (Altmann, 1974) was employed where, for each adult hour observed, the observer would focus on one adult and record each instance of third party reference as it occurred, as well as recording the complete hour of adult talk with a tape-recorder. In practice, the observer could unobtrusively follow the 'focal adult', ensuring that all her speech was recorded on tape, as well as via field notes. Support for the belief that the staff in general ignored the presence of the observer (who adopted a non-participatory stance throughout) comes from observation that, after the first week or so, the staff would 'lose their tempers' occasionally with the children in a natural fashion. The observer also recorded which child was addressed, who was being referred to, their respective ages, and the size and activities of the group or groups they were part of.[2]

Results
The proposal was that by attending to how she is referred-to in relation to other individuals, (e.g. as a friend or rival, as belonging to the same

or different groups, in a favourable or unfavourable light and so on) a child could build up a picture of how others perceive her as fitting into the social network, in greater detail than would be available in speech directed to her individually (that is via talk which does not refer to others). Overhearing contexts provide social structure information through exposure to the non-random patterns of role-relationship association, made available to the children through the adult's use of third party reference.

Analysis of the adults' examples of third party reference established that over 50% of the time, the adults would explicitly name the child referred-to and the primary function of the speech was directive (pay attention to X or behave like Y). Overhearing you own name being used by others with whom you are not directly involved with was not uncommon for children in this setting.[3] The first step for the social structure analysis was to identify whether the patterns recorded reflected in the adult's tendency to address and refer to certain children more often than others, and whether this pattern could be distributed in a fashion that might reflect elements of the social structure of the nurseries examined, and available to all overhearing children. The question asked was, were certain pairs of children being associated together as 'addressee-referred-to child pairs', in a greater than chance fashion (because they were friends, played together or fought/argued in a noticeable way)?

Furthermore, in order to establish whether any such 'bias' in the adult's third party reference utterances were not simply due to the fact that certain pairs of children tended to share the same attendance times at the nurseries, before undertaking the sociometric analysis for each nursery setting figures were calculated describing, (a) the attendance times for each child over the whole period, and (b) joint attendance figures for any possible child pair (the probability of their attendance together at the same time). The purpose of the analysis was to identify whether there was anything significant concerning the frequencies of particular 'addressee-referred-to child' pairings and to investigate whether the distribution of those frequencies might provide information relevant to a 'social structure' data picture of the nursery, which an overhearing child could be sensitive to, or aware of. Are there non-random associative patterns which could, from an 'ecological-utterance' view, form the basis for social-structural overhearing affordances?

Toward this end, matrices were drawn up from frequency data describing the number of occasions each child was addressed, and which of the other children was being referred-to, for each nursery. The examples from all the adults for a given setting were collated together.

For illustrative purposes here, the description of the procedure and findings will concentrate on the university nursery.[4] In this setting 29 children were present throughout the observational period (Table 6.1). Each row describes the number of times any of the other possible 28 children were referred-to when that one particular child was addressed. And so on for each row of the matrix.

Data Analysis

If we wish to know whether the observed frequencies (in Table 6.1) are associated together as addressee-referred-to child pairs to a degree significantly greater than chance, then it is necessary to compare this observed frequency matrix with an expected frequency matrix. This is equivalent to carrying out a 29 x 29 chi square analysis. An expected frequency matrix was calculated by working out the joint attendance figures for each pair of children. Dividing each entry in the attendance matrix by the average of all entries and then multiplying by the average of all entries in Table 6.1, yields an expected frequency matrix under the hypothesis that the frequencies are basically proportional to the time each pair of children attended the nursery together. However, it is possible that there is a tendency for high frequencies in certain cells of such a matrix, simply because these pairs of children were more often at the playgroup together on the same occasions. To control for this, the expected frequencies are conditioned on the observed marginal totals, while retaining the association structure (in terms of odds ratios) internal to the matrix of the expected frequencies. This allows for the calculation of expected frequencies (for each cell) while taking into account the probability that any two children were actually present together at the same time. The expected frequencies are generated by the iterative proportional fitting method described in Bishop, Feindberg, and Holland (1975) and written into the analysis program.

For this model the observed frequencies (Table 6.6) significantly depart from the expected frequencies (Table 6.2): $x^2 = 1140$ (d.f.617) $p < .001$.[5] Pairs of children are associated together as 'addressee-referred-to child' pairs, in the adults' utterances in a fashion which cannot be simply explained by a tendency to share the same attendance times at the nursery. Those cells which describe a positive association of addressee and referred-to child were identified using a procedure again described by Bishop, Feindberg, and Holland (1975).[6] Those cells with an observed frequency significantly in excess of chance (having a chi-value above this criterion)[7] were identified and shown in Table 6.3.

It should be noted, however, that because many cell frequencies are low it is not possible to assess those cells which were significantly 'less' than expected In a sense this excludes the 'negative' side of the sociometric picture (why certain children were not associated together to a degree that is significant). From the positive significant association data however, a sociogram or sociometric pattern (social structure indices) can be constructed. This is achieved by first identifying those child pairs where not only was there a significant addressee-referred-to child association, but additionally, when that same referred-to child was in turn an addressee, she was also significantly associated with the former addressee (now the referred-to child). For example, from Table 6.3, we can see that child pair 5–14 become significantly associated as, alternately, child pair 14–5. When all those 'reciprocating' addressee-referred-to child pairs are connected together then, for the university pre-school, we can identify six main sub-groups as shown in Figure 6.1.

Although group clustering data (who played together the most) was not recorded, this pattern certainly adheres to the author's observations of the naturally occurring groups in the nursery. It is clear that one can identify a picture of the social structure of the pre-school nurseries via the patterns of 'addressee-referred-to child' pairings. It is possible that, by attending to how she is referred-to in relation to other individuals, for example, as a friend or rival, in a favourable or unfavourable light, etc., a child could build up a picture of the social structure of the nursery she is part of. What is more, arguably it is a picture of how others (the adults) perceive her as fitting into the social network, arguably from the child's viewpoint a particularly significant source of information (especially as regards a comparison for her own social perceptions).

While it has not been possible to specify the dimensions upon which the adult preferences for particular addressee-referred-to child pairings might be based (e.g. group membership or friendliness, etc.), it has been possible to demonstrate that such a sociogram picture can be identified based on a measure of the positive association of 'addressee- referred-to child' pairs. Furthermore, for the nurseries examined, there is the suggestion of a link between the role relations of the children (e.g. who plays with whom the most often), which the adults may be sensitive to, and reflected in their preferences for addressing and referring to particular child pairs. For example, consider sub-group two in Figure 6.1.

We can consider first the 'strengths' of the chi-values for these significant reciprocating pairings, a source of possible relevant data lost when we consider only those results over the 1% chi-value. Returning to Table 6.3. the highest values (3.25 and 4.09) are found linking the two most talkative and boisterous girls in the nursery (Rhoda [14–9] and Lee [9–14]). The next highest (2.12 [14–5] and 2.37 [5–14]) are between Rhoda and the oldest girl in the playgroup, Lisa, and so on, through to the lowest figures linking Lee and Marie-Louise (1.16 [9–25] and 1.19 [25–9]). These values reflect a dimension of friendliness between the

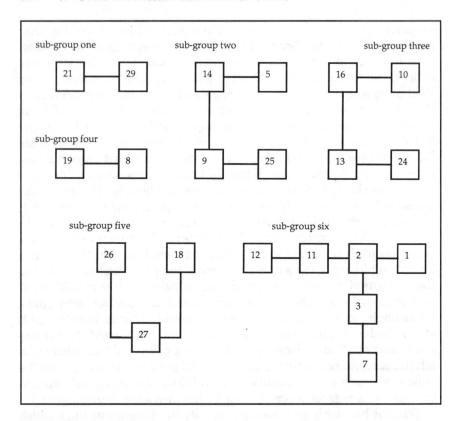

FIG. 6.1. Basic sociogram pattern

child groups. For example, the strongest bonds in this sub-group appeared to be between Rhoda and Lee, while the weakest (but still significantly strong) between Lee and Marie-Louise, for this sub-group. We can also identify relationships between sub-groups and other individuals which were significant in chi-value terms (from Table 6.3) in a 'one-way' fashion (not reciprocal), as in Figure 6.2. This is a typical example of these 'one-way' connections from the university nursery. Simply, the number of reciprocal and 'one-way' associations describe the children's relationships with each other in terms of the degree of friendliness or, in more precise terms, the groups they tended to remain with. We can also obtain some indication of the strengths of their relations (i.e. measured by how much time they spent with each other).

Additional support for this idea emerges from a comparison of the sub-groups identified across the two nursery settings studied, where the groups in the latter setting were not so clearly defined (compare with

TABLE 6.1 – Frequency of Addressee-Referred-To Child Occurrences

CHILD REFERRED-TO

	1	2	3	4	5	6	7	8	9	10	11	12	13	14	15	16	17	18	19	20	21	22	23	24	25	26	27	28	29	TOT
1	0	4	2	0	1	0	0	0	1	0	0	0	0	0	0	0	0	0	0	0	1	1	0	2	0	0	0	0	0	12
2	4	0	3	0	0	0	0	0	0	0	4	0	0	1	1	0	0	1	1	0	2	0	0	0	0	1	1	0	0	20
3	0	15	0	1	0	0	0	0	2	1	0	2	0	0	1	1	2	0	4	0	0	0	0	0	0	0	1	0	0	31
4	0	0	0	0	0	0	0	0	1	0	0	0	0	0	1	0	0	0	0	0	0	0	0	0	0	0	0	0	0	1
5	0	1	0	0	0	0	0	0	1	0	1	0	5	5	1	1	0	0	0	0	0	0	0	0	0	0	0	0	3	12
6	0	0	0	0	0	0	0	0	0	0	0	0	0	0	0	0	0	0	0	0	0	0	0	0	0	0	0	0	0	0
7	0	0	0	0	0	0	0	0	0	0	0	0	0	0	0	0	0	0	2	0	0	0	0	1	0	0	0	0	0	3
8	0	2	0	0	0	0	0	2	2	0	0	0	0	3	3	2	2	2	0	0	0	0	0	1	0	0	0	0	0	20
9	1	4	0	0	0	0	0	0	0	0	0	0	0	3	3	0	0	0	0	0	21	0	0	2	1	3	4	0	4	57
10	0	0	1	0	0	0	0	0	0	0	0	3	0	0	2	0	0	0	0	0	1	0	0	0	0	0	0	0	0	6
11	0	1	0	0	0	0	0	0	0	0	0	2	0	0	0	0	0	0	0	0	1	0	0	0	0	0	0	0	0	4
12	0	0	0	0	0	0	0	1	0	1	1	1	0	0	0	1	1	0	0	0	3	0	0	1	0	0	1	0	0	16
13	0	1	2	0	0	0	0	0	0	0	0	0	2	3	1	0	0	0	0	0	0	0	0	0	0	0	0	0	0	10
14	0	0	1	0	0	0	0	16	2	0	0	0	0	3	1	10	1	2	0	0	3	0	0	4	0	0	4	0	10	69
15	0	0	0	0	5	0	0	2	2	0	0	1	0	2	0	0	0	0	2	0	12	1	2	4	0	3	0	0	2	25
16	1	0	0	0	2	0	0	0	0	0	0	0	0	0	0	0	0	0	0	0	6	0	0	4	0	3	0	0	0	15
17	0	0	1	0	0	0	0	0	1	0	0	0	0	0	0	0	0	0	0	0	4	0	0	0	0	0	0	0	0	4
18	1	0	0	0	0	0	0	0	0	0	0	0	0	1	0	0	1	0	0	0	1	0	0	0	0	0	1	0	1	9
19	0	0	0	0	0	0	0	0	0	0	0	0	0	1	0	0	0	0	0	0	0	0	0	0	0	0	0	0	0	3
20	1	0	0	0	4	0	0	1	0	1	0	0	0	0	0	0	0	0	0	0	0	0	0	0	0	0	0	0	0	4
21	0	0	0	0	0	0	0	0	0	0	0	0	0	0	0	1	0	0	0	0	2	0	0	3	0	0	0	0	4	19
22	0	0	0	0	0	0	0	0	3	0	0	0	0	2	0	0	0	0	0	0	0	2	0	0	0	0	0	0	0	5
23	0	0	0	0	0	0	0	0	0	0	0	0	0	5	1	0	0	0	0	0	0	1	0	3	0	0	1	0	0	2
24	3	0	0	0	0	0	0	0	4	0	0	1	0	0	0	0	1	0	0	0	0	0	0	3	0	0	0	0	0	15
25	0	0	0	0	0	0	0	0	0	0	0	0	0	0	0	0	0	0	0	0	0	0	0	0	0	0	0	0	0	3
26	0	0	2	0	0	0	0	0	0	0	0	0	0	0	1	0	0	0	0	0	1	0	0	0	0	0	1	0	0	8
27	0	1	0	0	0	0	0	0	3	1	1	1	0	2	3	0	1	1	0	0	0	1	3	3	0	2	0	0	1	36
28	0	0	0	0	0	0	0	0	0	0	0	0	0	5	0	0	0	0	0	0	7	0	0	0	0	0	0	0	0	2
29	4	0	0	0	0	0	0	0	0	0	1	1	0	0	0	4	1	0	0	0	12	0	0	0	0	0	0	0	0	27
T =	13	32	12	1	12	0	0	6	37	3	8	13	8	41	23	29	9	5	6	4	57	3	8	22	2	11	17	1	32	438

Row label (vertical): C H I L D A D D R E S S E D

TABLE 6.2 – Expected Frequencies Matrix (adjusted given joint attendance figures)

CHILD REFERRED-TO

CHILD ADDRESSED	1	2	3	4	5	6	7	8	9	10	11	12	13	14	15	16	17	18	19	20	21	22	23	24	24	26	27	28	29	TOT
1	0	.9	.3	0	.4	0	0	.2	1	.1	.2	.3	.3	1.8	.5	.7	.3	.2	.2	.1	1.6	.2	.2	.6	.1	.4	.4	0	.9	12
2	.7	0	.8	.1	.6	0	0	.3	2	0	.4	.6	.4	3.4	1	1.2	.5	.3	.2	.2	2.8	.2	.3	1	.1	.5	.8	.1	1.5	20
3	.9	2.9	0	.1	.8	0	0	.4	2.9	.2	.5	.7	.7	4.2	1.7	1.8	1	.5	.8	.6	3.2	0	.5	1.8	.1	1.1	1.1	.1	2.3	31
4	0	.1	0	0	0	0	0	0	.1	0	0	0	0	.2	0	.1	0	0	0	0	.2	0	0	0	0	0	0	0	.1	1
5	.5	.9	.3	0	0	0	0	.2	1.3	.1	.2	.3	.2	1.8	.5	.6	.2	.1	.3	.1	1.8	.1	.2	.5	.1	.5	.4	0	.8	12
6	0	0	0	0	0	0	0	0	0	0	0	0	0	0	0	0	0	0	0	0	0	0	0	0	0	0	0	0	0	0
7	.2	.3	.3	0	0	0	0	0	.3	0	0	0	0	.5	0	.3	0	0	0	0	.8	0	1	0	0	0	2	0	.3	3
8	.6	1.5	.6	0	.6	0	0	1.9	0	.4	.5	.2	.3	3	1.1	1.2	.5	.3	.3	.1	2.8	.1	.3	1.1	.1	.5	.7	0	1.4	20
9	1.6	4.5	1.7	.1	1.9	0	0	.9	0	4	1.1	2	1	10	3.5	3.9	1.2	.7	.6	.6	6.4	.6	1.3	3.2	.3	2.1	2.3	.1	5	57
10	.2	.1	.2	0	.2	0	0	0	.5	0	.1	.3	.1	1	.3	.4	.1	0	.1	0	1.1	.1	.1	.3	.1	0	.4	0	.4	6
11	.1	.3	.1	0	0	0	0	.1	.4	0	0	.1	.1	.6	.2	.3	.1	0	.1	0	.6	0	.1	.2	0	.1	.1	0	.3	4
12	.4	1.1	.4	0	.4	0	0	.2	1.7	.2	.3	0	.5	2.5	.8	1.1	.3	.2	0	0	1.7	.3	.3	1.1	.1	.3	7	.1	1.4	16
13	.4	.9	.4	0	.2	0	0	.1	.9	.1	.2	.5	0	1.6	.4	.6	.2	.1	0	0	.8	.3	.1	.5	.1	.3	.3	.1	.8	10
14	2.1	5.6	1.8	.2	2	0	0	1	7.2	.5	1.4	2.1	1.3	0	4.3	5.5	1.2	.8	1.1	.7	11	.8	1.4	3.6	.4	2.1	3.4	.1	5.6	69
15	.6	1.6	.7	0	.5	0	0	.4	2.4	.2	.5	.7	.4	4.2	0	1.8	.4	.3	.2	.3	4.4	.2	.5	1.3	.1	.5	1.2	0	1.7	25
16	.4	1	.4	0	.3	0	0	.2	1.4	.1	.3	.5	.2	2.6	.9	0	.3	.1	.2	.1	2.7	.1	.3	.7	.1	.2	.7	0	1.2	15
17	.2	.3	.2	0	.1	0	0	.1	.4	0	.1	.1	.1	.5	.2	.2	0	.1	.1	0	.4	0	.1	.2	0	.2	.1	0	.3	4
18	.3	.7	.4	0	.2	0	0	.2	.8	0	.2	.2	.2	1.3	.4	.5	.3	0	.1	.1	.7	.1	.2	.6	0	.3	.2	0	.7	9
19	.1	.2	.2	0	.2	0	0	0	.2	0	.1	0	0	.5	.1	.2	.1	0	0	0	.8	0	0	.1	0	0	.1	0	.2	3
20	.1	.4	.2	0	.1	0	0	0	.4	0	.1	0	0	.6	.2	.2	.1	.1	.1	0	.6	0	.1	.1	0	0	.2	0	.4	4
21	.6	1.5	.5	.1	.6	0	0	.3	1.5	.2	.5	.5	.2	3.8	1.5	1.8	.3	.1	.6	.2	0	.1	.2	.8	.1	.4	1.2	0	1.4	19
22	.3	.5	0	0	.1	0	0	.1	.6	.1	.2	.4	.4	1.1	.3	.3	0	1	0	0	.5	0	.1	.5	.1	0	.1	.1	.5	6
23	.1	.1	.1	0	.1	0	0	0	.2	0	0	.1	0	.4	.1	.1	0	0	0	0	.1	0	0	.1	0	0	.1	0	.2	2
24	.5	1.1	.5	0	.3	0	0	.2	1.5	.1	.3	.6	.3	2.4	.9	1	.4	.2	.1	0	1.5	.2	.4	0	.4	.6	0	0	1.2	15
25	.1	.2	0	0	.1	0	0	0	.3	0	.1	.1	.1	.5	.1	.2	0	0	0	0	.5	.1	0	.1	.0	.1	0	0	.2	3
26	.3	.6	.4	0	.4	0	0	.1	1.1	0	.1	.2	.2	1.5	.4	.3	.3	.1	0	0	.8	0	0	.5	.1	0	.3	0	.3	8
27	.8	2.4	.9	.1	.8	0	0	.5	3	.4	.3	1.2	.5	6.1	2.1	2.8	.4	.2	.5	.3	6.8	.1	.7	1.7	0	.7	0	.1	2.6	36
28	.1	.2	.1	0	.1	0	0	0	.2	0	0	.1	.1	.3	0	.1	0	0	0	0	.1	.1	0	.1	0	.1	.1	0	.2	2
29	.8	2	.8	.1	.7	0	0	.4	2.9	.2	.5	1	.5	4.5	1.4	2	.6	.3	.4	.3	3.6	.3	.6	1.5	1	.3	1.2	.1	0	27
TOT =	13	32	12	1	12	0	0	6	37	3	8	13	8	41	23	29	9	5	6	4	57	3	8	22	2	11	17	1	32	438

TABLE 6.3 – Chi-square Values for Significant Cells

CHILD REFERRED-TO

		1	2	3	4	5	6	7	8	9	10	11	12	13	14	15	16	17	18	19	20	21	22	23	24	25	26	27	28	29	NCS
	1		3.2	2.8																				1.87							3
	2	4.2		2.6							5.6						1.4	1.6													5
	3			7.1	3.1						1.6	1.5						1.1		4.5											6
	4																														1
	5								3.2				1.6	2.4															2.4		3
	6																														0
	7																					2.6									1
	8																		3.2										3.8		4
	9								1.2																						3
	10												3.2	4.1												1.2					3
C	11			1.3					3.9				2.7			2.4									1.5				1.3		4
H	12											1.3	2.2											3.1							3
I	13													1.1											5.1						5
L	14					2.1										1.8															4
D	15					2.2										1.9									2.4	3.5			1.9		3
	16							5.7						1.5											3.9						2
A	17				1.9													6.6													5
D	18	1.2												1.9												1.2			1.6	6.1	3
D	19	2.5						4.5								2.2															1
R	20					10.3																									4
E	21													1.1	3.7							2.3				1.0			2.2		2
S	22													1.1								8.1									2
S	23													2.4										4.4							4
E	24		1.7						1.2							3.1								4.4					2.5		3
D	25								1.8					1.2																	3
	26			1.2																											6
	27																		1.5				2.3	2.7	1.1	1.4			1.2	1.3	1
	28																														
	29		3.5								6.9					1.4						4.4									3

CRITICAL VALUE FOR INDIVIDUAL CELLS = 1.007 (p <.01)
NCS = Number of critical cells.

the sociogram pattern shown in Appendix 1). In the local authority nursery there was a greater density of children (many more children at any one time), the style of the caretaking was consequently more restrictive, and the age-range more widespread (the youngest child started at 2 years of age). These factors made the formation of small, stable, close-knit groups a much less frequent occurrence.

There is, of course, a difference between identifying a form of 'verbal association social structure' in the adults' speech, social structural affordances available in the overheard talk, and demonstrating that the children do recognise and extract such affordances. However, what can be said is that simply through exposure to third party reference, the child is being provided with much more information about social relationships than could be available in 'dyadic' face-to-face communication. It was also very rare to notice any misunderstanding of the adult-to-child third party reference on the part of the addressed or referred-to child (e.g. for a child being referred-to thinking that she

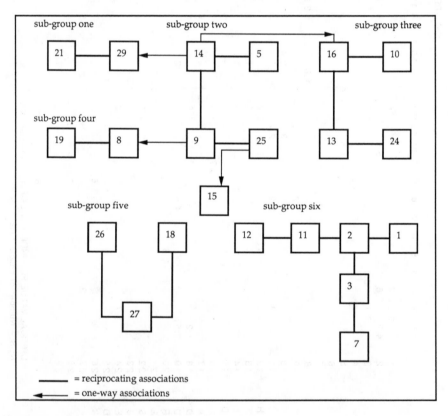

FIG. 6.2. Extended association sociogram pattern

was being addressed), notwithstanding the proviso that the absence of a given response, such as looking up on hearing one's name, does not necessarily indicate the child's lack of role-participation comprehension.

To continue, how can we identify whether children become sensitive to the 'attention structures' potentially available in the pre-school setting? We should remember also that observing how others refer to us when we are not directly involved in the ongoing conversation might be more significant to us as overhearers, due to the more 'objective' form such a statement appears to have. Consider the situation as adults where we ask someone in a roundabout way what they think of us or some behaviour we are exhibiting. Whatever credence we are going to give to a reply from such a request, is likely to hold less significance for us compared to the situation where we are inadvertent eavesdroppers on somebody else's comments about us. In the latter situation we can be more certain such a reply is what the addressee really thinks.

To summarise, this chapter has highlighted one dimension of a model of overhearing, a model which emphasises the importance of examining whether conversational contexts make available 'affordances' of talk to children who are developing social-cognitive participation skills. Having outlined the importance of overhearing as 'happenstance', chance or opportunity, the suggestion was made that the young child is being provided with lessons in what is likely to take place between people, and what is encoded, in the way that language is used, to convey or indicate a range of different social roles and relations. I then considered whether there are, in fact, 'structural/affordance' dimensions available in the speech that children overhear in pre-school settings. The answer is in the affirmative. There are non-random associative patterns provided by overheard adult-to-child utterances, the distinct ways in which children are addressed and referred-to in the pre-school. There exists an 'ecological utterance' basis for social structure information or sociometric overhearing affordances.

NOTES

1. Bandura (1969) favoured what he called sensory contiguity, this being an associative response connecting sensory events with symbolic coding processes that possess cue properties capable of eliciting overt responses corresponding to those that had been modelled. McLauglin (1971) points out that strictly speaking incidental learning is a misnomer as there is no experimental evidence which demonstrates that a distinct (that is qualitatively different) learning process occurs where there is no motive to learn.

2. In line with appropriate inter-observer reliability procedures, a second observer recorded 12 observational hours using the same procedure as the

first (the author). Adequate levels of agreement were obtained (by cross-checking field notes and verifying these with the tape-recordings) for the categories of interest, kappa co-efficients calculated where the number of category alternatives was small enough to permit analysis. Two independent observers also rated the forms of speech according to a speech coding category system (see Chapter 7) and adequate levels of agreement were reached (between 75–90%).

3. Linguistic description and details of the speech act functions of third party reference are reported in Forrester (1985, 1986).

4. Full details for both settings reported in Forrester (1986).

5. A similar analysis was conducted for the local authority nursery and again the association was significant, $x^2 = 1366$ $(d.f.468)$ $p.<001$.

6. This is done by dividing the square root of the critical value of the chi-square by the number of non-structural zero cells yielding a critical per-cell chi-value.

7. The standardised residual as calculated from the square root of the chi-square component for that cell.

CHAPTER SEVEN

Overhearing as
'Attention Focusing'

So far, an argument has been developed which places considerable emphasis on the provision of specific 'conversational affordances' within participation contexts, which the child is exposed to by virtue of overhearing talk. At this point, however, it is not clear whether such theoretical 'invariant' and 'transformational' social-cognitive affordances are made available primarily via non-verbal cues, intonational and linguistic/grammatical prompts, or are more generally related to the ongoing dynamics of conversational discourse. What is clear is that there are key practices and events in the child's overheard environment which are particularly 'attention-grabbing' often (for the older pre-school child) where exemplars of social practice, rule or convention are being demonstrated (e.g. Dunn, 1988). The second category of overhearing examined in this chapter considers aspects of overhearing contexts which are 'attention focusing'. I would like to turn first to one of the earliest and most consequential social practices the child will overhear, that is, name use, both her own and other peoples' names.

NAME PRACTICES AND
OVERHEARING NAME USE

In the philosophy of language and linguistics there is considerable debate, and interest, in the phenomenon of naming, that is the naming of things and proper names. Various cross-disciplinary interests contribute to our understanding of the more intricate aspects of naming. For example, theories of referentiality and formal content (e.g. Granger, 1982) can be set against ideas within positivism and phenomenology, where arguments often revolve around how it is that any object can be named and what this might imply. The problematic status of proper names is often cited. Students of deixis, particularly social honorofics (Levinson, 1983), point to some of the issues arising from the deictic and anaphoric use of proper names, where this helps to highlight the relationship between social interaction processes and the particular expression used. Finally, social anthropological and sociolinguist themes serve to remind us of the particularly ethnocentric nature of naming practices, and how such procedures serve a range of important social and institutional functions (Poole, 1985).[1] Here I would like to constrain the discussion on names and naming, to issues which highlight the relationship between overhearing name use (form the child's point of view) and the form, nature and significance of such practices for childrens' emerging social cognitive conversational skills.

CHARACTERISTICS OF NAME USE

Two themes in the philosophy of language serve as useful reference points for considering the ways in which psychology and linguistics have developed ideas of naming and names. From Locke (1690) to Montague (1970) there is a tradition which tends to view the practice of naming as an indication that indeed we possess an essential sense of 'the names of things' or more precisely cognise the extension of any given class of objects such that we can denote a general name for whatever it might be. In contrast, a second strand of thought, following Wittgenstein (1953) and Harrison (1974), suggests that much of this implicit 'mentalism' is somewhat misguided and what we should be concerned with are the social conventions which surround the circumstances where any given object or person is referred to by the use of a name. Harrison (1974), for example, argues that naming works along 'sortal principles' such that:

'what a child has to learn in learning his native language is not a set of correlations (between general names and Lockean abstract ideas) but an array of procedures, operations or practices which form the foundation upon which the conceptual scheme of the language is then erected' (p.135).

The former more 'essentialist' tradition appears to have had more adherents within cognitive (e.g. Rosch, 1975), and developmental psychology. Wales, Colman, and Pattison (1983), for example, utilise

Rosch's concept/category level schema when examining mothers' naming practices with different aged children. However, there are those who question the assumptions of this position. Carroll (1983) argues that while name-shortening processes operate 'in a lexical domain' (*Jay* for *Jimmy*) they are in effect behavioural or at least pragmatically determined. Similarly, in a study of the naming strategies of pre-school children, Mahalingam (1984) argues that rather than observing the emergence of a consistent labelling procedure (aligned to the acquisition of a concept/category), name learning was determined by functional context (i.e. the description and naming of objects was linked to their function). A commonplace example might be where a child will repeat (with particular stress on the name) another's name significantly 'attached' to an object on being offered a drink (but ... that's *Stephanie's* cup ... *Stephanie's* cup ... *Stephanie's*!). It is only in the recent past that research on names has looked in detail at the practice of using names. Frommer (1982), for example, suggests that the practice of naming people is closely related to perceptions of that individual's identity and in selecting a child's name parents opt for the one that will 'fit' the person they envisage their newborn becoming.

In the remainder of this chapter I would like to consider three ways in which overhearing name use can be characterised as an *attention focusing* device (where employed intentionally by speakers or otherwise). First, naming as sensitivity to social comment; second, as an 'attention orientation' strategy or procedure related to the acquisition and use of pronouns (by children), and third, naming as an attention focusing control technique for directing children.

SOCIAL SENSITIVITY TO NAME USE

One frequently cited effect found in introductory textbook in psychology is what is known as the 'cocktail party' phenomenon. There has been no difficulty in demonstrating that where people are in 'earshot' of others who are using their names in a conversation they are not directly involved in, then this is particularly attention focusing for the person concerned. A corollary of this phenomenon has been commented on by Bond (1989), with respect to hearing impaired adolescents watching two other people signing. In such contexts, overseeing another using the sign for your name or initials, elicits a very strong demand for an explanation of why you are talking about her. There are distinctions which can be made with reference to the kind of information which is made available in such contexts. For example, while I might ask one of my colleagues for an opinion on a recently completed article, the kind of reply will be quite distinct from where I might inadvertently overhear a couple of my colleagues (that is in a context where I know they assume I am not present) conversing about my work. I am more likely to surmise that what is now being said about me by X is more 'objective' and less contaminated by the social pressures intrinsic to direct questioning (or at least under a different set of exigencies).

In other words there are a number of quite different 'overheard' dimensions to contexts where one's name is used by others. For the young child, there are likely to be potentially rich forms of presuppositional information (social, emotional and cognitive) made available to an overhearing infant, communicating a great deal about how those closest to her perceive, accommodate to, and otherwise view her as a person. One everyday practice which lends support to this observation is where parents report their growing recognition (toward the end of the child's second year) that they can no longer talk about the infant and use her name as if she wasn't there. Parents awareness of their child's sensitivity to her proper name is built into the matrix of the changing practices and social significance of naming. For example, we are all familiar with situations where one child is being told off, and her sister is being referred-to as an example of how to behave, the way her name is employed will convey quite different information (and significance) compared to contexts where she is being asked to take off her sister's coat (as it doesn't belong to her). It is clearly difficult to do justice to the kinds of subtle distinctions which are built into our everyday understanding and use of naming practices.

Given the gaps in the literature and the possible importance of this topic to my argument about models of social-cognitive development, participation and overhearing, an investigation was conducted into the earliest indications of the young infant's social sensitivity to overhearing name use (where he/she overhears his/her name being used by other people engaged in dialogue). As an exploratory step in identifying the affordances of conversations with reference to role of overhearing name use, this investigation sought to highlight the earliest indications of the young infant's social sensitivity to overhearing name use.

INFANT'S RESPONSIVENESS TO NAME-REFERENCE CONVERSATIONAL AFFORDANCES

Method

Procedure
A longitudinal observational study was carried out with 5 mother-child-child triads in a naturalistic laboratory setting (furnished with various toys, picture books and games). Each triad comprised a

mother with an older child (approximately 4–5 years) and a young infant (average age 11 months at the beginning of the study). The mothers and their children were recorded once every six weeks over a period of six months. The mothers were asked to act as they normally would when at home with their children, with the only proviso being that, where possible (where their actions would fit into the context of what was going on), they should converse with the older child about the infant, using names and appropriate forms of reference (his/her, he/she). A split-screen recording set-up was employed, where three cameras allowed for the recording of all the participants throughout the sessions (approximately 30–40 minutes in length). The mothers tended to read to or play with the older children throughout the sessions.

Results

If the young infant responded at all to overhearing their mother's use of their name, it was with looks towards the speaker and not towards the other participant who was being addressed by her. The responses were coded either as a 'look' (without other noticeable head movement) or as a 'turn and look'. All responses are summed as TL in Table 7.1.

TABLE 7.1
Infant Responses to Reference (%)

Age	Sess. No.	Resp.	S1 (male)		S2 (male)		S3 (male)		S4 (male)		S5(female)	
			N	P	N	P	N	P	N	P	N	P
11.0m	1	TL	9	-	2	4	5	2	7	7	5	-
		V	-	-	-	-	-	-	-	-	-	-
12.5m	2	TL	18	-	3	0	5	-	-	-	4	-
		V	-	-	-	-	2	-	-	-	2	-
14.0m	3	TL	4	-	-	-	14	-	5	-	35	-
		V	-	-	-	-	-	-	-	-	10	-
15.5m	4	TL	59	-	-	6	57	14	33	-	58	-
		V	18	-	-	-	-	-	19	-	50	-
17.0	5	TL	40	6	46	2	40	25	56	16	65	3
		V	20	-	21	-	13	25	31	-	29	5

TL = Turns and looks   N = Names
V = Vocalization accompanying turn   P = Pronouns

Interestingly, the infants did not look towards the mother (who has just mentioned his/her name) until about 14–15 months old (see Figure 7.1). At this age there was also a sudden increase in the amount of vocalisation (on the part of the infant) accompanying the 'turn and look'. Commonly, the infant's vocalisation would begin only after her mother had used her name (in her talk with the other older toddler). Furthermore, it is interesting to note that we do not appear to be highlighting a gradual appearance of this response of looking, rather a sudden (comparatively speaking) onset. The decreasing frequency of naming and reference over time by the mothers, reflected the observation (more than any other factor) that by 14–15 months the infants were becoming more mobile. Once they were walking, their movements and their tendency to vocalise a great deal more reduced the number of opportunities the mother had for employing third person reference in the way desired (see Figure 7.2).

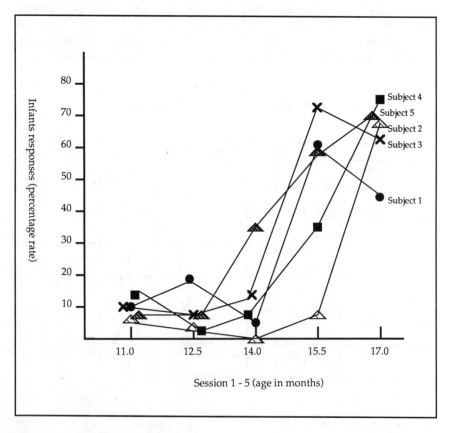

FIG. 7.1. Infant response rate (%)

However, the most striking aspect of the study (and not clear from the summary here) is that when the young infants began to respond in a non-random fashion to self-reference by others, the intonational characteristics of name or pronoun reference (by the mother) were significantly marked. The intonational patterning as a constituent part of 'motherese' (Snow & Ferguson, 1977) may not have a direct bearing upon the acquisition of language (Gleitman, Newport, & Gleitman, 1984), but nonetheless may be a significant factor in providing the infant with considerable exposure to conversational affordances. In particular, the rising intonational contour of speech addressed to others may signal to an overhearing infant that a change in turn is about to occur (see Sachs, Brown, & Salerno, 1976).

One final observation of the study was that towards the end of the period (when the infants were 17 months old) there were an increasing number of instances where the children would imitate overheard

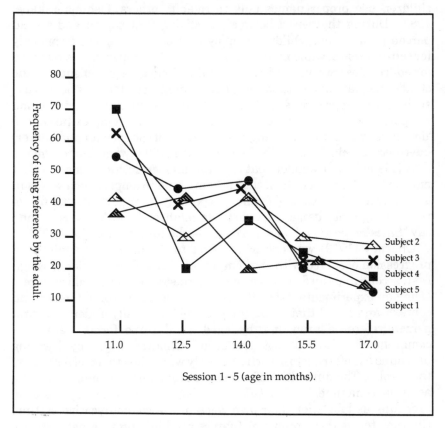

FIG. 7.2. Reference frequency by adults (%)

utterances of their mothers (talking to the other child), and in particular words or phrases which were spoken in a 'sing-song' fashion. More often than not they would imitate such words in a similar 'musical style' and would do so two or three times, usually without looking at anyone else (i.e. for themselves).

NAMING AND PRONOUNS

The second category of overhearing as 'attention focusing' is the relationship between naming and pronoun use. Cruttenden (1979), has pointed out that, where adults would typically use pronouns, children will often use proper names, and Durkin (1987) suggests that the complexities inherent in pronoun use are avoided by the use of names. Further, before first person pronoun use or named self-reference, children use proper names only to refer to others (Oshima-Takane, 1988). During the period between acquiring first person and second person pronoun use, children employ first person pronoun forms only for self-reference, while name use (along with kinship terms) is reserved for addressees (Strayer, 1977). One of the obvious requirements for the child's adequate understanding of deixis and deictic terms is how to use such words appropriately, that is, given the spatial, proximal and temporal dynamics of any ongoing interaction. The complexities of the 'deictic centre' (e.g. the shifting role-relations of the speaker and hearer) have been succinctly described by Levinson (1983) where he comments that it is no small wonder that children master deictic terms at all. It may be for this reason then, that parents tend to employ such words in a very 'attention focusing' fashion, especially their early deictic use of the child's proper name (e.g. where an adult will speak to a child and say "Susie's a good girl then, isn't she?"—the infant being Susie).

Charney (1979) was one of the first to document the age-related progression observed with the comprehension and production through first, second and third person pronoun forms with 2–4 year old children. Using an experimental task situation, she varied person reference and context, and found that while the youngest only fully understood first person reference pronouns, by aged 4 all three forms were fully comprehended (though not produced). Children begin by learning pronouns as referring to speech roles only when they themselves occupy those roles. The difficulties of pronoun reversal or pronominal shifting as it is sometimes called (I/You shifts), are overcome by treating pronouns as labels for their own roles in the communicative setting. Charney terms these pronouns (names used in a pronominal fashion), 'person in speech-role-referring pronouns'.

However, this leads, as Chiat (1981) points out, to the counter intuitive notion that children may pick up the correct use of 'I' to refer to herself as speaker, without understanding that when others use the word 'I', it refers to themselves. Chiat (1981) stresses that the child must discover the form 'I' from other's speech (from contexts where 'I' refers to speakers other than themselves) and suggests that the subjects in Charney's (1979) study used 'my' in a rote-learning fashion as part of an unanalysed whole containing 'my' which corresponds to a complex concept including the notion of 'self'.

The progression one observes with pre-school children, Chiat (1981) suggests, demonstrates that only gradually does the child establish that the concepts (names vs. pronouns) are linguistically distinct, and that pronouns encode roles in the communicative setting while names label individuals. Interestingly, Bonnett (1983) suggests that the appearance of proper names in the young child's vocabulary should be recognised as including the act of summoning on the child's part. That is, the capacity to summon is to be understood as the child simultaneously referring to the roles of sender and receiver during the speech act. In an attempt to make sense out of some rather ambiguous results in her earlier data, Chiat (1982) looked for comparative data from adult usage of third person pronouns. It was this category of pronoun which was always the most difficult for the young children to produce (by age 4), even though comprehension was adequate by age 3 (Chiat, 1981). Her adult study draws attention to the plurifunctional nature of pronouns where the normal deictic function of pronouns is independent of their impersonal, hypothetical or perspective shifting function. For example, one friend can comment to another about her own behaviour along the lines of "She's crazy, your friend!", here referring to herself in the third person. Chiat's (1982) main proposal is that the patterns of errors we observe when children are learning pronouns is a result of the child 'imitating' pronouns correctly as speech role deictics, while also 'imitating' them incorrectly (reversing them in the wrong contexts) as perspective shifting devices.

While such error patterns might point to some of the potential problems (for the child) of observing and overhearing others use personal pronouns and other deictic terms, such contexts are also facilitating. The role of overhearing and the acquisition of first and second person pronoun forms was investigated by Oshima-Takane (1988). By comparing children who had exposure to others using personal pronoun forms with those without such experience Oshima-Takane (1988) established that acquisition is facilitated by overhearing and observing talk, not specifically involving them. Although the data then are somewhat difficult to interpret, there is little doubt that overhearing and observing others plays a part in the acquisition of deictic terms. This is further supported by Fox (1980) who has highlighted the problems hearing-impaired children have with deixis, where they are constrained by face-to-face interaction dynamics. What can be said is that young children's extensive exposure to naming practices is closely related to the sequence in which they learn pronouns, which in turn will be facilitated by whatever opportunities they have for overhearing speech by others.

NAMING AS A CONTROL TECHNIQUE

The third characteristic form of naming is where it is realised as a 'control technique'. Schaffer and Crook (1978) have documented this use of proper names in adults' talk to young children where it fulfils a directive function. Part of the interest in this area arose out of earlier controversies with regard to the role of motherese (e.g. Newport, Gleitman, & Gleitman, 1977; Wills, 1977) where it was argued that the particularly marked way in which adults used proper names (most often in place of pronouns) was taken to indicate the pedagogic potential of motherese. Durkin, Rutter, and Tucker (1982a) and Durkin, Rutter, Room, and Grounds (1982b) carried out cross-sectional and longitudinal studies of the incidence of proper name use during the child's second year. Durkin et al. (1982b) suggest that not only are the forms of proper name use syntactically and pragmatically deviant, but they are also inconsistently employed. They conclude by suggesting that not only is the adult-to-child use of proper names different (from adult forms) but arguably more difficult.

Likewise, Durkin et al. (1982a) argue that rather than facilitating language learning (the motherese hypothesis), proper name use by adults fulfils the primary communicative functions of orienting the child's attention or instructing her to act. They report that one of the most common instances where proper name use was employed inappropriately was where the child's proper name use was used as if the child was not present as in "look, Dolly is staring at Kenny (the child)". In contrast, Conti-Ramsden (1989), in a study looking at the proper naming practices of language impaired and non-impaired children interacting with their mothers, found no instances of inappropriate pragmatic use or syntactic form. Again, Conti-Ramsden (1989) sought to tease apart the motherese hypothesis (by examining proper name use), but in her study she found that the variability in form and function was considerably greater than reported in earlier work. However, attention-orienting, and employing names as instructions to act, was once more one of the primary functions of the adults proper name use. In particular, when in 'teaching contexts' (rather than free play) the amount of proper name use increased considerably.

This brings me then to a consideration of adult-to-child talk where children will be exposed to name use and name reference in a fashion quite distinct from their earlier experiences of overhearing name use. Group addressing speech (overhearing and listening to talk where you are being addressed by another and treated as part of a group) involves quite striking, and highly controlling, forms of name use. A study of group addressing speech can help articulate the relationship between naming practices, overhearing and 'attention focusing' control purposes of adult speech to children. The rest of this chapter outlines a study of group addressing speech conducted in parallel with the earlier reported study of third party reference in pre-school contexts.

GROUP-ADDRESSING SPEECH AND OVERHEARING NAME USE

Although group addressing speech normally amounts to only 2–3% of all adult-to-child utterances in the pre-school, exploratory observations by the author in a pre-school context suggested that this form of talk may be a very salient form of speech for the young child to overhear. The forms of address are related to function ("*Everyone* come into the book corner ... and ... The *rest of you* come out and play"); form of reference are more likely to be overheard in groups than in other contexts ("Are *you all* finished, right clap for Michael"); adults appear to be using this form of talk for specifically 'management' functions and it is most likely that this is the first context where the young child will overhear forms of talk where she is being treated as a member of a group. Many of these issues are interrelated.

Despite the recognition that adult's talk to children in classroom settings is the primary mechanism through which teaching and learning take place (Edwards & Mercer, 1986) few studies have looked closely at the form and content of 'group talk' or more specifically here, adult-to-child group addressing speech. Group addressing speech is more often than not, preceded by attention getting words (such as Look! or Right!), is significantly louder than other speech, rarely contains more than a few propositions and, by definition, will often contain group labels such as everybody, everyone, all of you, the lot of you, etc. Group addressing speech can be considered from at least two perspectives; first, as a form of language intrinsically linked to social interactions involving more than two people and secondly, from the speaker's point of view, as one of the major forms of 'management talk' particularly used in classrooms. As a 'polyadic' (multi-participant) language form, group addressing speech is a special kind of 'co-addressee-referree' speech, in that both the individuals addressed and referred-to are one and the same (e.g. "Right everybody, I want you all to go and tidy up!").

While Tanz (1980), Brener (1983) and others have drawn attention to the late acquisition of deictic terms, which involve the presence of third parties in conversational contexts, there is no available information on young children's comprehension of group addressing speech itself. Studies have, however, drawn attention to the role of group addressing speech as management talk (McHoul, 1978; Payne & Hustler, 1979; Pimm, 1987). From the speaker's angle, it can be argued that although there are a number of people involved, the 'group' is being treated as 'one other' participant in a form of speech akin to the 'dia' logic of dyadic encounters. Payne and Hustler (1979) looked at adult-to-child talk in a classroom of 9–10 year old children and propose that group addressing speech is particularly facilitative as a 'cohorting' or group control method. Group management is maintained by a peculiar form of 'two-party' dialogue, with the group participating as one party, the teacher the other. Similarly, McHoul (1978) has suggested that group addressing speech is one of many methods internal to the forms of 'cohorting' or collective control used by teachers to counteract pupil inattention and over-participation.[2] More recently Schaffer and Liddell (1984) compared adult talk across dyadic and polyadic settings (with pre-school children) and found that the latter contained a significant amount of management talk, much of it group addressing speech. The principle aim of this study here was to highlight aspects of the form and function of adult-to-child group addressing speech in the pre-school context and consider the role of such talk for the overhearing child.

Method

Setting and Procedure

The design, setting, procedure and criteria for inter-observer reliability were as in the previous chapter, that is, the data for the analysis below were collected alongside third party reference material. Along with the collection, coding and analysis of the group addressing utterances, the size and activities of the group were also recorded. In addition a frequency count of all adult-to-child directed speech was extracted from the tape-recordings, the whole process taking approximately 2.5 hours for each hour of taped observation. Around 500 examples of adult-to-child group addressing speech were collected and 925 examples of adult-to-child 'dyadic' (dialogue) speech were randomly selected from the audio-tapes. This made possible comparison of various factors described below (speech function across group addressing and third person reference speech for example). All speech examples were coded according to various categories ranging from the linguistic form the utterance might take, the speech act performed by the language, and a number of other relevant indices (details in Appendix 2).

Language Analysis.

The group addressing, third party reference and dyadic 'dialogue' utterances were coded in line with Searle's (1969) speech act category system. While problems with Searle's system have been highlighted (see Levinson, 1983)[3] for an initial analysis of speech forms, amended versions have proved useful to other workers in developmental pragmatics and is a valuable technique if care is taken to recognise some of the implicit assumptions in such an outline (e.g. Ervin-Tripp, 1977). Searle (1969) developed and proposed five basic types of actions which performed when any speech act occurs:

1. Representatives ... which commit the speaker to the truth of the expressed proposition (e.g. concluding).
2. Directives ... which are attempts by the speaker to get the addressee to do something (e.g. requesting or questioning)
3. Commissives ... which commit the speaker to some course of action (e.g. promising).
4. Expressives ... which express a psychological state (e.g. thanking.)
5. Declaratives ... which affect immediate changes in the institutional state of affairs (e.g. christening, etc).

The preliminary pilot work suggested that approximately 70% of the speech acts employed with adult-to-child group addressing speech performed a directive function. Thus, while adopting Searle's (1969) system, the 'DIRECTIVE' category was expanded somewhat in order to examine in more detail the plurifunctional nature of group addressing. On the basis of the pilot study examples five sub-categories were created:

(a) MODELLING DIRECTIVES:
"You can all see that she is being a good girl."
(b) POSSESSIVE DIRECTIVES:
"Look you boys, that belongs to the 'sunshine group', so put it back."
(c) ACTION DIRECTIVES:
"Sit down the rest of you!"
(d) ATTENTION DIRECTIVES where the group is instructed to pay attention to a referred-to child or children:

"Look at those boys and girls over there."

(e) REQUESTS or (information directives) where the group is asked for information concerning the referred-to child:

"Do any of you know where those boys went?"

While more than one 'speech act' could be operating in the utterance context (e.g. the example in the (d) above (taken from the transcripts) was both a directive to pay attention to somebody, and a request for the group to adopt their behaviour); in most circumstances one primary function of the speech was paramount and the level of inter-observer reliability obtained reflected this (between 75–90%).

Results
See Table 7.2

(a) *The amount and form of group addressing speech.*   Table 7.2 provides a representative sample of group addressing speech where either the group (i) or an individual (ii) is being referred-to. The data in Table 7.3 below summarise the amount of group addressing speech children are typically exposed to in the pre-school setting.

While the frequency and overall proportion of group addressing to all adult-to-child talk appears low, various factors suggest that group addressing speech is a particularly salient form of language for the young child to overhear. For example, the tape-recordings reflected the fact that group addressing speech would normally occur at significant 'breakpoints' in the sequential pattern of adult-child conversation, there would normally be a raising of the pitch of the adult's voice, and increase in loudness and particular stress on the language used to refer to or address the group. An amusing example of this:

"When I say EVERY, I mean EVERY BOY and GIRL in this group!" (should go and tidy up now)

was used with particular pedagogical stress when one of the caregivers was attempting to get all the children to tidy away some toys. Group addressing speech was also relatively syntactically simple (normally no more than two propositions per sentence), with a low number of words per utterance, and highly directive. This speech form is qualitatively more significant in the pre-school context than descriptive figures alone might suggest.

With regard to the form of group addressing speech, the way in which the adults would *address* children of this young age, that is, either explicitly ('Right everyone ...') or implicitly ('I don't want to see anyone

TABLE 7.2
Examples of Group Addressing Speech

(i) *Group addressing—group referring:* where the group being addressed (implicitly or explicitly) and the group being referred-to (implicitly or explicitly) are the same group of children.

Everyone sit down
Everyone come into the book corner
I was driving along and there was some people from the nursery on the bus!
Right, boys and girls, come over here

Well, someone's telling lies, that's all I can say
Right, are you all exhausted?
I thought I asked some of the children to help
Let me see you all lying down on the floor like little bunnies
Every time someone brings a toy in there's a fight
I don't want to see anyone on the heaters
Just a wee minute, boys and girls
The rest of you come out here and play
I want every boy and girl in the playgroup to come and pick up the straws

(ii) *Group addressing—individual reference:* where the group is being addressed (either implicitly or explicitly) and one individual in that group is being referred-to.

Why is Phanos crying?
Right, girls, come out and play just like Yinka
I know where Gary Sinclair's granny lives
Now, where is Mohammed ... sit down everyone
Everyone except Eliah
The only girl to say thankyou was Fifa
If Lee's not feeling well, the rest of you come out to play
We'll just have Ian
I said Gary ... the rest of you come with me
What about Craig Stuart ... right, clap for Michael
Clever girl ... clap for Fifa, give Fifa a big clap
Was it Kieran who was making that noise?

... '), while both types were employed equally often (58:42%) different patterns are identifiable.

When the speech was highly directive there was much greater use of explicit group addressing forms and correspondingly when the speech acts were fulfilling a representative function very few explicit forms were in evidence. A closer analysis of the directive speech act forms of group addressing revealed that it was commonly employed where the adults were directing the children to act in some way (clearly indicating who was to do whatever)—see Table 7.4(a). In contrast the implicit form was likely to be overheard where the adults already had the group's attention, and they were directing it to something or other (for example, to try and behave like another child or attend to what the speaker was doing).

TABLE 7.3
Adult-to-Child Group-addressing speech

Pre-school	A (University)	B (LEA - nursery)
No. of children (mean daily attendance)	14	22
No. of adults	2	4
Observational hours	50	56
No. of adult-to-child utterances	13,100	10,200[a]
Speech rate per hour (mean for adults)	130	45
Adult-to-child groups addressing utterances	242	291
Rate per hour	4.84	5.19

[a]Approximate no. calculated from 10% of recordings

Regarding the forms of *reference* a child would overhear when being addressed as part of a group, there was a greater amount of reference by name in the group addressing contexts (specifying the child referred-to clearly by name) compared to third party reference contexts, where only one individual is being addressed and one referred-to—see

TABLE 7.4
For and Function of Group-addressing Speech

	% data		
Pre-school setting	A (p)	B (p)	d.f.
(a) Forms of address used			
(1) by speech act function	<0.001	<.001	2
(2) by directive speech act funtion	<0.001	<.001	4
(b) Forms of reference used			
Group-addressing vs third party reference	<.001	<.01	2

Table 7.4(b). Interestingly, in contrast to third party reference, there is little personal pronoun reference used in group addressing contexts. The adults either specifically point out a child by name or use a distinct identification form of reference (such as *this boy* or *that girl*).

(b) The Function of Group Addressing Speech. While having already pointed to the directive function of group addressing speech in these pre-school settings, this aspect of the talk can be highlighted in greater detail by comparing group addressing speech with third party reference and 'dyadic' dialogue forms of adult-child talk, as in Table 7.5 below. By doing so we also wish to investigate whether there are particular aspects of the speech which arise out of the increased number of participants involved (i.e. dialogue—'dyadic', third party reference—'triadic' and group addressing speech—'polyadic').

Looking across these forms of speech (from dyadic to group) there is both a rise in the directive function and a corresponding fall in the proportion of group addressing 'representative function' speech—see Table 7.5.(a). Not surprisingly, group addressing speech is not used for expressive functions (e.g. welcoming or thanking). Group addressing speech as a linguistic medium for expressing the speaker's psychological

TABLE 7.5 (a)
The Function of Adult-child Speech in the Pre-school

Type of speech	Group-addressing	Third party reference	Dialogue
Representatives	18.5[a]	31.5	31
Directives	74.0	62.0	51
Commissives	7.5	5.0	11
Expressives	—	1.5	7

[a]All scores are percentages

TABLE 7.5(b)
The Directive Function of Adult-child Speech in the Pre-school

Pre-school	A			B		
Speech forms	GA	TPR	DIA	GA	TPR	DIA
Modelling directives	3[a]	4	10	5	4	8
Possessive directives	7	3	6	6	3	9
Action directives	77	51	38	80	54	43
Attention directives	1	16	7	—	10	11
Information directives (requests)	12	26	39	9	29	29
N	242	621	262	291	520	233

[a]Percentage scores
GA = Group-addressing speech   TPR = Third-party reference   DIA = Two-party dialogue

state would be a rare speech act in the pre-school context (beyond humorous asides). In sum, it would appear that as the number of participants in these forms of 'conversation' increase the function of the adult's speech takes on a much more directive nature.

A closer examination of the more detailed function categories of directive group addressing speech revealed a significantly increased use of the 'action directive' function (in comparison to the other forms of speech) and almost no use of the 'attention' or 'information' directive (requests)—see Table 7.5(b). In other words, asking a group collectively to pay attention to another group or attempting to elicit information from them (as a group) was rarely the function of adult-to-child group addressing speech in this context.

Summarising this section on the form and function of group addressing speech, it is necessary to step back and ascertain what these results might mean for the relationship between overhearing and developing social-cognitive participation skills. What is implied for the young pre-school child as listener in group addressing contexts? Exposure to group addressing speech can be seen as a unique situation where participation can be optional, that is, either as a possible 'next speaker' participating listener or as a more passive 'overhearing listener'. As a member of the group she has to simultaneously comprehend that as part of the group, she can fulfil the role of participating listener as in the dyadic encounter (and probably will be the next speaker representing the group), while at the same time perceiving her potential role as only one of many 'overhearing' listeners. In effect, there is the possibility (unlike dyadic encounters) of being freed from certain participation requirements. Somebody else in the group can make the necessary reply, not her. In fact, one skill to be acquired is how to recognise situations where it would be wiser to 'stay mum'. Another is to know that as a group member you are a ratified member of a participation context which has quite different social participation rules (to those previously encountered). Consider where a group is addressed by an adult (a typical example):

"Does anyone know what day it is?"

This form of address has been shown to elicit more hand raising etc than explicit directives for participation (McHoul, 1978; Payne & Hustler, 1979). Leaving aside the importance of such a language medium for instruction and 'cohorting processes', from the pre-school child's point of view arguably a reply by her is significant in that it might set her apart from the group as somebody who 'knows the answer', or the group might consider that her response represents an answer for the whole group. Payne and Hustler (1979) suggest that this is the case with older children, and while these younger children have yet to attach any particular importance to collective 'answering', arguably the pre-school context provides 'baseline' lessons in such discourse scenarios. Compare this context with a situation where an adult may say:

"Which one of you girls was being naughty?"

Now the young child can either remain silent (and be grouped with everyone else as a potential 'naughty girl') or she can assert that she is not one of the naughty girls. Arguably, exposure to group addressing contexts will provide participant lessons in role identity changes within and apart from the group (e.g. identity as a group member separated from the teacher compared to individual identity within the group and so on). At the present time little is known of the role-relational processes operating in pre-school groups, and how children learn participant role skills. Overhearing classroom talk does appear to have a bearing upon the way in which children will contribute to discussions in the class. Orsolini (1988) recorded over 5000 turns of talk in a classroom of 4–5 year olds and found that children were much more likely to offer relevant information (and extend the topics introduced by the teacher), where the teacher was expanding on a contribution previously offered by another child. She also notes that the way the children began to discuss topics with each other followed a similar pattern; high relevance to a preceding utterance initiated a subsequent relevant contribution by another child. Establishing topic/discourse cohesion extends across successive turns at talk, interdependent with circumscribed management procedures in such contexts. Again, the child as overhearer is being provided with demonstrative lessons about role-relations, participant status, what might be needed to introduce warrantable topics and other key elements for successful participation.

The group addressing results above have also highlighted the specific forms of group addressing speech that will be overheard by the child. It would not be surprising for the young child (particularly the 3 year old), to find it difficult to participate successfully as a group member when a range of possibly confusing terms are used by the adults. For example, on occasion, the adult speaker is a fundamental part of the group ("All of us can now ..." and "Sometimes we do this ... ") at other times separate ("Everyone ... All of you ... I want you all" ... and so on) and most confusingly, sometimes part of the group and yet apart ("We tidy up now, don't we children?"). Pimm (1987) has pointed out how confusing this must be for older children (learning mathematics) and the examples recorded here suggest that such forms of address are not uncommon in the pre-school.

However, it may be less confusing for the child than an orthodox linguistic analysis would suggest. The findings above have highlighted the relationship between group addressing *form* and *function*, in that explicit indicators of group membership (Everybody ...) will be overheard when the group is being 'managed' for particular purposes. Further, as a young child there is a much greater possibility that you will overhear your own name (or an identifying tag) as a member of a group compared to reference forms commonly used in other dialogue contexts: however, the way in which your name is used (the accompanying stress and intonation) marks it in a quite distinct way. Such accompanying markers make available in a 'direct' way, information which indicates the current dynamic role-relation 'affordances' for this conversational context.

Finally, the functional analysis of group addressing speech highlights the very 'management' orientation of the talk. It appears that forms of speech which are 'extra dyadic' contain a higher proportion of directives than commonly found in other adult-child dialogue. Group addressing speech is particularly facilitative as a 'cohorting' mechanism, evidenced in the observation that the main kind of directive function is the 'action' form where the adult is trying to specifically change the group's behaviour in some way. These results largely support previous 'management' conceptions of group addressing speech (Payne & Hustler, 1979). There are numerous amusing examples where the adults themselves use the 'overhearing' context for their own and possibly the childrens 'group identity' ends, for example:

(Adults to each other in loud voices and with particular emphasis on 'they', 'children' and 'nobody', etc.)

"They're lovely dancers, aren't they Cathy?"

"Very tidy, these children, don't you think?"

"Nobody will get any sweets if they carry on like this, will they Brenda?"

A case has been put here for paying more attention to the relationships between language forms overheard in multi-party interactions and the skills necessary for successful participation (in groups). Previous research which has focused upon discourse differences across the school and home setting (Wells, 1983), understandably centred around parent-child and teacher-child comparisons. Commonly reported problems of children who enter infant school without any pre-school experience may arise, not so much out of the lack of opportunity for peer-peer interaction, but because some infants have had little exposure to being treated as part of a group.

Various questions emerge out of this attempt to examine the 'attention orienting' nature of overhearing, whether as name use, overhearing as social sensitivity or what it might mean to be addressed as a member of a group. Isolating the subtleties of 'overhearing contexts' and how participant role-relation affordances might be made available to the child through exposure to other's talk will be complex. In this chapter the importance of overhearing name use has been established. In the final chapter I will return to a consideration of some ways in which these factors have a bearing upon the framework outlined in Chapter 5.

NOTES

1. In an ethnographic study of infancy within the Bimin-Kuskusmin tribe in Papua New Guinea, Poole (1985) describes the highly complex naming practices before and after the 'giving of female names' to the child around the age of 2. The argument here is that by examining naming practices one can gain insight into a people's ethnopsychology as in the act of linking a person with a label the individual is particularised or identified in relation to other people.

2. These points are not restricted only to 'social' aspects of classroom contexts. For example, Campbell (1988) points out that despite the emphasis upon the cognitive aspects surrounding learning to read (particularly in classrooms), reading communicates to the child the importance of a range of other interactional skills. In reading as an activity, 'the teacher conveys messages, often implicitly from which children learn about conversational rights, the importance of classroom interactions, oral reading as a shared activity, and the nature of reading' (p.377). Clearly the understanding of such contexts is not restricted to the child who is actually called upon to read, again implicating the role of overhearing and observing in such group contexts.

3. Levinson's (1983) main criticism is that Searle's speech act category system is better understood subsumed under the conversational analysis approach.

CHAPTER EIGHT

Overhearing as Conversation Monitoring

INTRODUCTION

Two aspects of overhearing have now been considered, overhearing as happenstance and overhearing as attention focusing. A third distinguishing characteristic or context of overhearing, is overhearing as conversation monitoring or 'tracking'. Attention has already been drawn to the distinction between overhearing as participant and as contributor. An additional dimension to such a contrast is overhearing as bystander in either a ratified or non-ratified participant role (Goffman, 1981). The suggestion was made that participation in conversation will be facilitated (and in part depend upon) the degree of exposure the infant and young child has to opportunities for watching and overhearing others engage in talk. In this chapter the aim is to examine the relationship between overhearing as conversation monitoring and subsequent participation, principally by reporting on two experiments which utilised the significance of overhearing name use (for the young child) as a method for examining conversational participation skills. The significance of these studies is best understood against the background of available research which has looked at children's conversations, research which has examined contexts 'beyond the dyad' (two-party dialogue).

Ervin-Tripp (1979) analysed over 700 videotaped examples of dyadic, triadic and polyadic conversations involving older and younger siblings, friends' and adults' interactions with children in naturalistic contexts. In line with Sacks et al.'s (1974) assumptions on the importance of gaining the floor in multi-party conversations, it is hypothesised that to be able to participate requires the possession of fairly sophisticated information processing abilities. Ervin-Tripp (1979) reports that across 'dyadic—triadic' contexts, younger children were significantly worse at successfully timing interruptions. In other words, the ability to synchronise conversational turn-taking appropriately (here taken as the avoidance of excessive overlapping) increase over time (age) and is easier to accomplish in dyads than triads (and polyads).[1]

In dyadic contexts younger children found it easier to anticipate the correct point for their own completions or answers in conversations with partners, suggesting that the very presence of a non-participating third person (in triadic encounters) made the monitoring of their own conversations more problematic. Ervin-Tripp (1979) also suggests that older children, when interrupted as part of a triadic encounter, are less likely to ignore overlaps, irrespective of whether they were interrupting or being interrupted. Twenty-five per cent of the time older children would attempt to rebuff the challenge, whereas the younger children would rarely do so. Remedies would commonly take the form of increased volume of their own talk, immediate repetition or repetition immediately after the interrupter had finished talking.

Although concerned primarily with older children's group conversational abilities, Dorval and Eckerman (1984) report a study of pre-school children's conversational skills and suggest that pre-school children lacked certain kinds of 'triadic' conversational skills because of problems of processing speed. Their argument is based on the suggestion that as appropriate and prompt turn-taking in triads or groups requires (a) recognising 'transition relevant pauses' in the talk; (b) understanding what is said quickly enough to reply before someone else attempts to, and (c) recognising cases where a response is called for from a particular member of a group, then it is to be expected that pre-school children will find it difficult to participate fully in multi-party conversational contexts. There data would support such a suggestion, that is where compared with older children's conversational participation skills.

In contrast, other work suggests that children's early conversational skills are more sophisticated. Craig and Gallagher (1983) investigated the role of gaze and proximity as non-verbal turn-regulating mechanisms in young children's conversations and using naturalistic videotaped settings they looked at 'non-simultaneous' language events across dyadic and triadic grouping of familiar 4-year-old children (i.e. ignoring interruptions). They found differences in speaker/listener gaze across contexts relative to changes in turns at speaking, which indicated that in triadic contexts the child who was not the 'non-next speaker' listener, decoded the turn allocation gaze cues of the current speaker, and would often respond appropriately (i.e. by not interrupting or turning towards the 'next speaker' other listener).

Additionally, Craig and Gallagher (1983) point out that the speaker gaze patterns were more variable within dyads. There were many more examples of looking at self, or at objects around about. While this might imply that there are more demands placed upon speakers in triadic contexts, it may equally reflect the fact that within dyadic encounters any speech at all can be taken (as far as the listener is concerned) as intended for her. Craig and Gallagher (1983) comment that no two children engaged in dialogue to the exclusion of the third party present for any substantial period of time (again which might be taken to reflect difficulties children might have at this age in maintaining topics, relevance and so on).

In a separate analysis of the same subjects Gallagher and Craig (1982) analysed the pattern of overlaps occurring across the spontaneous speech within these contexts. They wanted to investigate the extent to which their subjects could integrate linguistic and pragmatic information so as to anticipate 'transition relevant pauses'. Coding verbal/verbal and verbal/non-verbal overlap behaviours (e.g. interrupting talk with gestures) they found that 'internal sentence' overlaps tended to occur at points in the speaker's sentence where the rest of what she was going to say was to be anticipated in some way. This, they suggest, implies an integration of 'desire for next turn' with knowledge of the language (structure of sentences and so on). Further, Gallagher and Craig (1982) also propose that 'sentence initial' overlaps (two children overlapping precisely at the beginning of a turn at talk) do not reflect any lack of discourse skill, but rather the recognition by the children of each other's attempts to dominate what is going on. There was a clear tendency for some children to dominate the conversation until a competitor made sustained attempts to 'gain the floor'. All of this they suggest reflects 'interactive competence rather than conversational inadequacy' (p.74).

In a longitudinal study (1 year) of children aged between 2–3 years, Dunn and Shatz (1989) examined whether young children attend to, or understand, the topic of speech not addressed to them, by analysing their intrusions into conversations between mothers and older siblings. Three points are worth noting in this study. First, they suggest that relevant intrusions were much more likely if the preceding speech was about the child who made the interruption. Second, they implicate the importance of role relations between the adults and children in this study where they comment 'to intervene in other's conversations with a comment that is relevant and/or provides new information involves a challenge that differs from that of responding to speech addressed to oneself, or from initiating a conversation on a topic of one's choice' (p.408). Third, they suggest that conversational situations that offer opportunities to intrude in other's talk 'fosters children's abilities' although in what particular way is left unspecified.

One final study related to the concerns of this chapter was conducted by Craig and Washington (1986) looking at the turn-taking behaviours of 4-year-old children in triads. They found that most of the utterances were 'non-simultaneous' (very few interruptions) and that turn-allocation was regulated much more by the speaker than by the listener (e.g. self-selection). In addition, they report that turn allocation was most affected by proximity (whoever was standing next to the current speaker was likely to be the next speaker and not the other remaining members of the triad) and that conflicting bids (for next speaker) were more likely to occur where the speaker's gaze was focused on one listener, but happened to be very close to the other.

What is important is that such proximity effects might indicate that while children of this age are good at detecting intonation affordances of conversational contexts, they are much less skilled at providing them, and initially they use proximity rather than intonational emphasis and volume, to indicate or provide the appropriate conversational affordance (display of the intention to interrupt). This study emphasised that if you wish to 'self-select' as a listener, you must carefully monitor the conversation and if you are somewhat distant from the speaker it is simply much harder to do so.

Craig and Washington (1986) also stress that quite distinct conversational role patterns were discernible for the three possible roles (speaker; listener-next-speaker and listener-non-next-speaker). Importantly, when speaker cues about possible turn-exchanges were present, the listener-non-next-speaker was more consistently watching the speaker than was the other listener, and when no speaker cues were being displayed the listener-non-next-speaker appeared much less attentive. They comment:

'Most turn-exchange behaviours occurred alone, although many combinations were possible. This lack of redundancy in marking the direction of the turn-exchange, like non-explicit selections of the turn-exchange behaviours overall, underscores the need for careful monitoring of the other participants in the interaction' (p.193).

A STUDY OF CHILDREN'S
RESPONSES TO NAME USE
BY OTHERS

Few child language studies then, have considered the relationship between overhearing talk, conversation monitoring abilities and participation skills. During the observational study reported earlier (where addressee-referree association patterns were identified), it came to the author's attention that the way in which the referred-to child responded to overhearing her name being used by another, indicated that she was monitoring the conversation taking place between the speaker and the addressee. Given there is no reason to believe that a young, about to be referred-to, child will be paying much (if any) attention to a conversation she is not involved with, while also recognising that overhearing (suddenly) her name being used by somebody else is likely to be noticeable (attention-orienting), then we might expect a fairly high proportion of looks towards the speaker (whoever has just mentioned her name) when her name is used. For the child concerned this might be to establish whether she is being addressed, or if it is perfectly clear from the intonation that she is not, then possibly a look to ascertain what is being said about her.

However, it appeared that the child understood something of the communicative intention in the speaker's act of referring to the third party (the child herself) and would turn to observe the addressee's response, as if to see if he/she had 'got the message'. For example, the speaker would say to the addressee, 'Christine, that's a nice hat Katie's wearing, isn't it?', and the referred-to child Katie, if she responded at all, would look at the addressee to see if she would look at her hat or respond in some other way. Explicit evidence of this kind, that is, a response which indicates that the young child is not only paying attention to overheard conversations but is monitoring them quite closely, is clearly important for any developing model of the role of overhearing and conversational participation abilities. The first step was to look at the behaviour in a more systematic fashion (than the previous field notes recorded during the earlier study), and to establish the extent of this conversational monitoring skill with pre-school children. The aim of the first experiment was simply to examine the referred-to child's response to name use in a group conversational context.

(a) Experiment 1: Monitoring name use by others
Method

Design

In designing this experiment two considerations were paramount. First to examine the non-random pattern of the referred-to child's response (in other words, the tendency to show a higher proportion of looks towards the child being addressed, compared to looks towards the speaker). Second, by comparing responses to third party reference forms with responses to two-party (dyadic) dialogue, to highlight the significance (with reference to the conversation monitoring skills of the referred-to child) of overhearing your own name being used by others with whom you are not participating. While these utterance contexts are not directly comparable, it is necessary to establish whether children within hearing distance of a conversation, have a tendency to look at other children who are being spoken to by an adult, even though they themselves are not being referred-to in any particular way. This would serve to underscore the important nature of the 'referred-to' child's response when she overhears her name being used.

Setting

This experiment was conducted in a quiet room at the University of Strathclyde's pre-school playgroup. To enable video analysis, two tables were placed together in a 'V' shape and the experimenter positioned at the apex and for each group of children, two children sat at the tables on either side of him. This ensured that when the experimenter addressed child A, (the addressed child), and referred to child R, (the referred-to child), child R (if she was going to respond with a look at the addressed child) would be seen to turn her head clearly towards the addressed child (and away from the speaker). This set-up circumvented problems during the analysis over coding whether the referred-to child looked towards the speaker or the addressee (see Figure 8.1). Such a response, of course, was the behaviour under examination. The referred-to child was always nearest the experimenter, the addressee furthest away, and for any third party reference utterance, 'addressee-referred-to' child pairs were always seated together at the same table. Approximately half-way through each session each pair of children at a table would exchange places allowing each child in the group to be the 'referred-to' subject.

Subjects and Procedure

Nine children from the University playgroup took part in this experiment. Their ages ranged from 3;5 to 4;5 (average 4;0). The children

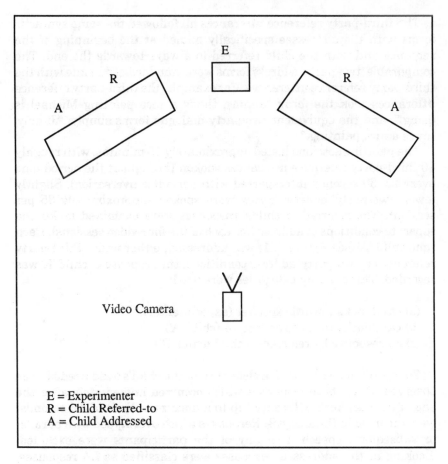

E = Experimenter
R = Child Referred-to
A = Child Addressed

FIG. 8.1. The experimental set-up

were observed in groups of four (with three of the children taking part more than once) over four separate occasions. Only two of the children in the final group appeared to have language difficulties, all the rest were very comfortable with the experimenter and each other. To facilitate an appropriate context within which as many examples of naturally occurring third-party reference utterances could be spoken, the children were asked to draw some animal shapes, (templates were provided) and then paint them in. This allowed the experimenter to include numerous examples of third-party reference in his speech to the children such as:

"Jamie, that's a nice painting Katie's doing."

The third-party reference utterances all followed the same syntactic forms with the addressee specifically named at the beginning of the sentence and with the child referred-to always towards the end. The comparable 'two-party' address forms were standardised in line with the third-party reference utterances. For example, the third-party reference utterances took the form: "Jimmy, that's a nice painting Michael is doing.", and the equivalent two-party dialogue forms simply: "Jimmy, that's a nice painting."

The painting sessions lasted approximately 15 minutes, with roughly 40 third-party reference utterances spoken throughout the period (one every 25–30 seconds interspersed with normal conversation). Slightly fewer 'two-party' address forms were spoken (approximately 35 per session). The referred-to childs' responses were examined under the separate conditions of address (for each of the four video sessions). Each time child 'A' (see Figure 8. 1) was addressed, either under third-party reference or 'two-party' address conditions, the response of child 'R' was recorded. Three coding categories were used:

(a) child looks towards speaker (experimenter).
(b) child looks towards addressee (child 'A'). ·
(c) no response by referred-to child (child 'R').

For a look to be recorded, a clear turn of the child's head needed to be observed. Only those responses which occurred immediately after the end of the speaker's utterance (up to a maximum limit of 3.5 seconds) were included in the analysis. Responses which overlapped with parallel or subsequent speech from any of the participants were excluded. 'Looking at the addressee' responses were classified as LA responses, 'looks at the speaker' as LS responses. After each video session the experimenter analysed each tape (coding responses according to the above categories) in conjunction with an independent observer. The level of inter-observer reliability was around 95% (kappa co-efficients .79). Disagreements were either resolved via playback of the tapes, or where agreement could not be reached, those responses were excluded from the analysis (only two such occasions occurred).[2]

Results
The main comparison of interest is the ratio of responses with either looks at the addressee or looks at the speaker across the third-party reference and two-party dialogue conditions. In order to control for possible confounding effects of individual or session analysis,[3] Mantel-Haenszel (1959) chi-square tests were carried out highlighting the non-random pattern of the referred-to child's response described in

TABLE 8.1
Percentage Response Rates for Language Forms

Forms of response	Third party reference	Two-party dialogue
Looks at speaker	8	14
Looks at addressee	53	15
No response	39	71

Table 6.1 (individual analysis, x^2 = 4.62; d.f. = 1; p<0.001; session analysis, x^2 = 8.18, d.f. = 1; p<0.001).

Employing this analysis entailed dropping out a considerable amount of data. Nevertheless, this did not obscure the overall conclusion, that is, the odds of looking at the addressee under the 'third-party reference' condition are 4–5 times the odds of looking at the same addressee under the 'two-party dialogue' condition. Simply, these results demonstrate that when a child overhears his/her name being used, there is a high probability that he/she will respond by looking towards the person being addressed. For children of this age range (3;4 to 4;6) there is little evidence that they are at all confused regarding speaker-addressee role (they do not mistakenly believe that they are being addressed by name), which is interesting given the findings of the observational study in Chapter 5. There the overhearing young infants did not exhibit any interest in others using their names until around 14 months, and their earliest responses was by turning and looking at the speaker.

The results of this experiment highlight the existence of a conversation monitoring skill which may be well established by the time children are four years old. It is well documented that children's conversational skills in dyadic contexts appear to be quite sophisticated even by 18 months (Stern, 1974; Trevarthen & Hubley, 1978). When a child of 3 years overhears her name being used by others with whom she is not directly participating, she either shows little interest or responds in a fashion which suggests that she is monitoring the conversation in some way. Under these circumstances less than 10% of the time will she look towards the speaker (Table 8.1).

Furthermore, comparing responses to third-party reference with two-party dialogue provides an indication of how often children within listening distance of ongoing dialogue respond in a non-verbal fashion to the participants involved. Around 70% of the time (Table 8.1) no response is apparent from children who are within listening distance of two other people engaged in a conversation. Introducing the child's name into the conversation leads to a dramatic increase in the proportion of occurrences where the referred-to child looks at the child being addressed by the adult. Overhearing your own name being used by those with whom you are not directly involved with is of considerable importance to the young child. The odds of a child referred-to by name looking at the child being addressed during or immediately after a third- party reference utterance are 4–5 times the odds of a nearby child looking at the same addressee during normal two-party dialogue.

The non-random response pattern (the LA response) highlights the fact that the child was not reacting to name use in this context as a straightforward reaction to naming as simply an attention orienting device, but at least half of the time must have been monitoring the ongoing conversation in a relatively sophisticated fashion. Analysis of the timing of the response for the participants in this context revealed that on, by far, the majority of occasions where the child looked towards the addressee this would occur not at, or immediately after, overhearing his/her name being used, but after the completion of the speaker's sentence. This would indicate a sensitivity to the turn-taking procedures such that they would turn to look, just before the appropriate turn-change pause indicative of speaker change.

Why exactly does the referred-to child turn towards the child being addressed? The observational study of adult-child use of third-party reference in the pre-school setting suggested that the ways in which particular children are addressed and referred-to together in the adult's third party reference utterances, could be an important source of information concerning the social relationships between the children. It seems reasonable to argue that the referred-to child does not merely look towards the addressed child simply because it is the latter's turn in the conversation. We might expect to observe the same phenomenon with the two party dialogue forms if this was the case. Rather, the fact that she has been referred-to is, for her, significant. It is much more likely that the referred-to child could be seeking information regarding the way in which she is paired with the addressed child.

Consider then the hypothesis that the referred-to child may tend to view any information conveyed by the addressed child's response (any reply to the speaker's act of reference) as significant in some way. Here, from the referred-to child's point of view, is a relatively rare situation where there is every likelihood that somebody (and increasingly more importantly a peer) is going to comment upon an activity or some other attribute directly related to her. From this 'sensitivity to social information' hypothesis, differential rates of the referred-to child's 'looking at the addressee' response could be predicted with respect to the probability that an answer is likely to be forthcoming from the child being addressed by the speaker. By using a question versus statement comparison across third-party reference forms it should be possible to establish the degree of sensitivity to name reference.

(b) Experiment 2: Conversation Monitoring and Developing Participation Skills

In order to look in more detail at the child's response to name overhearing, a second experiment was conducted with three aims. The first concerned why the referred-to child looked at the addressee after overhearing her name being used by the speaker. In line with a "seeking social information" hypothesis this experiment employed a question versus statement third-party reference comparison. For example, in a question format (e.g. "Lee-Ann, do you like Katie's painting?") the child addressed is being specifically asked for a comment about the referred-to child. In contrast, the participation demands upon the child when replying to a statement form (e.g. "Lee-Ann, that's an interesting picture Katie's doing") are not so compelling, that is, beyond minimal constraints of politeness. The previous experiment showed that there were numerous occasions where the children would simply ignore statements made by and between others. If the referred-to child is (a) monitoring the ongoing conversation, (b) skilled enough to recognise the distinct conversational demands associated with the use of these speech forms, and (c) likely to respond to her name use by others in a fashion which indicates her sensitivity to social information about herself, then response rates should be higher in the question-format context.

The second aim of this experiment was to examine the emergence of the 'looking response' as a potential developmental indices of conversation monitoring skills. As children get older, we could expect to find an increase in the 'looking at addressee' response to name overhearing, reflecting their increasing sensitivity to the circumstances surrounding social referencing. The child's growing knowledge of the likelihood that the child being addressed may make a relevant response in relation to the speaker's act of reference. The third aim was to replicate the effect reported in the first experiment with different children in a separate setting.

Method

Design
The design of the experiment above was again employed, adapted however, for two third-party reference conditions. This allowed for comparisons between: (a) third-party reference questions and two-party dialogue; (b) third-party reference statements and two-party dialogue;

and (c) third-party reference questions and third party reference statements. Three pre-school age groups were examined with an increase in the number of subjects in each group. This second experiment took approximately three months to run and was carried out in a different pre-school day nursery setting in Glasgow. It was carried out in the staffroom of the nursery and the physical layout, material and so on, followed the format established in the first experiment.

Subjects and Procedure
Twenty-four children participated in this study in three age groups (youngest age range 2;5–3;5: middle range 3;6–4;5: oldest group 4;6–5). For each age band two sub-groups were established, with four children in each group for the duration of the study. All children were familiar with each other for at least six months prior to the experiment and were predominantly social economic class three, with approximately equal numbers of boys and girls. While the procedure followed the format set out in the previous experiment, certain alterations were incorporated into the procedure.[4] To ensure that the introduction of the test sentences occurred in a natural fashion and in a sufficient number, the format of the utterances would vary slightly in content, while maintaining their essentially similar format. For example, a third-party reference question might vary between: "Jamie, do you like Katie's painting?" and "Jamie, do you like Katie's doll (on her painting)?"

All third party forms were standardised, with the addressee named at the beginning and the referred-to child towards the end of the utterance. The grammatical structure of the examples was constant throughout, with only the slight changes in form specified above.[5] Three types of test sentences were employed:

(a) third-party reference questions, "Jamie, do you like Katie's painting?"

(b) third-party reference statements, "Jamie, that's a nice picture Katie's doing."

(c) two-party dialogue utterances, "Jamie, that's a nice picture."

Data Analysis
For each session (n = 24) the referred-to child's responses were coded according to the format of the previous experiment. However, preliminary analysis of the oldest age group of children revealed the necessity for an additional coding category: a 'verbally appropriate response'. As our interest is primarily concerned with evidence of the child's ability to monitor the conversation of others with whom she is

not directly participating (and not looking at responses *per se*), it became apparent that while some of the older children were failing to respond to the speaker's act of reference to them with a 'look' (at the addressee or speaker), they did produce verbally relevant responses to the speaker's utterance immediately after, and by way of comment upon, the ongoing conversation.

For example, when the speaker would say to the addressed child, "Jamie, do you like Katie's painting?", before the addressee replied, or if there was no reply, the referred-to child, Katie, would typically comment: "Well, I think it's good anyway!", without necessarily looking at the addressed child or the speaker. For this reason, in addition to the three coding categories defined above (Experiment 1), a 'verbally appropriate response' category was included, defined as a response where the referred-to child does not respond with a look towards either the addressee or speaker, yet makes a verbal response relevant to the ongoing conversational context.

Verbally appropriate responses were of three types:

(a) a comment about the referred-to child or her painting (that is, herself: e.g. "Well I like mine anyway!").

(b) a comment with reference to the addressed child's potential reply: for example, "No!" (anticipating that the addressed child was about to comment negatively) or,

(c) a comment on the speaker's act of addressing the addressed child: for example, "She won't like it!"[6]

Results.

(1) Children's Responsiveness to Name Reference. It is clear from Table 8.2 that in terms of overall response rate the referred-to child, when overhearing his/her name being used by others with whom he/she is not directly involved, will tend to respond with a 'look' either towards the addressee or speaker. This increasing responsiveness or social sensitivity is evident for both forms of third- party reference (questions and statements). With the 'two-party' address there is simply a consistent low response rate.

If the analysis is restricted to the 'looking' response alone, then we find a 10% rise for all language forms across the younger age groups, followed by either a slight fall (third-party reference questions and two-party dialogue forms) or a small increase (third-party reference statements) across the middle and older child age groups. However, if the 'verbally appropriate responses' of the older-aged children are included we highlight the importance of overhearing name use, that is with regard to conversational participation and responsiveness. What

TABLE 8.2
Referred-to-child's Percentage Response Rate

Language Form	Total Responses			Looking at addressee			Looking at speaker		
	TPRQ	TPRS	TPD	TPRQ	TPRS	TPD	TPRQ	TPRS	TPD
AGE GROUPS									
2;5 - 3;5 (n = 8)	45	41	22	34	23	12	11	18	10
3;6 - 4;5 (n = 8)	66	52	33	56	47	23	10	5	10
4;6 - 5;5 (n = 7)	79	69	30	65 (42	47 32	14 16)*	14	22	16

*Looks only (not including verbally appropriate responses)
TPRQ = Third-party reference questions
TPRS = Third-party reference statements
TPD = Two-party dialogue

we seem to have evidence for is a change in form as regards conversational monitoring skills in the pre-school age range, or more strictly a change in those behaviours from which we can infer that the conversation is being monitored by the referred-to child.

At the youngest age (2;3–3;5) the child, if she responds (note around 50% of the time they do not respond at all), will turn and look at either the child being addressed or the speaker. While this response rate may appear low, it is nevertheless twice the rate observed where the child is merely responding to a conversation going on nearby in which no explicit reference is made to her or him. Between the ages of 3;5–4;5, this responsiveness increases by as much as 20% under the third-party reference question condition and by around 11% with the third-party statement condition. Finally, with the older age group (4;6–5;5) one can identify a transitional stage for conversation monitoring abilities. The children are moving from what is arguably a non-verbal indication of conversation monitoring skills, towards a recognition of the conversational affordances made available through name use, such that they interrupt and comment at a 'relevant' juncture in the ongoing conversation. For the third-party reference condition the 'looking' response rate, although falling by 10%, is supplemented by a 23%

'contribution' from the inclusion of the verbally appropriate response category (Table 8.2). As an example of the verbally appropriate response, and as a reminder of the context the children were in (Figure 8.1):

Speaker: Anne-Marie, do you like David's space-ship? (in his picture) and then interjecting before the child addressed answers:
David: (the referred-to child) *"Well, I like it anyway"* (stress on I!).
Anne-Marie: *"em ... it's all right."*

A similar pattern of results is seen with the statement forms of third-party reference (Table 8.2), where verbally appropriate responses account for 15% of the monitoring responses in this category. For the oldest age group, while there is the same propensity for the referred-to child to react with a looking response as there was with the middle age range children, this does not increase, and what emerges in parallel, and as an alternative to the 'looking response', is the tendency to break into the conversation with an appropriate comment.

Analysis revealed consistent effects for third-party reference questions (TPRQ) versus two-party dialogue (TPD) for all age groups x^2 = 19.6; 35.3; 51.6, all d.f. 1, p <0.01). However, third party reference statement versus two-party dialogue comparisons highlighted significant differences only for the two older age categories (x^2 = 15.2 (d.f. 1. p <0.05); x^2 = 35.3 (d.f.1. p <0.01)). In terms of developmental changes, TPRQ responses were significantly greater than TPD (T = 10, p <0.01) and TPRQ significantly greater than TPRS (T = 53.5 p <0.01). These effects were found to be consistent whether verbally appropriate responses were included or excluded (that is where looks only were analysed).

(2) Conversation Monitoring Skills. An initial analysis of the 'looking-at-addressee' (LA) response, using Mantel-Haenszel and Cochran tests, revealed no significant effects for any of the comparisons, principally due to the low number of absolute frequencies (or cells) of interest. Nevertheless, in line with the argument developed here, and with what was found previously (in Experiment 1), comparable predictions can be made. We should observe a higher proportion of LA responses with the third-party reference condition, that is compared with the two-party condition (i.e. comparison of proportions of responses). Furthermore, as the 'looking at speaker' (LS) response is primarily a random response (that is in line with the hypothesis that there is no reason for expecting the referred-to child to look at the speaker more often in one compared with any other condition) we would not expect to find any significant differences with regard to the response

rates across the comparisons of interest to us. And in line with the hypothesis that children will become increasingly sensitive to the distinct participation demands of being addressed with questions or with statements, we should find significant response rate differences across these utterance forms.

Percentage response rates for the two forms of looking responses (LA and LS) were calculated for the categories concerned and sign tests comparing the percentage rates for the looking response categories calculated. This was carried out within each age group, across the conditions. Comparison of the patterns across the LA and LS response rates to name overhearing support the hypothesis that the reason an affect was observed in the previous experiment was due to the higher proportion of LA responses after exposure to third-party reference language forms, that is compared to two-party dialogue. No equivalent pattern can be observed for the LS responses for any of the possible language comparisons. This LA effect can be found for all age groups for our original comparisons (TPRS vs. TPD as in the previous experiment) and for third-party reference questions versus two-party dialogue (Table 8.3).

With regard to the 'seeking social information' hypothesis and the third-party question vs. statement comparison, although the data might indicate a tendency for a higher response rate with the question forms of third-party reference, no significant differences were discernible. Between group analysis revealed that for the LA response rates significant effects were found between third-party reference questions and two-party dialogue $(T = 6, p < 0.01)$, third-party reference statements and two-party dialogue $(T = 10, p < 0.001)$. There was also

TABLE 8.3
Sign-test Comparisons for Response Forms

Age group	Language forms	Response forms	
		Looks at addressee	Looks at speaker
2;5 – 3;5	TPRQ v TPD	$P<0.05$	n.s.
	TPRS v TPD	$P<0.01$	n.s.
	TPRQ v TPRS	n.s.	n.s.
3;6 – 4;5	TPRQ v TPD	$P<0.01$	n.s.
	TPRS v TPD	$P<0.01$	n.s.
	TPRQ v TPRS	n.s.	n.s.
4;6 – 5;5	TPRQ v TPD	$P<0.01$ (*$P<0.01$)	n.s.
	TPRS v TPD	$P<0.01$ (*$P<0.01$)	n.s.
	TPRQ v TPRS	n.s.	n.s.

*Verbal responses excluded
TPRQ = Third-party reference questions
TPRS = Third-party reference statements
TPD = Two-party dialogue

evidence of an age trend where comparison was made between third-party questions and statements, although the absence of any effect in the analysis above suggests caution in interpretation (follow-up tests revealed that the source of the age effect can be traced to differences between responses to these language forms for the children aged between 3;6 and 4;5 years—see Figure 8.2).

What is clear is that the referred-to child's conversation monitoring response increases over the age ranges studied (i.e. becomes more marked). No corresponding increase is apparent where children are simply responding to ongoing conversation which does not explicitly refer to them. There is a distinct change in the manner of how this monitoring is reflected. Although there is clearly something of a 'ceiling effect' with the looking response, arguably a more interesting indication of monitoring is the appearance of interruption (i.e. the 'verbally appropriate response'). For the older age group of children (4;5–5;5) this accounts for around 20% of monitoring response forms under third-party reference conditions. This was not the case for the younger age groups where in comparison to the 40 examples recorded with the older children, only two instances of such interruption occurred.

SUMMARY

While these results lend support to the argument that young children's monitoring skills are not as limited as has previously been suggested (Dorval & Eckerman, 1984; Ervin-Tripp, 1979) other aspects of this study are worth noting. First, attention needs to be drawn to the distinction between: (a) the emergence of overall increased responsiveness to other people's conversations—an indication of the influence of overhearing as happenstance—and (b) the emergence and development of conversational monitoring skills of a participative nature. Consider Figure 8.2(a) where the probability of a response to both forms of third-party reference can be plotted alongside the likelihood of responding to overheard 'two-party' dialogue. Across age groups this overall responsiveness to overheard conversations, which contain explicit reference to the referred-to child, clearly increases. However, turning to Figure 8.2(b) and considering as a proportion of all responses recorded, only those responses which might be taken as indicative of conversation monitoring abilities (looks at the addressee and verbally appropriate comments), while there remain differences between two-party dialogue and both kinds of third-party reference, there is not only some indication of a ceiling 'effect' but possibly some sign of a decrease in responsiveness for the older aged children.[7] By the time a child is between 3–4 years old, 75% of occasions where she is

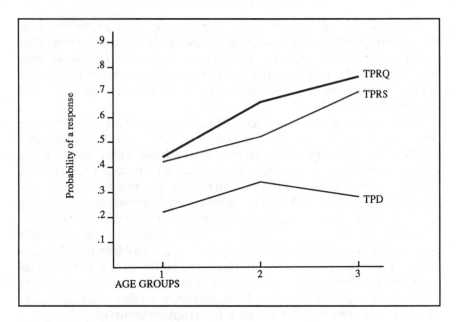

FIG. 8.2(a). All Responses/All Exposures

exposed to overhearing others using her name, her response is indicative of waiting to see in what way the child addressed is going to respond (to the speaker's act of reference), by looking at or interrupting him/her.

The progression from non-verbal listening skills (the LA response) to the use of the speaker's act of reference as a way of breaking into the conversation highlights the importance of naming in this context. There are two issues here. One is that we cannot necessarily assume (as is the case in a number of conversational analysis studies) that there is a premium on 'gaining the floor' and thus a tendency for the children to use every opportunity possible to interrupt. It may be just as important for the children to learn when it would be advantageous not to interrupt and remain silent. The other is the act of naming which forces or demands that a comment be made by the referred-to child. Analysis of other naturally occurring circumstances during the session where the children were referred-to pronominally (and where there was no adult participant), did not often result in interjection by the latter. The results here, however, do implicate the facilitative role of the child's sensitivity to 'naming' for the acquisition of conversation participation skills in that the immediacy of such socially-charged encounters warrants a comment by the referred-to person. Use of their name demands that they participate in a conversation in which they were not actively involved.

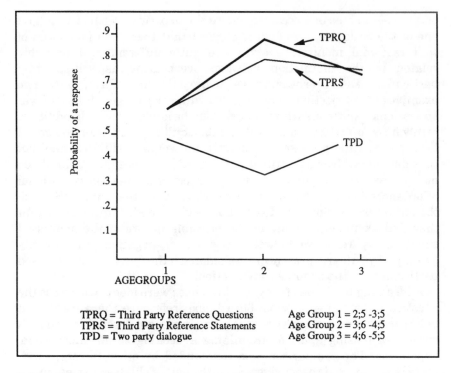

FIG. 8.2(b). Looks at Addressee + VAR/All Looking Responses + VAR

From the age of 2;5 to 4;5 the ability to monitor conversations in 'multi-party' contexts is expressed non-verbally. Between the ages of 4;6–5;5 children becomes significantly more sophisticated in their monitoring skills such that they can anticipate a forthcoming response from the child addressed by the speaker and pre-empt such a comment by use of an appropriate interjection. It was noteworthy that all such interjections by the referred-to child were relevant to the ongoing topic and not attempts to change the discussion or take over the floor, interrupt by introducing a new topic, or whatever. Interesting also (with reference to their ability and the timing and detection of turn-taking indices—intonation and so on) was the observation that the referred-to child would more often than not comment without actually looking up to see what the addressed child was doing.

In fact, only two examples were recorded where a 'look' occurred along with a 'verbally appropriate' response. While this to some extent reflects the exigencies of the task they were doing (painting—they appeared to be very engrossed in what they were doing such that to stop, look up and comment might only occur when a particularly striking event occurred—such as one occasion where the experimenter had to tell off one of the children), two factors suggest that these two indicators of conversational monitoring skills are quite different and arguably related to the distinction between overhearing as self-selecting participant and overhearing as non-participant. First, only two examples of interjection were recorded with the younger children (over 16 sessions—subsequently excluded from the analysis) who, in addition, rarely interrupted any talk involving the adult experimenter and one of their peers. Unless spoken to directly, the younger children may not consider themselves as 'ratified participants' or more likely, simply do not possess the requisite skills for recognising the conversational affordances made available when somebody uses their name. Second, the nature of the older children's interjections made it quite clear that they had an understanding of the probable nature of the addressed child's likely response (whether positive or negative) and already (simply by their presence) considered themselves as ratified participants in the ongoing conversation.

Addressing the issue of why no differences were identified across the question and statement forms of third-party reference, there are at least two reasons which suggest that it was simply not a sensitive enough method of teasing apart or examining a 'seeking social information' hypothesis. The comparison was confounded by other factors. First, there is an inherent responsiveness on the part of children to treat much of adult-to-child 'statement' talk as directive in nature (Dore, 1979) particularly in pre-school and classroom settings (Emiliani, Zanni, & Cargetti, 1981). Such talk is treated in much the same way as a question: if an adult makes a statement directed at you then clearly even at a minimal level of politeness constraints, you need to make a relevant reply (see also Becker, 1988a). Second, although there are studies which have successfully employed question/answer comparisons to tease out subtle aspects of speaker selection or turn-taking mechanisms (Berninger & Garvey, 1981), the effect of using names appears to be of such significance that other aspects of the talk become secondary. The videotapes highlighted numerous occasions where although adult-to-child talk was of more interest than other child-child talk, the use of names in adult-talk was particularly attention orienting, that is in a way which either offer a 'not to be missed' opportunity to enter the talk or which demanded or warranted a 'social pre-emptive' comment on the part of the child who was about to be commented upon.

In summary, for all age groups the referred-to child rarely responded to overhearing her name immediately it was mentioned, suggesting that children of 3 years of age are sensitive to the pragmatics of turn-taking (nuances of intonation, gaze direction and so on) in and accompanying the speaker's use of their name in conversations they are not directly involved with. Instead the referred-to child turned to look at the addressed child (or makes a verbally appropriate response) before the addressed child began to reply to the speaker indicating their knowledge that a reply was warranted. The timing of the response also revealed a sophisticated degree of precision. There was on average a 2.5 second switching pause (turn transfer) between the end of the speaker's sentence and the beginning of the addressed child's response. 1–1.5 seconds after the completion of the speaker's sentence the child, who had been referred-to, began to turn towards the child addressed and is already looking when the addressed child subsequently speaks—see Forrester (1988) for details. She does this whether she is under 3 or over 5 years, suggesting that this ability is acquired relatively early and is well established by the end of the pre-school period. Although only 50–60% of the time children aged 2.5–3.5 respond to name-referring in the fashion reported, they do so with the similar manifestations of their sensitivity to the fine-tuned timing of turns at talk, indicative of their recognition of conversational affordances.

This is further borne out by the observation that when the addressed child did not respond to the speaker, the referred-to child normally waited for 4–5 seconds, as if to make certain that no reply would be forthcoming. Only after such a gap would they resume what they were doing (painting). This might suggest that young pre-school children have some understanding of the 'switching pause' patterns of turn-transfer procedures in talk, and in this context, only 'gives up' on the expected reply after a significant (in pause switching terms) period to time has elapsed. This sensitivity to the turn-taking timing precision of conversations argues against any suggestion that children have problems in group conversational contexts because of constraints linked to processing speed (Dorval & Eckerman, 1984). Not only can they anticipate the turn-patterns, but can do so from overhearing alone (that is without having to look up) and with sufficient skill such that they can time their own interruptions appropriately.

The two experiments reported in this chapter highlight the conversation monitoring skills of young pre-school children. It has also been possible to demonstrate a relationship between overhearing name use and subsequent participation in conversation. This skill not only builds upon earlier conversation monitoring abilities (the younger child's looking response) but also, in the manner in which it is exhibited—the timing of the interrruption—highlights the affordance like nature of conversational contexts. The final chapter takes up these and other related issues, alongside a consideration of the overhearing model within the context of the eco-structural framework.

NOTES

1. A number of studies have looked at triadic and polyadic patterns of talk in adults conversations. Goffman (1976), although arguing that the two-party face-to-face dialogue is the dominant form of encounter in any triadic or multi-party grouping, draws attention to the skills involved in moving to and fro between 'ratified participants' and bystanders, an essential element for overall group cohesion. Harrigan and Steffan (1983) and Goodwin (1981) have provided some empirical data concerning the subtleties of turn-taking timing in multi-party conversations. Bennett (1981) and Tannen (1980) examining group conversations have all reported on the self-selected turn allocation procedure described by Harrigan (1985), that is, interruption.

2. With regard to validity, that is whether the 'turn and look' could be considered as a conversationally related behavioural response, it was not possible to undertake commonly used 'validity' indicators with children of this age. For example, in similar adult non-verbal interaction studies (Von Cranach & Vine, 1973), following the experiment a person being addressed by a speaker is usually asked whether they felt or knew that they were being 'looked at' at that time, in that context. However, for the response in question here, the timing, consistency, frequency and the directional precision of its manner indicate that it was directly related to the conversational exchange.

3. Finding a significant association in a chi-square merely because the data are all 'piled' on top of each other—either from individual subjects or over sessions.

4. The painting game was altered in light of the fact that the youngest age group had difficulty in drawing out the shapes before filling them in. For all age groups, drawings were provided and the children were instructed to colour them in.

5. Full details of procedure in Forrester (1988).

6. During the analysis, five video sessions were randomly selected from the total (24) and analysed by independent observers. Adequate levels of inter-observer reliability were obtained for the categories of interest (79–90%, kappa co-efficient 0.70–0.81), each video analysis taking approximately 1.5 hours.

7. There is, of course, considerable difference between the ease of simply turning and looking at another compared to where one begins to interject into a conversation—particularly into another conversation which is taking place between one of your peers and an adult.

CHAPTER NINE

Investigating and Understanding Young Children's Social-cognitive Skills: A Synopsis

Threads of the various arguments outlined earlier can now be reconsidered and a preliminary evaluation of the eco-structural framework attempted. I began by suggesting that despite the increasing proliferation of research and interest in social-cognitive development, the contemporary models supporting the more popular research strategies are unlikely to provide the necessary conceptual and methodological tools for understanding young children's social-cognitive skills. There is something paradoxical, of course, in making such a suggestion. On the one hand social-cognitive developmental research, at the time of writing, is a major paradigm within developmental psychology and of considerable interest to many outside the discipline (e.g. cognitive scientists, linguists, clinical psychologists and so on). On first appearances there is a sense of considerable optimism and enthusiasm and a growing number of researchers and educators are turning towards this sub-discipline. On the other hand, and possibly related to its current popularity, it has not yet engaged in that level of critical self-analysis indicative of more secure domains within the social sciences. There is a history of critical comment within developmental social cognition (from Shantz, 1975 on) however, and understandably in the early days, this was more concerned with establishing what should come within the domain of enquiry or how social-cognitive development might be defined.

In Chapter 1 historical elements and complementary interests within social-cognitive developmental research were identified, and together these have helped define, demarcate and contribute towards explaining why there is such interest in this field. My aim though was not simply to describe these elements, but to place them with regard to the influence of the most dominant contemporary metaphor, 'symbol-manipulating' representational information processing. Some problems arising from the overemphasis on this guiding frame of reference were outlined: Why has there been so few attempts to justify the separation of 'individual and social'? Will concern with the formal aspects of developmental psycholinguistics constrain the investigation of the relationship between language and social cognition? Why do we limit the potential of our models by simply accepting the underlying philosophical assumptions of mainstream cognitive science? Does the methodological solipsism of the information processing approach not assume a questionable notion of cognitive separability?

Others have raised similar doubts (Feldman & Bruner, 1987), but here my concern centred around two issues germane to the study of children's social-cognitive skills. The first was the suggestion that dominant theoretical views of social-cognitive development cannot adequately accommodate participatory aspects of children's social-cognitive development (participating in conversations). The second matter was more a question of emphasis: if we wish to study how the young child learns to successfully participate in the social world, then what might facilitate our investigations is a framework which encourages the development of models which change the emphasis away from 'in the head' predications, towards conceptions of social-cognitive interaction, and participation scenarios constitutive of the social practices between humans.

Three groupings or themes within the literature on children's social-cognitive development were identified (individualistic; interactionist and a third subsuming language, conversational studies and research on children's social-cognitive skills). There was a threefold intention inherent in reviewing the field in this fashion. One was simply expediency: to better understand a burgeoning research domain by comparing and contrasting various identifiable strands. A second aim was to highlight various theoretical positions in the area so as to facilitate an evaluation of the current 'state of the art'. The third goal was more ambitious: to critically review the research field with reference to one overarching question, are the theoretical perspectives within social-cognitive development research appropriate for the study of children's participative social-cognitive skills? Chapter 2 considered the individualistic constructivist and representational approaches (the Piagetian and the information processing positions).

Any discussion of Piaget and the myriad of examples and instances where Piagetian ideas have found expression, is always problematic in the sense of the potential ambiguity or 'misreading' of one's criticisms. Piaget's writings were both voluminous and wide ranging, covering epistemology, sociology, philosophy of science, child psychology, education and semiotics. Care needs to be taken in identifying and directing discussion at particular aspects of Piagetian theory while recognising that Piaget will always deserve another (and many) readings. Within developmental psychology (and education) although there have been isolated attempts to articulate his formulations on language acquisition (Howe, in press) and sociology (Mays, 1982), the significance of his ideas is most clearly seen in the uptake of the 'logico-mathematical' conception of cognitive development. The precision and clarity of formal-operational constructions of cognition and development (Piaget, 1952) facilitated the analysis of certain aspects of mathematical thinking, and importantly, developmental indices of that thinking.

The question though is the appropriateness of considering social-cognitive development along formal operational constructions (Youniss, 1978). Part of the difficulty is that formal mathematical models cannot easily accommodate social or socially produced interaction phenomena. An important sense in which such formulations are 'motivated towards closure' is the prescriptive nature of the explanatory accounts realised (see Chapter 2). In other words, there is an overemphasis on descriptions and constructions permissible only within certain clearly specified boundaries. This might help account for the observation that constructivist Piagetian accounts have tended to concentrate on certain forms of cognitions (solving physics problems; inferential processing), arguably activities commonly only conducted very occasionally in everyday life. Neo-Piagetians themselves (e.g. Chapman, 1986) recognise such limitations and have started to move towards considering and integrating some of Piaget's sociological writings with social-cognitive development. At the time of writing it is not clear where these developments will lead.

Understandably, given the close correspondence of representational and constructivist approaches in psychology, various proponents of the information processing view have subsumed Piagetian constructivism within their concerns, incorporating variations of his terminology (e.g. schema) with little circumspection. As the decade progresses, however, there is every likelihood that commentators will be re-evaluating and calling into question the theoretical prominence of information processing psychology. Since the early 1960s the dominant theoretical position has, without question, been that particular combination of 'operational behavourism' (the methodology of experimental psychology) and computational/symbol-manipulation metaphors. More recently this has taken expression in re-formulations of 'brain as representation' and the rise of parallel distributed processing or connectionism. What is not clear is whether the cracks appearing in the ediface of cognitive psychology (e.g. Bruner, 1990; Costall, 1986; Parker, 1989) are Kuhnian paradigmatic fissures or simply marginalised commentaries of those with a closer kinship to disciplines boundering psychology.

Within social-cognitive development research the information processing approach has taken a number of expressions, ranging from adaptations of the script idea, through 'processing constraint' conceptions and onto schema-theoretic models (Chapter 2). One approach (the theory of mind view) has developed into a distinct and firmly established social-cognitive paradigm with at least six sub-themes identified within its domain (see Astington & Gopnick, 1991). It is not easy to reach an adequate evaluation of this literature, and identifying reasons why this particular area has grown so rapidly might help highlight problematic issues germane to information processing developmental psychology, broadly conceived. First, there is the implicit commitment to Kantian conceptions of the significance of propositional attitudes, and the position accorded to the individuating subject. Leaving aside the controversial nature of such assumptions (Descombes, 1980; Sinha, 1988), what is problematic here is that certain kinds of questions appear to be excluded. For example, why do we not ask, under what circumstances does the child recognise that the sanctioned use of a 'mental state' word or verb is now appropriate? And correspondingly, within what set of criteria and under what conditions are we led to infer (from what the child says) that she can now be said to possess a 'theory of mind'?

In other words, it is too rarely recognised that the parameters and potential of any given model are facilitated and *constrained* by its particular pre-theoretical assumptions. Williams (1989) reminds us that the relation between underlying philosophical position and instantiated theory, helps determine both the domain of a model and the subsequent analysis. And so when one recognises that continental philosophy and post-modernist criticism have articulated alternatives to the privileged status of the 'epistemic subject', it may now be time to consider deriving or constructing investigative approaches where the adoption of one or other guiding theoretical framework requires a parallel level of argument and analytic interpretation. This is not yet a common practice in developmental psychology.

When, as a second issue bearing upon the 'theory of mind' literature, the 'concept/category' foundation stone of cognitive psychology (the *cogito* or *logos*) is complementarily supported by the methodological inheritance of Piagetian experimental child psychology, there is in place methods, techniques and a whole genre of institutional practice particularly amenable to the investigation of deception, false belief, second and third order inferential processing and so on. This is not to say that such investigations cannot provide valuable insights for our understanding of children's social-cognitive development (Baron-Cohen, 1989; Whiten, 1991), only that considerable caution should be exercised regarding the implicit assumptions of this particular variety of information processing psychology.

Arguably two of the more difficult issues germane to all information processing approaches to social-cognitive development are the observations that our experience is not that of 'constructing' our representational worlds in order that we may act, and the fact that while appearing to be essentially concerned with process and change the information processing metaphor remains methodologically static. The theory rests upon assumptions about stable sets of events, and ultimately may be unable to incorporate 'dynamic interaction' within its formulations. Again, its commitment to each individual's possession of requisite 'symbol manipulating' representational processes may yet prove to be an insurmountable barrier to the development of alternative, conceptually richer accounts of social interaction.

Interactionist social-cognitive development was defined with reference to approaches which maintain, or are at least emergent from, social-interaction constructs. Within this broad category the Genevan school was distinguished from two other more directly 'social interactionist' approaches (Mead and Vygotsky), in that the former, despite its emphasis on a *social* social cognition (Durkin, 1986) maintains a Piagetian explanatory formulation. Unfortunately, in the Genevan school, there remains some distance between general principles such that 'social interaction establishes the fabric of development', and the specifics of how and why children provided with opportunities to interact with peers perform better on certain kinds of tasks, compared to where they had to work on their own. Doise (1985) recognises the difficulty of highlighting the nature of the processes which enhance social-cognitive development, and increasingly where the concern is with social-cognitive competencies and skills, the emphasis has moved to considerations of the social-discursive contexts of such learning (Doise, 1990). But it is not clear whether there remains a tendency to consider the facilitative nature of interaction for learning along a somewhat oversimplified dimension of conflict versus cooperation. Additionally, an adequate analysis of process is likely to involve the utilisation of conversational analysis and related ethnomethodological principles. The juxtaposition of a Piagetian inspired explanatory account of social-cognitive development with the inductive approaches of conversational analysis might be one future direction for this theme of research.

Vygotsky and Mead are again, like Piaget, theorists who will for many years inspire researchers within and beyond developmental psychology. Social-cognitive developmental research influenced by Vygotsky has grown in recent years, facilitated by a variety of powerful and influential ideas: the zone of proximal development, the word as a single unit of meaning, the emphasis on mediational processes and so on. There remains though a gap between the complexities of Vygotsky's philosophical ideas and the way in which Vygotskian models have been taken up (Heckhausen, 1987; Wertsch et al., 1985). Vygotsky's ideas on the emergence of self-regulatory behaviour and his emphasis on language and 'signs as tools', needs to be understood with reference to his threefold formulation of development (genetic; mediational and individual). As Wertsch (1985) reminds us, only the latter level of analysis (how it might be that cognitive development emerges and is derived from interactions on the social plane) has been addressed within developmental psychology. An adequate evaluation of Vygotsky's work (or more particularly the way in which his work has found expression) is not yet possible given that it is not clear whether we are dealing with only circumscribed parts of the theory. Where we are, certain quite fundamental problems arise. Sinha (1988), for example, cogently argues that Vygotsky's perspective, while emphasising the importance of the social interaction context for social-cognitive development, only submerges the epistemic subject. How, also, are we to understand the 'zone of proximal' development: as a travelogue metaphor of development with an ever decreasing horizon somewhere beyond the sight of adult-child partners, or as a yet to be realised 'formal predictive' theory? Care needs to be taken to carefully consider the analytic basis for whatever aspect of Vygotsky's framework is being taken up. Only by doing so are we likely to benefit from the considerable insights he proffered.

Within the literature it is also possible to identify the influence of Mead, both directly (Fine, 1981) and indirectly, through his influence in social and clinical psychology. Beyond some of the problems implicit in Mead's conception of the self, cognition and the relation of such to the generalised other (e.g. the somewhat odd relation between attitudinal stances and the perlocutionary force of utterances), Mead holds an interesting yet curious position astride social theory and social psychology. Mead's symbolic interactionism was both anathema to behaviourism (given his conception of the relation between self and society) and yet unwieldy and imprecise for cognitive psychology. He will remain a source of ideas for those concerned with social cognition and social-cognitive development, not least for his attempts to conceptualise relations between thinking, language and symbolised gesture.

The suggestion was made then, that social-cognitive developmental theories fail to incorporate or integrate social-theoretic with individualistic approaches not least because the models proposed maintain the pre-eminence of individual cognition as the central construct. This itself works against formulating adequate conceptions of 'dynamic' social interaction, essential where the aim is to study the young child's developing participative social-cognitive skills. This proposal helped lead into a discussion of research work which has considered the relationship between language studies (child psycholinguistics) and social-cognitive development. This third theme in the literature was evaluated alongside research which addresses the issue of social-cognitive skills because of the emphasis I wished to place on the conversational context and its importance for the child's dynamic engagement with the social world. Again, a number of points can be reiterated and others expanded.

At least three themes within the research on language and social cognition were highlighted: the formalist, the pragmatic-constructivist and the social-semiotic. The point was made that as yet this emerging literature has not coalesced into a distinct research paradigm, but is better viewed as shared points of contact between these themes and developmental social cognition research. Further, the identifiable meta-theoretical incompatibility between these elements reminds us that integration is not the aim, rather the more comprehensive theories within each domain seeks to establish the parameters of its concerns by reference to 'external' and tangential theoretical positions (Karmiloff-Smith, 1990; Sinha, 1988).

It was also noted that the scope of developmental social cognition research has been established or at least partially marked out with reference to measurement and assessment criteria of those who define social-cognitive skills. There has been little concern, however, over the way such definitions have been employed. As yet we do not adequately distinguish between the terms, *abilities* and *skills*, and use of words such as 'competencies' serve only to obfuscate the overarching aim of many favoured definitions: external validation and realisable assessment criteria. Clearly, there is considerable value in employing adequate and appropriate performance measures; however, only where there is a well argued theoretical basis for such indices and not simply a 'fits best' taxonomy of social skills and cognitive behaviours placed together cheek-by-jowl (Strain, Guralnick, & Walker, 1986).

An important proposal of this book is that wherever else developmental social-cognitive processes and phenomena might be located, the site for their uncovering is the conversational context. Cognitive development is simply not possible without the child engaging in conversation, and social-cognitive skills are increasingly being defined with respect to communicative competence. Dialogic processes are coming under greater scrutiny from many areas within developmental and educational psychology, and within social-cognitive development no theoretical perspective would consider dispensing with considerations of interaction, and by implication the social-discursive 'conversational' processes inherent to them. Discussion of conversation and conversational contexts is fraught with difficulty though. For example, the study of the conversational context within infancy studies of early communicative development is a different enterprise compared to work directed at examining conversational processes in the classroom, and again both very different from models of relevance and communication in pragmatics. Models, methods and techniques have also taken on a myriad of forms (from the communicational to the inductive ethnomethodological) and we are in danger of losing the considerable benefits realisable through the study of talk. Another related problem is that there is a tendency either to subsume the study of language use as part of conversation or to equate language comprehension and production as equivalent to conversational skills.

One answer to the first problem is to clearly specify the appropriate level of analysis when studying conversation. There are at least three aspects to consider: conversation as models (of learning; of social interaction; of the role of overhearing; or whatever); conversation as medium (information being made available both to participants and analyst about whatever topics are being discussed and the ongoing process of the talk itself); and conversation as criteria (that is, one measure of assessment of social-cognitive skills is performance in conversational participation). Such a framework is suggested in Forrester (1991).

Addressing the second problem is more difficult. Following Wittgenstein (1953) there has long existed a tradition within philosophy of language, sociolinguistics and social psychology which has taken to task the excessive formalist tendencies of psycholinguists and other students of language (Billig, 1987; Halliday, 1973; Harre, 1979; Labov, 1972; Potter & Weatherall, 1987). Such efforts to remind us of the social basis of language have been somewhat muted, in part because the theories and models proposed remain 'static' in the sense of not incorporating the dynamic and participative nature of engagement in talk (as activity). While recognising the social basis of language there remains a tendency to view language itself as an object (now a social semiotic object): not as an interactive, dynamic and potentiating activity which has to be managed and produced by participating individuals. Arguably, and in line with the considered insights of the ethnomethodologists, there is the possibility that we can develop models of conversation and conversational activity which will allow new ways of considering children's developing social-cognitive skills, as well as avoiding the terminological and theoretical confusion engendered by the contiguity of language and conversation.

One of the subsidiary aims outlined in the first chapter has been fulfilled. The major themes, theories and research studies have been brought together and evaluated with reference to the question: can the current theoretical frameworks provide the necessary concepts and 'tools' for studying social-cognitive development, where this is conceived as being centred around children's conversation participation skills. The doubts expressed prepared the way for proposing an alternative view, the eco-structural framework. The phrase serves to remind the reader of the contributory aspects of the ecological perspective, as well as corresponding structural elements of conversation/participation contexts. I think it important to emphasise that this is best viewed as an orienting framework, a conceptual matrix which provides points of reference from where various models and theories of social-cognitive development might be developed. If anything the framework seeks to maintain and articulate its diversity as much as potential points of correspondence. Another important aim of this framework is that it may help articulate the criteria (appropriate set of substantiating constructs) we might wish to employ when deciding to use this, and not that, particular metaphor or model for specific research topics.

There are two ways in which I think it valuable to assess the scope, salience and applicability of this framework: analytically, in the sense of evaluating its potential advantages and identifiable problems, and with reference to the 'test-case' outlined earlier, the relation of overhearing contexts to children's developing participative social-cognitive skills. There are five elements to the framework: the ecological perspective, conversational analysis, Goffman's micro-sociological analysis of participation contexts, the problematic nature of identity and representation and finally issues of intentionality and implicature.

Since the mid 1960s, the ecological approach to visual perception has provided a valuable alternative critique to the representational assumptions of mainstream information processing psychology (particularly perception). Gibson's (1966, 1979) focus was on the symbiotic relationship between active perceiver and environment. His terminology of 'animal-environment' coupling, resonation and 'direct' perception was derived from a 'realist' alternative to Euclidean geometry, ecological optics. In recent years the formal basis for this approach has become firmly established in perceptual-motion research and related areas of applied perceptual psychology. Particular aspects of this approach might be very beneficial for attempts at understanding children's participative social-cognitive skills, especially the affordance construct.

The notion of affordance, although a term often over-used, misconstrued and applied in somewhat dubious contexts, is important within the framework in that it serves to emphasise the dynamic nature of the child's interaction with the world (social or otherwise). It also emphasises a particular sense of potential and possibility. What needs to be remembered is that affordances offer, or have the potential for, sets of actions: they do not determine them. As suggested earlier, the notion of an affordance and affordances structures, pre-eminently addresses both the centrality of dynamic participation, and interaction and conversations as 'potentiating' contexts. Care must be taken though to avoid a certain form of 'naturalism' and associated appeals to evolutionary processes as being a sufficient explanatory account (Michaels & Carello, 1981). In other words, there is an unwarranted tendency to frame discussion of the affordance metaphor along innate and 'behavioural-ecological' lines, such that the cultural basis of affordances is overlooked. Gibson (1979) talks of affordances as 'offerings of the environment', and the potential of such in that many unrealised affordance forms have yet to be taken advantage of. This should help remind us or at least serve to highlight the suggestion, that those affordances which *are* utilised, are produced and recognised by those that employ them as cultural phenomena instantiated in particular contexts. As infants we inherit a matrix of cultural-specific affordance structures. Subsequently, as older children and adults we contribute towards the production of those very affordance structures, utilising and making them available to each other as 'to be recognised' structural forms. Representations can themselves be conceived as social semiotic or socially produced affordance structures.

One way in which this proposal bears fruit is with reference to the second element in the framework, conversational analysis and the insights of the ethnomethodologists. If the predominant orientation of our sensory-cognitive processes leads to our engaging in constructivist conversational practices which build upon our skills in detecting and extracting affordances, then what form do such structures take? From Garfinkel (1967) through Sacks et al. (1974) and beyond, conversational analysts have been recording, transcribing and describing the myriad patterns and structures of talk employed by participants in conversation. Notwithstanding recent commentaries which throw light on certain questionable assumptions in this approach (Cameron, 1989), one useful definition of ethnomethodology is the analysis of the ways in which social interaction provides for the demonstration of the rationality of accounts of social interaction.

This is important for two reasons, the idea of conversational structuration and with reference to the philosophical basis of identity and representation. Leaving aside the latter for the present, structuration was described as the production of affordance-like conversational structures by participants for co-participants, the making available of structural patterns of talk which allow our predisposed 'perceptually biased' cognitions to take expression and function. Not only do we utilise such in our everyday interactions, but it is encumbent on the young child to learn to recognise and produce such affordance-like structures in conversations. Overhearing and observing others interacting will help by providing examples: however, at this point we need to establish that such structures exist, and that participants are in fact oriented towards them. As indicated earlier, the detailed work of Schegloff and Sacks (1973), Brown and Levinson (1978), provide excellent examples of participants' demonstrations and orientations of ongoing rational 'to be noticed and produced' behaviour (how to close a conversation, politeness constraints and so on).

However, we need to be careful to distinguish our role as analyst, and our own recognition of ourselves as participants. In other words, one particular advantage of the ethnomethodological legacy is that if participants themselves are not oriented to the production and recognition of realisable and to be realised affordance structures, then on what grounds can we infer their existence? An adequate conceptualisation of what is involved in identifying the affordances of talk may require an 'internal' account of conversational participation, somewhat at odds with the methodological tradition of developmental psychology. The question why we might require an 'internal' account derives first from the recognition that it is questionable whether one can establish what anyone knows 'extra-discursively'. Ascertaining whether another knows anything can only be established with reference to our own participation in that particular social-discursive context broadly conceived. Simply, we lack an adequate account of what it is to be 'inside' any conversational context. Bringing together the benefits of the affordance metaphor and the insights of the conversational analysts can facilitate the development of models appropriate for studying children's participative skills.

A third construct in the eco-structural framework is Goffman's micro-sociological approach to the study of participation contexts. Despite the marginalised status of Goffman's work within sociology and psychology, various aspects of his work are important, particularly given their richness and underdeveloped status: the doctrine of natural expression, his emphasis in describing participant roles in interaction and his formulations of the dynamics of participation. Goffman was careful to stress the reality status of the social world: worlds are not simply socially constructed, but exist as institutional forms of life to which are actions are always oriented, and within which are actions and behaviours are to be read. At the same time, however, he stressed that our 'natural expressions' are not simply instinctual, but are socially produced displays. Again, the correspondence with affordance structures might be drawn out here in that recognisable displays of expressive behaviour and role enacting can be considered as an interdependent part of conversational dynamics. For example, consider our ability to recognise the important difference between 'acting-out' and 'acting-at', such that one's public display and validation of role authenticity is manifested in the embracing of a somewhat playful (thus confident) stance to that conventional and institutionalised form of behaviour being expressed. Such observations again serve to underscore the cultural basis of social affordance structures, again similar to Goffman's notion of frames. The advantage of viewing such as having a close correspondence with the affordance metaphor, is in his emphasis on the micro-behavioural level of social interaction. Goffman was careful to stress that the 'institutional frame' of talk, is not simply a pre-determined expression of socially instituted life, but is a dynamic form of activity 'in regard' to those institutions. Finally, within this section I noted the value of Goffman's taxonomy of participant roles and the warrantable status of interactants. Such a categorisation helps move away from the 'speaker-centrism' of much interactional analysis, accentuating the interdependent nature of speaker, addressee and onlooking participants.

The fourth construct of the framework can be viewed as an attempt at circumventing problems which derive from the favoured philosophical assumptions of contemporary social-cognitive developmental research (e.g. overemphasis on the epistemic subject—Sinha, 1988). The account of representation proposed in Chapter 5 sought to argue that representational processes are themselves inherently dynamic: produced, re-presented and promoted in social-discursive processes (including both 'talk' and 'text'). Furthermore, understanding the production of representational phenomena may be facilitated by a consideration of narrativity in line with elements of the conceptualist tradition of identity, as Reason (1984) suggests. Specifically, it is only through the narrative construction of those material presuppositions which underlie and support conversational behaviour (themselves derived from conventions of everyday social practice) that a warranted and justifiable account of representational activity is realisable. The relevance of such to the insights of the ethnomethodological oriented conversational analysts is articulated in their recognition of identity as being 'chronically open to challenge ... [and that] social identities are so vulnerable that we lose sight of any substantial, content-full identity in the obsession with making provision for and displaying a rational social world' (Reason, 1984, p.21). The point to be emphasised is that there are sufficiently developed alternative formulations of representation and identity (beyond Cartesian and Kantian accounts) which can accommodate conceptions of the child's dynamic engagement with the social world.

The fifth aspect of the eco-structural framework considers the role of intentionalitiy and implicature, and the ways in which these ideas have been examined within social-cognitive developmental research. Why this is important derives from the realisation that contemporary theories have not adequately addressed the problem of the inaccessibility of intentional states, and what might be involved in investigating children's knowledge and displays of such. The gap which needs to be bridged is the relationship between participation, regularities of talk, and the rationalist analysis of implicature, and its importance for the possibility of successful communication to exist at all. Interestingly, Grice (1982) himself recognises that a principled defence of the rationalist position in pragmatics (and the argument that communication itself is not possible without participants displaying and providing for the recognition of intention—i.e. implicature) rests ultimately upon interpretative evaluation (not logic). That aside, and in line with my emphasis on children's participative conversational skills, the suggestion was made that our conceptions of intentionality would benefit from moving away from an overconcern with utterance interpretation and onto considering what might be involved in the dynamic display of implicature produced (and oriented to) by participants during the accomplishment of talk. I touched on one or two studies on the child's earliest displays and recognition of intention, and both Dore (1983) and Ryan (1974) provide important pointers regarding how we might proceed. Arguably though, they remain constrained by the privileged position of the individuating subject. Possibly Goffman's outline of the doctrine of natural expression might help us to conceptualise appropriate notions of intention and implicature: as display behaviours 'to be read' by other participants. This element of the eco-structural framework certainly raises some of the more vexing questions for our understanding of the relationship between cognitive (i.e. rationalist) and social (participative) development.

Having reiterated and summarised the earlier review and the theoretical underpinnings of the eco-structural framework, its utility and applicability can be further evaluated with reference to the 'test-case' outlined in the previous three chapters (6–8). I began by asking, are their affordances of talk, and can we consider the role of the child as overhearer, where exposure to overhearing contexts might have a bearing on young children's developing social-cognitive skills? Goffman's (1981) outline of participant roles served as a useful starting point, particularly where supplemented by McGregor's (1983) insights into the unrealised and overlooked role of the listener in talk. Furthermore, the difficulties of accommodating and understanding the predictability and projectibility of talk (for participants) can be overcome by employing the affordance construct. Gibson's most significant contributions were his demonstrations of the mutuality of perception and motion. Affordances can only be recognised, made available and produced as dynamic formulations. What then is the relation between overhearing (for the young child) and the acquisition of social-cognitive participative skills?

Overhearing was characterised as having, or operating in, at least three domains: as happenstance, as 'attention focusing' and as conversation monitoring. I started with overhearing as happenstance, and made the case for at least two further distinctions to this theme, as exposure to participation contexts and as opportunities for perceiving sociometric affordances. Regarding exposure, overhearing and overseeing can be characterised as examples of, and lessons in, what is likely to occur between humans and arguably will contribute towards learning and detecting the affordances of social interaction. When seated near others on that well known Clapham omnibus, our fascination with what we hear is not simply 'nosiness', but rather, is based on our recognising that our interactions with others never loses a sense of potential. Eavesdropping (particularly for children) provides 'free lessons' in the kinds of social practices which take place between others, and through the mechanics of listening itself, examples and expressions of the conversational affordances which make communication and interaction possible at all. The young child learns to recognise the opportunities germane to specific forms of social interaction, and the related social conventions and norms required for the appropriate patterns of talk displayed.

The second way in which overhearing as 'happenstance' was considered was with reference to overhearing patterns of third-party reference in pre-school contexts. By examining the way in which adults would address children, and in doing so be more likely to refer to particular members of their peer group, it was possible to highlight non-random associative patterns of name reference. There are 'social structure information' affordances of a 'referential/linguistic' form available to overhearing children in such environments. Using the methods described in Chapter 6 (e.g. sociometry) one can begin to identify social information affordances available in overheard talk, affordance structures which reflect the network of social groups within these contexts. While the question remains as to whether the children themselves were cognisant of such associative patterns, identifying the existence of such is an important first step in demonstrating one way in which the eco-structural framework can aid our investigations.

The analysis of 'attention focusing' function of overhearing and how this might relate to emerging social-cognitive skills started with a brief summary of research on naming and naming practices. In the literature on intentionality and in research on the acquisition of deictic terms (pronouns and so on), name and naming studies have been tied to a diverse range of interests (e.g. object categorisation in philosophy of language; name acquisition in developmental psycholinguistics). Curiously, few studies have specifically examined name use, and my specific concern was the relationship between overhearing (for the child) other's use of your own name and how this might relate to social cognitions. Two studies were reported, the first examining the young child's earliest sensitivity to name use by others, the second group addressing speech where the child is being treated and spoken to as a member of a group. A few points can be made.

First, the child only begins to exhibit any specific response to name overhearing around the fourteenth or fifteenth month and one way in which this sensitivity should be considered is with reference to participation dynamics. That is, this is the first clearly 'non-random' speech event taking place between others the child is not involved with, to which she pays a lot of attention. It is clearly an 'attention focusing' instance of an overhearing context. Second, it was noteworthy that the child's earliest responses to naming were where the intonational contours accompanying use were particularly marked. When we consider also, the fact that the only other situation where the infants appeared to be utilising overheard talk was when they would imitate specific occurrences of the mother or other toddler's talk which had been spoken in a 'sing-song' fashion, then arguably specific sound patterning may be another 'affordance structure' available to, and utilised by, the young infant. This would accord to some extent with research which has emphasised the affordance or 'higher order' sensory information available via auditory channels (Bower, 1977) and there may be considerable scope for the argument that intonational patterns provide the 'invariant' and 'transformational' structures necessary for the child's emerging participative skills.

The study of group addressing speech highlighted a number of the relationships between overhearing and participation contexts. The forms of address and reference associated with these speech contexts were significantly marked (e.g. occurring as particular break points in the adults speech) and (for the overhearing child) provided outline lessons in group participation parameters of interaction. For example, it was noted that as a group participant the child has to comprehend that there are a number of possible role relations realisable, in part determined by whether she engages in responses and replies to the adult's overtures. Exposure to group addressing contexts provides such lessons in role identity changes within and apart from the group. Together these studies highlight some of the subtleties of overhearing contexts, and implicate the presuppositional social practice basis of language use in such circumstances. For example, use of explicit and implicit address forms is related to whether you happen to be a member of a large or smaller group, marking for the child opportunities for deciding whether to opt in or out of the group (and pre-empting requisite role participant demands).

The third characteristic form of overhearing was conversation monitoring. The importance of this study was that the demonstration of a relationship between overhearing name use by others and subsequent participation by the referred-to child in the conversation. Again, the framework provides pointers towards understanding the role demands of such contexts by differentiating participant, overhearing participant along constructs of 'ratification' or not. The experiments used the child's response to name use as a method of studying conversation participation skills, the first demonstrating the non-random nature of their response to name use and highlighting their sensitivity to the stuctural affordances of the talk they were monitoring (i.e. indicated by the precise timing of their looking response). The second experiment examined how monitoring abilities of this nature develop, and in addition attempted to examine factors which might influence the nature of their response (the seeking-social information hypothesis). Notwithstanding insufficient evidence in support of the latter, what was particularly striking in this study was the child's participation (i.e. interruptions) following name use by others. The older children not only engaged in the talk so as to pre-empt potentially challenging social comments on their own behaviour, the form of their response was such that it was manifestly related to their sensitivity to, and utilisation of, the structural predictability of talk and turn-taking. Their recognition and use of the structural affordances made available by other's talk (and particularly the social markedness of naming) not only highlights the sophisticated nature of their participative skills, but also points towards the confrontational and 'role-demanding' nature of the conversational context itself. The potential ambiguity of participant status where you are simply present and overhearing others engaging in talk changes the minute your name is used. This immediately establishes your position as a 'ratified' partner and demands or warrants a certain level of participation.

A few concluding comments can now be made. Theoretically, the eco-structural framework argues for a move away from constructs predicated upon cognitive representations as essentialist attributes of 'private' individual minds, and towards conceptual elements which emphasise the social-discursive nature of representational processes, particularly the role of conversation. The five principle elements of the framework (the ecological perspective; conversational analysis; participation role; identity and representation and the role of implicature/intentionality) provide a meta-theoretical matrix or foundational base for the development of models and conceptions of children's participation and interaction skills, principally by accentuating engagement. The framework is first and foremost an attempt to formalise the active and participatory nature of the child's social-cognitive development. For example, it indicates how dynamic aspects of everyday interaction and conversation can be modelled from an 'internalist' perspective without sacrificing the benefits of certain formal methods (e.g. by utilising the affordance metaphor). It can be noted in passing that despite the advances in research on conversation and discourse we still lack an adequate model of what it is 'psychologically' to be dynamically engaged 'in' a conversation (see Levinson, 1983, for a similar point). The eco-structural framework also proposes that conceptions of representation and identity might be better formulated with recourse to ideas of narrativity and related constructive processes of conversational engagement. The question is posed as to how it is that the young child begins to recognise implicature, and clearly there is a need to examine the correspondence between learning to display intentionality and the orientation of participants towards the 'affordance structures' of conversation.

An additional aspect of the framework is that the considerable insights accruing to the work of the conversational analysts can be harnessed to the methodological requirements for theory development in developmental social cognition research, principally through the role of the 'affordance' construct and conversational affordances. The affordance construct offers a range of potentially powerful research ideas which cut across a number of the limitations of the information processing metaphor. In particular the focal concern with movement, action and the essentially dynamic nature of conversational contexts can be re-formulated along lines of investigation currently somewhat cumbersome for cognitive approaches. There has been considerable difficulty in harnessing the numerous insights of the conversational analysts (in large part given their particular ethnomethodological orientation) along lines which can be utilised by developmental psychologists in ways which go beyond the descriptive (Ervin-Tripp, 1979; McTear, 1985). By conceiving of participation as an 'internal' psychological activity where the emphasis is upon the dynamics of action, movement, and with an orientation to ongoing development and so on, combined with the formal, conceptual and methodological techniques and procedures accruing to the ecological perspective, we may be in a better position to examine the young child's developing social-cognitive participative skills.

In order to move away from somewhat restrictive individualistic accounts of representation, we may have to consider alternative accounts, for example, conceptions based upon narrativity. It is clear that this is a considerably complex issue and one which raises a number of unresolved and vexing metaphysical and theoretical issues (Feldman & Bruner, 1987; Parker, 1989; Sinha, 1988). One point emphasised earlier was that much of present day research cannot adequately address a range of important questions in this area, because insufficient attention has been paid to nature of the (often constraining) underlying theoretical views. Not least the importance of this is that the presuppositional frameworks underlying whatever models we employ (be they Piagetian; computational or social-semiotic) help determine the kinds of conceptual tools and analysis realisable in the research. Of course there is more than a little ambivalence to such a critique in the philosophy of language, social theory and developmental psychology itself, particularly given that it is no easy task to walk a tightrope between the requirements and demands of a scientific psychology, while recognising the particular kinds of constraints such 'discourses' hold us to (Parker, 1989; Sinha, 1988).

Understanding how young infants and children become competent social beings remains a considerable puzzle. There is little doubt that the influence of the more dominant theoretical perspectives within cognitive and developmental psychology will continue, in large part because they have contributed significantly to specific problems within child development research. The purpose here has been to argue that as far as social-cognitive development research is concerned, the key questions to be addressed centre around the child's participative skills within social interaction and conversation. Viewed in this way, contemporary theories appear to constrain the development of appropriate investigative 'tools' for conceptual and methodological reasons. Possibly the most serious way in which they are restrictive is that they do not easily accommodate concepts and models which move the research emphasis as far as possible away from 'in the head' formulations. This is not to say, of course, that individualistic theoretical constructs are in anyway unimportant or somehow incorrect. Rather, if we wish to understand social-cognitive development as a participative skill, then we would benefit considerably from predicating our theoretical positions upon social-theoretic constructs as far removed from the 'epistemic subject' as possible. This monograph is one example of how such a project can be initiated.

Appendix 1

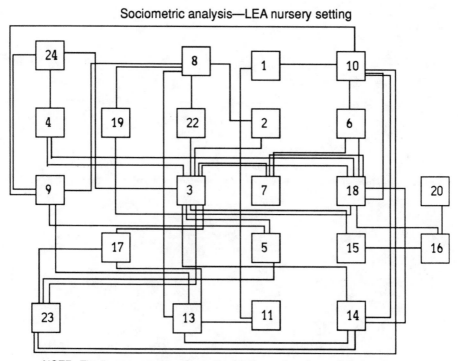

Sociometric analysis—LEA nursery setting

NOTE: The lines represent reciprocating 'address-referee' associations only

Appendix 2

1. What is the size of the group (being addressed and referred-to)?
2. Is the group being addressed by implication or explicitly?
3. What is the primary speech act function?
4. If a directive, what is the sub-category function?
5. Is the group being referred to, or a specific individual?
6. If an individual, what is the size of the group he/she is in?
7. If the group being addressed and the group being referred to are not part of the same group, what are the respective sizes of each group?
8. If the group being addressed and referred to are the same group, what is the primary activity of the group?
9. If as 7, above, what are the primary activities of each group?
10. If a specific individual is being referred to, what form of language is used (e.g. name, identifier, pronoun, by implication)?

References

Abernethy, B. (1990). Expertise, visual search and information pick-up in squash. *Perception, 19,* 63–77.

Abromvitch, R. (1980). Attention structures in hierarchically organized groups. In D.R. Omark, E.E. Strayer, & D.G. Freedman (Eds.), *Dominance relations.* Hillsdale, N.J.: Lawrence Erlbaum Associates Inc.

Altmann, J. (1974). Observational study of behaviour: Sampling methods. *Behaviour, 49,* 227–267.

Anderson, J.R., & Bower, G.H. (1973). *Human associative memory.* London: Winston.

Argyle, M. (1969). *Social interaction.* London: Methuen.

Astington, J.W. (1988). Promises: Words or deeds? *First Language, 8,* 259–270.

Astington, J.W., & Gopnik, A. (1988). Knowing you've changed your mind: Children's understanding of representational change. In J.W. Astington, P.L. Harris, & D. Olson (Eds.), *Developing theories of mind.* Cambridge: Cambridge University Press.

Astington, J.W., & Gopnik, A. (1991). Theoretical explanations of children's understanding of the mind. *British Journal of Developmental Psychology, 9,* 7–33.

Astington, J.W., Harris, P.L., & Olson, D.R. (1988). (Eds.), *Developing theories of mind.* Cambridge: Cambridge University Press.

Atkinson, M. (1986). Learnability theory. In P. Fletcher & M. Garmen (Eds.), *Language Acquisition.* 2nd Edition. Cambridge: Cambridge University Press.

Bandura, A. (1969). Social learning theory of indentifactory processes. In D.A. Goslin (Ed.), *Handbook of socialization theory and research.* Chicago: Rand-McNally.

Bandura, A., & Barab, P.G. (1969). *Conditions governing non-reinforced imitation.* Unpublished manuscript. Stanford University.

Bandura, A., Grusec, J.E., & Menlove, F.L. (1966). Observational learning as a function of symbolization and incentive set. *Child Development, 37,* 499-506.

Bandura, A., Ross, D., & Ross, S.A. (1961). Transmission of aggression through imitation of aggressive models. *Journal of Abnormal and Social Psychology, 63,* 575-582.

Baron, R.M. (1980). Contrasting approaches to social knowing: An ecological perspective. *Personality and Social Psychology Bulletin, 6,* (4), 591-600.

Baron-Cohen, S. (1989). The autistic child's theory of mind: A case of specific developmental delay. *Journal of Child Psychology and Psychiatry and Allied Disciplines, 30,* (2), 285-297.

Barton, E.J. (1986). Modification of children's prosocial behaviour. In P.S. Strain, M.J. Guralnick, & H.M. Walker (Eds.), *Children's social behaviour: Development, assessment and modification.* New York: Academic Press.

Beal, C.R. (1988). Children's knowledge about representations of intended meaning. In J.W. Astington, P.L Harris, & D. Olson (Eds.), *Developing theories of mind.* Cambridge: Cambridge University Press.

Beal, C.R., & Lockhart, M.E. (1989). The effect of proper name and appearance changes on childrens reasoning about gender constancy. *International Journal of Behavioural Development, 12,* (2), 195-205.

Bearison, D., Magzannen, S., & Filardo, E. (1984). *Socio-cognitive conflict and cognitive growth in young children.* Paper presented at the Jean Piaget Society Annual Symposium. Philadelphia.

Beattie, G. (1983). *Talk: An analysis of speech and non-verbal behaviour in conversation.* Milton Keynes: Open University Press.

Becker, J. A. (1988a). The success of parents' indirect techniques for teaching their preschoolers pragmatic skills. *First Language, 8,* 173-182.

Becker, J.A. (1988b). "I can't talk, I'm dead": Preschoolers spontaneous metapragmatic comments. *Discourse Processes, 11,* 457-469.

Bem, D. J. (1972). Self-perception theory. In L. Berkowitz (Ed.), *Advances in Experimental Social Psychology (Vol. 6).* New York: Academic Press.

Bennett, A. (1981). Interruptions and the interpretation of conversation. *Discourse Processess, 4,* 171-188.

Berthenthal, B.I., & Bai, D.L. (1989). Infants sensitivity to optical flow for controlling posture. *Developmental Psychology, 25,* (6), 929-935.

Berninger, G., & Garvey, C. (1981). Questions and the allocation of construction and timing of turns in child discourse. *Journal of Psycholinguistic Research, 10,* 403- 420.

Billig, M. (1987). *Arguing and thinking: A rhetorical approach to social psychology.* Cambridge: Cambridge University Press.

Bishop, Y., Feindberg, S., & Holland, P. (1975). *Discrete multivariate analysis.* Cambridge, Mass.: M.I.T. Press.

Bloor, D. (1983). *Wittgenstein: A social theory of knowledge.* London: Macmillan.

Bond, D. (1989). *Personal communication: Royal School for the Deaf.* Margate, England.

Bonnett, C. (1983). L'utilisation des noms de personne et l'apparition du nom propre chez le jeune enfant. *Psychologie Schiweizerische Zeitschrift für Psychologie und ihre Anwendungen, 42,* (2-3), 107-126.

Bower, G., Black, J.B., & Turner, T.J. (1979). Scripts in memory for text. *Cognitive Psychology, 11,* 177-220.

Bower, T.G.R. (1977). *A primer of infant development.* San Francisco: Freeman.

Bowlby, J. (1959). *Child care and the growth of love.* London: Fontana.

Brackett, D. (1983). Group communicating strategies for the hearing impaired. *Volta Review, 85,* 116-128.

Brackett, D., & Donnelly, J. (1982). *Hearing impaired adolescents' judgements of appropriate conversation entry points.* Paper presented at the American Speech-Language Association Convention. Toronto, Canada.

Brener, R. (1983). Learning the deictic meaning of third person pronouns. *Journal of Psycholinguistic Research, 12,* 235-262.

Bretherton, I., McNew, S., & Beeghly-Smith, M. (1981). Early person knowledge as expressed in gestural and verbal communication: When do infants acquire a "theory of mind"? In M.E. Lamb & L.R. Sherrod (Eds.), *Infant social cognition.* Hillsdale, N.J.: Lawrence Erlbaum Associates Inc.

Bronfenbrenner, U. (1979). *The ecology of human development.* Cambridge, Mass.: Harvard University Press.

Brown, P., & Levinson, S. (1978). Universals in language usage: Politeness phenomena. In E. Goody (Ed.), *Questions and politeness: Strategies in social interaction.* Cambridge: Cambridge University Press.

Brown, R. (1988) *Group Processes.* London: Blackwell.

Bruner, J.S. (1975a). The ontogenesis of speech acts. *Journal of Child Language, 2,* 1-19.

Bruner, J.S. (1975b). From communication to language—a psychological perspective. *Cognition, 3,* 255-287.

Bruner, J.S. (1983). The acquisition of pragmatic commitments. In R.M. Golinkoff (Ed.), *The transition from pre-linguistic to linguistic communication.* Hillsdale, N.J.: Lawrence Erlbaum Associates Inc.

Bruner, J.S. (1990). Culture and human development: A new look. *Human Development, 33,* (6), 344-355.

Bruner, J. S., & Sherwood, V. (1976). Early rule structure: the case of peekaboo. In J.S. Bruner, A. Jolly, & K. Sylva (Eds.), *Play—its role in development and evolution.* New York: Penguin Books.

Bryant, P.E. (1982). The role of conflict and agreement between intellectual strategies in children's ideas about measurement. *British Journal of Psychology, 73,* (2), 243-251.

Bryant, P.E. (1985). Parents, children and cognitive development. In R.A. Hinde, A.N. Perret-Clermont, & J. Stevenson-Hinde, (Eds.), *Social relationships and cognitive development.* Oxford: Clarendon Press.

Bryant, P.E., & Trabasso, T. (1971). Transitive inferences and memory in young children. *Nature, 232,* 456-458.

Buck-Morss, S. (1975). Social-economic bias in Piaget's theory and its implications for cross-cultural studies. *Human Development, 18,* 35-49.

Butterworth, G., & Light, P. (1982). *Social cognition: Studies in the development of understanding.* Brighton: Harvester.

Butterworth, G., Harris, P.L., Leslie, A.M., & Wellman, H.M. (1991). Perspectives on the child's theory of mind, part 1; editorial preface. *British Journal of Developmental Psychology, 9,* 1-6.

Cambell, R. (1988). Learning about reading during pupil-teacher reading interactions. *Cambridge Journal of Education, 18,* 377-386.

Cameron, D. (1989). *Rules, power and communication.* Paper given at the "Conversation, Discourse, Conflict" Conference. Trinity College, Dublin, March.

Campos, J.J., & Spendberg, C. (1981). Perception, appraisal, and emotion. In M. Lamb, & Z. Sherrod (Eds.), *Infant social cognition.* Hillsdale, N.J.: Lawrence Erlbaum Associates Inc.

Carey, S. (1985). *Conceptual change in childhood.* Cambridge, Mass.: M.I.T. Press.

Carroll, J.M. (1983). Nameheads. *Cognitive Science, 7,* (2), 121-153.

Cartwright, D.O., & Zander, A. (1968). *Group dynamics. 3rd Edition.* New York: Harper.

Chandler, M. (1985). Social structures and social cognitions. In R.A. Hinde, Perret-Clermont, & J. Stevenson-Hinde (Eds.), *Social relationships and cognitive development.* Oxford: Clarendon Press.

Chandler, M. (1988). Doubts and developing theories of mind. In J.W. Astington, P.L Harris & D. Olson (Eds.), *Developing theories of mind.* Cambridge: Cambridge University Press.

Chandler, M., Fritz, A.S., & Hala, S. (1989). Small scale deceit: Deception as a marker of two, three and four year old's early theory of mind. *Child Development, 60,* 1263-77.

Chapman, M. (1986). The structure of exchange: Piaget's sociological theory. *Human Development, 29,* 181-194.

Charney, R. (1979). Speech roles and the development of personal pronouns. *Journal of Child Language, 7,* 3-69.

Chase, I.D. (1980). Social processes and hierarchy formation in small groups: A comparative perspective. *American Sociological Review, 45,* 905-924.

Chase, I.D. (1984). Reported personal communication in social conflict in early childhood. In G.J. Whitehurst (Ed.), *Annals of child development (Vol. 1).* London: Jai Press.

Chiat, S. (1981). Context-specificity and the generalizations in the acquisition of pronominal distinctions. *Journal of Child Language, 8,* 76-91.

Chiat, S. (1982). Adult use of pronoun forms. *Journal of Child Language, 9,* 359-347.

Chomsky, N. (1957). *Syntactic structure.* The Hague: Mouton.

Chomsky, N. (1959). Review of Skinner's verbal behaviour. *Language, 35,* 26-58.

Chomsky, N. (1965). *Aspects of a theory of syntax.* Cambridge, Mass.: M.I.T. Press.

Chomsky, N. (1988). *Language and problems of knowledge: The Managua lectures.* Cambridge, Mass.; London: M.I.T. Press.

Clark, A.J. (1987). Connectionism and cognitive science. In J. Hallam & C.S. Mellish (Eds.), *Advances in Artificial Intelligence.* London: Wiley.

Clark, H.H., (1982). The relevance of common ground: Comments on Sperber and Wilson. In N.V. Smith (Ed.), *Mutual knowledge.* Academic Press.

Clark, H.H., & Carlson, T. (1981). Context for comprehension. In J. Long & A. Baddeley (Eds.), *Attention and performance IX.* Hillsdale, N.J.: Lawrence Erlbaum Associates Inc.

Clark, H.H., & Clark, E. (1977). *Psychology of language.* Holt, Rhinehart, & Winston.

Clark, H.H., & Haviland, S.E. (1977). Comprehension and the given-new contract. In R.O. Freedle (Ed.), *Discourse production and comprehension.* Hillsdale, N.J.: Lawrence Erlbaum Associates Inc.

Clark, H.H., & Lucy, P. (1975). Understanding what is meant from what is said: A study in conversationally conveyed request. *Journal of Verbal Learning and Verbal Behaviour, 14,* 56-72.

Clark, H.H., & Marshall, C.R. (1981). Definite reference and mutual knowledge. In A.K. Joshi, I. Sag, & B. Webber (Eds.), *Elements of discourse understanding.* Cambridge: Cambridge University Press.

Clark, H.H., & Schaefer, E.F. (1987). Concealing one's meaning from overhearers. *Journal of Memory and Language, 26,* 209-225.

Clark, N., Stephenson, G.M., & Rutter, D.R. (1986). Memory for a complex social discourse: The analysis and prediction of individual and group recall. *Journal of Memory and Language, 25,* 295-343.

Cochran, W.G. (1954). Some methods of strengthening the common chi-square test. *Biometrics, 25,* 383-399.

Collins, R. (1988). Theoretical continuities in Goffman's work. In P. Drew & A. Wootton (Eds.), *Ervin Goffman: Exploring the interaction order.* Polity Press: Cambridge.

Collis, G. (1990). *In (the) front of the car: Complex prepositions and noun phrases.* Paper given at the 1990 Child Languge Seminar. Canterbury: University of Kent.

Conti-Ramsden, G. (1989). Proper name usage: Mother-child interactions with language-impaired and non-language-impaired children. *First Language, 9,* 271-284.

Collis, G.M., & Schaffer, H.R. (1975). Synchronization of visual attention in mother-infant pairs. *Journal of Child Psychology, Psychiatry and Allied Disciplines, 16,* (4), 315-320.

Combs, M.L., & Slaby, R. (1977). Social skills training with children. In B.B. Lahey & A.E. Kazdin (Eds.), *Advances in child clinical psychology (Vol. 1).* New York: Plenum.

Corter, C., Abromvitch, R., & Pepler, D. (1981). The role of the mother in sibling interaction. *Child Development, 54,* 1599-1605.

Costall, A. (1986). Evolutionary gradualism and the study of development. *Human Development, 29,* (1), 4-11.

Coulthard, R.M. (1977). *An introduction to discourse analysis.* London: Longman.

Craig, H.K., & Gallagher, T.M. (1983). Adult-child discourse: The conversational relevance of pauses. *Journal of Pragmatics, 7,* 347-360.

Craig, H.K., & Washington, J.A. (1986). Children's turn-taking behaviours: sociolinguistic interactions. *Journal of Pragmatics, 10,* 173-197.

Cruttenden, A. (1979). *Language in infancy and childhood.* Manchester: Manchester University Press.

Damon, W. (1981). Exploring children's social cognition on two fronts. In J.H. Flavell & L. Ross (Eds.), *Social cognitive development: Frontiers and possible futures.* Cambridge: Cambridge University Press.

Datta, S.B. (1983). Patterns of agnostic interference. In R.A. Hinde (Ed.), *Primate Social Relationships.* Oxford: Blackwell Scientific Publications.

Descombes, A. (1980). *Modern French philosophy.* London: Blackwell.

Descombes, A. (1986). *Objects of all sorts: A philosophical grammar.* London: Blackwell.

Dickson, W., Hess, R., Miyake, N., & Azuma, H. (1979). Referential communication accuracy between mother and child as a predictor of cognitive development in the United States and Japan. *Child Development, 50,* 53-59.

Doise, W. (1985). Social regulations in cognitive development. In R.A. Hinde, A.N. Perret-Clermont, & J. Stevenson-Hinde (Eds.), *Social relationships and cognitive development.* Oxford: Clarendon Press.

Doise, W. (1990). The development of individual competencies through social interaction. In H.C. Foot, M.J. Morgan, & R.H. Shute (Eds.), *Children helping children.* London: Wiley.

Doise, W., & Mugny, G. (1979). Individual and collective conflict of centration in cognitive development. *European Journal of Social Psychology, 9,* 105-108.

Doise, W., & Mugny, G. (1984). *The social development of the intellect.* Oxford and New York: Pergamon Press.

Doise, W., & Mugny, G. (1985). Recherches sociogenetiques sur la coordination d'actions intedependentes. *Revue Suisse de Psychologie Pure et Appliquée, 34,* 160-174.

Doise, W., Mugny, C., & Perret-Clermont, A.N. (1975). Social interaction and the development of cognitive operations. *European Journal of Social Psychology, 5,* 367-83.

Donaldson, M. (1978). *Children's minds.* London: Fontana.

Dore, J. (1979). Conversational acts and the acquisition of language. In E. Och & B. Schiefflen (Eds.), *Developmental Pragmatics.* New York: Academic Press.

Dore, J. (1983). Feeling, form and intention in the babies transition to language. In R.M. Golinkoff (Ed.), *The transition from pre-linguistic to linguistic communication.* Hillsdale, N.J.: Lawrence Erlbaum Associates Inc.

Dorval, B., & Eckerman, C.O. (1984). Developmental trends in the quality of conversation achieved by small groups of acquainted peers. *Monographs of the Society for Research in Child Development, 49,* 1-72.

Drew, P., & Wootton, A. (Eds.). (1988). *Ervin Goffman: Exploring the interaction order.* Polity Press: Cambridge.

Duncan, S., & Fiske, D.W. (1977). *Face-to-Face Interaction.* Hillsdale, N.J.: Lawrence Erlbaum Associates Inc.

Dunn, J. (1988). *Social understanding.* London: Basil Blackwell.

Dunn, J., & Kendrick, C. (1982a). The speech of two and three year olds to infant siblings: Babytalk and the context of communication. *Journal of Child Language, 9,* 579-595.

Dunn, J., & Kendrick, C. (1982b). *Siblings: Love, envy and understanding.* Oxford: Basil Blackwell.

Dunn, J., & Munn, P. (1985). Becoming a family member: Family conflict and the development of social understanding. *Child Development, 56,* 480-492.

Dunn, J., & Shatz, M. (1989). Becoming a conversationalist despite (or because of) having an older sibling. *Child Development, 60,* 399-410.

Durkin, K. (1986). *Language development in the school years.* London: Croom-Helm.

Durkin, K. (1987). Minds and language: Social cognition, social interaction and the acquisition of language. *Mind and Language, 2,* 105-40.

Durkin, K. (1988). Language development and social cognition: Editorial introduction. *First Language, 8,* 89-102.

Durkin, K., Rutter, D., & Tucker, H. (1982a). Social interaction and language acquisition: Motherese help you? *First Language, 3,* 107-20.

Durkin, K., Rutter, D., Room, S., & Grounds, P. (1982b). Proper name usage in maternal speech: a longitudinal study. In C.E. Johnson & C.L. Thew (Eds.), *Proceedings of the second international congress for the study of child language.* Washington, D.C. : University Press of America.

Eckerman, C.O., & Stein, M.R. (1982). The toddler's emerging interactive skills. In K.H. Rubin, & H.S. Ross (Eds.), *Peer relationships and social skills in childhood.* New York: Springer-Verlag.

Eckerman, C.O., & Whatley, J.L. (1977). Toys and social interaction between infant peers. *Child Development, 48,* 1645-1656.

Eco, U. (1979). *The role of the reader. Explorations in the semiotics of texts.* London: Hutchinson.

Edmundson, W. (1990). Poverty of stimulus or poverty of theory? Abstracts of the 1990 Child Language Seminar. *First Language, 10,* 255-270.

Edwards, D., & Mercer, N. (1986). Context and continuity: Classroom discourse and the development of shared knowledge. In K. Durkin (Ed.), *Language development in the school years.* London: Croom Helm.

Edwards, D., & Middleton, D. (1988). Conversational remembering and family relationships: How children learn to remember. *Journal of Social and Personal Relationships, 5,* 3-25.

Eisenberg, N. (1986). *Altruistic emotion, cognition, and behaviour.* Hillsdale, N.J.: Lawrence Erlbaum Associates Inc.

Eiser, J.R., & Stroebe, W. (1972). *Categorization and Social Judgement.* London: Academic Press.

Emihovich, C., & Miller, G.E. (1988). Talking to the turtle: A discourse analysis of logo instructions. *Discourse Processes, 11,* 183-196.

Emiliani, F., Zanni, B., & Cargetti, F. (1981). From interaction strategies to social representation of adults in a day nursery. In W. Robinson, (Ed.), *Communication and development.* New York: Academic Press.

Emler, N.P., & Hogan, R. (1981). Developing attitudes to law and justice. In S.S. Brehm, S.M. Kassin, & F.X. Gibbons (Eds.), *Developmental social psychology.* Oxford: Oxford University Press.

Ervin-Tripp, S. (1979). Children's verbal turn-taking. In E. Ochs & B. Schieffelin (Eds.), *Developmental pragmatics.* New York: Academic Press.

Ervin-Tripp, S., & Mitchell-Kernan, C. (1977). *Child discourse.* New York and London: Academic Press.

Farr, R. (1981). The social origins of the human mind: A historical note. In J. Forgas (Ed.), *Social cognition: Perspectives on everyday understanding.* London: Academic Press.

Farr, W.F., Braines, D.F., Aquirre-Hauchbaum, T., & Salvador, F. (1986). Impact on children when one parent disparages the other. *Medical Aspects of Human Sexuality, 20,* 45-56.

Feagans, L., Robinson, J. A., & Anderson, R. (1988). Maternal attributions to a handicapped and non-handicapped twin. *First Language, 8,* 183-197.

Feldman, C., & Bruner, J. (1987). Varieties of perspective: An overview. In J. Russell (Ed.), *Philosophical perspectives on developmental psychology*. London: Basil Blackwell.

Fine, G.A. (1981). Friends, impression management and preadolescent behaviour. In S.R. Asher, & J.M. Gottman (Eds.), *The development of children's friendships*. Cambridge: Cambridge University Press.

Fisher, I.E. (1976). Dropping remarks and the Barbadian audience. *American Ethologist, 3*, 227-242.

Fiske, S.T., & Taylor, S.E. (1984). *Social cognition*. New York: Random House.

Flavell, J.H. (1977). *Cognitive development*. Englewood Cliffs, N.J.: Prentice-Hall.

Flavell, J.H., & Ross, L. (1981). *Social cognitive development*. Cambridge: Cambridge University Press.

Fodor, J. (1983). *The modularity of mind*. Cambridge, Mass.: M.I.T. Press.

Forgas, J.P. (1981). *Social cognition: Perspectives on everyday understanding*. London: Academic Press.

Forrester, M.A. (1985). *Adult-to-child third party reference in the pre-school*. Paper presented at the Child Language Conference. Nottingham, 1985.

Forrester, M.A. (1986). *Polyadic language processes and the pre-school child*. Unpublished PhD thesis, University of Strathclyde.

Forrester, M.A. (1988). Young children's polyadic conversation monitoring skills. *First Language, 8*, 201-226.

Forrester, M.A. (1989). Adult-to-child group addressing speech in the pre-school. *Child Language, Teaching and Therapy, 5*, 64-78.

Forrester, M.A. (1991). A conceptual framework for investigating learning in conversations. *Computers in Education, 17*, 61-72.

Fox, D.S. (1980). *Teacher-child discourse interaction and the language of pre-school learning impaired children*. Doctoral dissertation. Teachers College, Columbia University.

Frommer, M. (1982). *Names. Etc.; 39*, 106-108.

Furnam, L.N., & Walden, T.A. (1990). Effects of script knowledge on pre-school children's communicative interaction. *Developmental Psychology, 26*, 227-233.

Furth, H.G. (1978). Young children's understanding of society. In H.McGurk (Ed.), *Issues in childhood social development*. London: Methuen.

Gallagher, T.M., & Craig, H.K. (1982). An investigation of overlap in children's speech. *Journal of Psycholinguistic Research, 11*, 63-75.

Garfinkel, H. (1967). *Ethnomethdology*. Englewood Cliffs, N.J.: Prentice-Hall.

Garton, A. (1984). Social interaction and cognitive growth: Possible causal mechanisms. *British Journal of Developmental Psychology, 2*, 269-274.

Garvey, C. (1977). *Play*. London: Fontana/Open Books.

Garvey, C. (1984). *Children's talk*. Oxford: Fontana.

Garvey, C., & Berninger, G. (1981). Timing and turn-taking in children's conversation. *Discourse Processes, 4*, 27-57.

Gazdar, G. (1979). *Pragmatics: Implicature, presupposition and logical form*. New York: Academic Press.

Gelman, R., & Spelke, E. (1981). The development of thoughts about animate and inanimate objects: Implications for research on social cognition. In J.H. Flavell & L. Ross (Eds.), *Social cognitive development*. Cambridge: Cambridge University Press.

Gibbs, R. (1986). Skating on thin ice: Literal meaning and understanding idioms in conversation. *Discourse Processes, 9,* 17-30.

Gibson, J.J. (1966). *The senses considered as perceptual systems.* Boston: Houghton Mifflin.

Gibson, J.J. (1979). *The ecological approach to visual perception.* Boston: Houghton Mifflin.

Giddens, A. (1988). Goffman as a systematic social theorist. In P. Drew & A. Wootton (Eds.), *Ervin Goffman: Exploring the interaction order.* Polity Press: Cambridge.

Ginsburg, H., & Opper, S. (1983). *Piaget's theory of intellectual development.* London: Prentice-Hall.

Givon, T. (1984). Deductive vs. pragmatic processing in natural language. In W. Kintsch, J.R. Miller, & P.G. Polson (Eds.), *Method and tactics in cognitive science.* Hillsdale, N.J.: Lawrence Erlbaum Associates Inc.

Gleitman, L., Newport, E.L., & Gleitman, H. (1984). The current status of the motherese hypothesis. *Journal of Child Language, 11,* 43-80.

Goffman, E. (1963). *Behavior in public places: Notes on the social organization of gatherings.* New York: Free Press.

Goffman, E. (1967). *Interaction ritual: Essays on face-to-face behavior.* New York: Doubleday Anchor.

Goffman, E. (1976). Replies and responses. *Language in Society, 5,* 257-313.

Goffman, E. (1979). *Gender advertisements.* London: Macmillan.

Goffman, E. (1981). *Forms of talk.* Hillsdale, N.J.: Lawrence Erlbaum Associates Inc.

Golinkoff, R.M. (1983a). *The transition from pre-linguistic to linguistic communication.* Hillsdale, N.J.: Lawrence Erlbaum Associates Inc.

Golinkoff, R.M. (1983b). The pre-verbal negotiation of failed messages: Insights into the transition period. In R.M. Golinkoff (Ed.), *The transition from pre-linguistic to linguistic communication.* Hillsdale, N.J.: Lawrence Erlbaum Associates Inc.

Goodwin, C. (1981). *Conversational organization: Interaction between speakers and hearers.* London: Academic Press.

Graddoc, D., Cheshire, J., & Swann, D. (1987). *Describing language.* Milton Keynes: Open University Press.

Granger, G. (1982). The notion of formal content. *Social Research, 49,* (2), 359-462.

Gresham, F.M. (1986). Conceptual issues in social competence assessment. In P.S. Strain, M.J. Guralnick, & H.M. Walker (Eds.), *Children's social behaviour: Development, assessment and modification.* New York: Academic Press.

Grice, H.P. (1957). Meaning. *Philosophical Review, 66,* 377-88. Reprinted (1971). In D. Steinberg & L. Jakobvovits (Eds.), *Semantics: An interdisciplinary reader.* Cambridge: Cambridge University Press.

Grice, H.P. (1981). Pre-supposition and conversational implicature. In P. Cole (Ed.), *Radical pragmatics.* New York: Academic Press.

Grice, H.P. (1982). Meaning revisited. In N. Smith (Ed.), *Mutual knowledge.* London: Academic Press.

Guralnick, M.J. (1986). Peer relations of young children. In P.S. Strain, M.J. Guralnick, & H.M. Walker (Eds.), *Children's social behaviour: Development, assessment and modification.* New York: Academic Press.

Guralnick, M.J. (1990). Peer interactions and handicapped children's development. In H.C. Foot, M.J. Morgan, & R.H. Shute (Eds.), *Children helping children*. New York: Wiley.

Habermas, J. (1970). Introductory remarks to a theory of communicative competence. Reprinted in H.P. Dreitzel (Ed.), *Recent Sociology, No. 2*. London: Macmillan.

Hacker, P.M.S. (1972). *Insight and illusion: Wittgenstein on philosophy and the metaphysics of experience*. London: Oxford University Press.

Halliday, M.A.K. (1973). *Explorations in the function of language*. London: Edward Arnold.

Hake, D.F., & Olvera, D. (1978). Cooperation, competition and related social phenomena. In A.C. Catania & T.A. Brigham (Eds.), *Handbook of applied behaviour analysis: Social and instructional processes*. New York: Irvington.

Harre, R. (1979). *Social Being*. Oxford: Blackwell.

Harrigan, J.A. (1985). Listeners' body movements and speaking turns. *Communication Research, 12*, 233-253.

Harrigan, J.A., & Steffan, J.J. (1983). Gaze as a turn exchange signal in group conversations. *British Journal of Social Psychology, 22*, 167-178.

Harrison, B. (1974). On understanding a general name. In M.P.M. Richards (Ed.), *The integration of a child into a social world*. Cambridge: Cambridge University Press.

Hartup, W.W. (1970). Peer interaction and social organization. In P.H. Mussen (Ed.), *Carmichael's manual of child development (Vol. 2)*. New York: Wiley.

Haviland, S.E., & Clark, H.H. (1974). What's new: Acquiring new information as a process of comprehension. *Journal of Verbal Learning and Verbal Behaviour, 13*, 512-521.

Heber, J. (1971). The influence of language training on seriation in 5–6 year old children initially at different levels of descriptive competence. *British Journal of Psychology, 68*, 85-95.

Heber, J. (1981). Instruction versus conversation as opportunities for learning. In W.P. Robinson (Ed.), *Communication and development*. London: Academic Press.

Heckhausen, J. (1987). How do mothers know? Infants chronological age or infants performance as determinants of adaptations in maternal instruction. *Journal of Experimental Child Psychology, 43*, 212-226.

Higgins, E.T. (1981). Role taking and social judgment: Alternative developmental perspectives and processes. In J.H. Flavell & L. Ross (Eds.), *Social cognitive development*. Cambridge: Cambridge University Press.

Higgins, E.T., Ruble, D.N., & Hartup, W.W. (Eds.). (1983). *Social cognition and social development*. Cambridge and New York: Cambridge University Press.

Higgins, E.T., & Wells, T. (1986). Social construct availability and accessibility as a function of social life phase: Emphasising the "how" versus the "can" of social cognition. *Social Cognition, 4*, 201-206.

Hinde, R.A. (1979). *Towards understanding relationships*. London: Academic Press.

Hinde, R.A., Perret-Clermont, A.N., & Stevenson-Hinde, J. (1985). *Social relationships and cognitive development*. Oxford: Clarendon Press.

Hinton, A. (1981). *Associative memory*. London: Academic Press.

Hobson, P. (1991). Against the theory of "theory of mind". *British Journal of Developmental Psychology, 9,* 33-54.

Hollos, M. (1977). The comprehension and use of social rules in pronoun selection by Hungarian children. In S. Ervin-Tripp & C. Mitchell-Kernan (Eds.), *Child discourse.* New York and London: Academic Press.

Hoffman, M.L. (1981). Perspectives on the difference between understanding people and understanding things: The role of affect. In J.H. Flavell & L. Ross (Eds.), *Social cognitive development.* Cambridge: Cambridge University Press.

Hoffman, M.L. (1982). Development of pro-social motivation: Empathy and guilt. In N. Eisenberg (Ed.), *The development of pro-social behaviour.* New York: Academic Press.

Howe, C. (in press). *Language learning: A special case for developmental psychology.* Hove: Lawrence Erlbaum Associates Ltd.

Howe, C., & Ogura, T. (1988). *Structure and sequence in play and early language: An investigation of the Piagetian viewpoint.* Proceedings of the 1988 Child Language Conference. Warwick University.

Humphrey-Jones, C. (1986). Make, make do and mend: The role of the hearer in misunderstanding. In G. McGregor (Ed.), *Language for hearers: Language and communication library (Vol. 8).* London: Pergamon Press.

Ignjatovic-Savic, S. (1985). Commentary on Wertsch, J. and Sammarco, J.G. (p.291-293). In R.A. Hinde, A.N. Perret-Clermont, & J. Stevenson-Hinde (Eds.), *Social relationships and cognitive development.* Oxford: Clarendon Press.

Isen, A.M., & Hastorf, A.H. (1982). Some perspectives on cognitive social psychology. In A.M. Isen & A.H. Hastorf (Eds.), *Cognitive social psychology.* The Hague: Elsevier.

Ingram, D. (1989). *First language acquisition.* Cambridge: Cambridge University Press.

Jahoda, G. (1982). The development of ideas about an economic institution: A cross-national replication. *British Journal of Psychology, 21,* 337-358.

Johannson, G. (1973). Visual perception of biological motion and a model for its analysis. *Perception and Psychophysics, 14,* 201-211.

Johnson, C.N. (1988). Theory of mind and the structure of conscious experience. In J.W. Astington, P.L Harris & D. Olson (Eds.), *Developing theories of mind.* Cambridge: Cambridge University Press.

John-Steiner, V. (1987). *Notebooks of the mind: Explorations of thinking.* New York: Harper and Row.

Jordan, R. (1989). An experimental comparison of the understanding and use of speaker-addressee personal pronouns in autistic children. *British Journal of Disorders of Communication, 24,* (2), 169-179.

Jordan, R. (1992). In D. Messer & G. Turner (Eds.), *Critical influences on language development.* London: Macmillan.

Karmiloff-Smith, A. (1979). *A functional approach to child language.* Cambridge: Cambridge University Press.

Karmiloff-Smith, A. (1990). Piaget and Chomsky on language acquisition: Divorce or marriage? (Keynote address—1990 Child Language Seminar). *First Language, 10,* 255-270.

Keller, M., & Reuss, S. (1984). An action theoretical reconstruction of the development of social cognitive competence. *Human Development, 27,* 211-220.

Kintsch, W. (1982). Memory for text. In A. Flammer & W. Kintsch (Eds.) *Discourse processing*. London: North-Holland.

Kintsch, W., & van Dijk, T. (1978). Toward a model of text comprehension and production. *Psychological Review, 85,* (5), 363-394.

Kirkpatrick, J., & White, G.M. (Eds.). (1985). *Person, Self and Experience.* Berkeley, CA: University of California Press.

Kohlberg, L. (1966). A cognitive-developmental analysis of children's sex-roles and attitudes. In E.E. Maccoby (Ed.), *The development of sex differences.* Stanford: Stanford University Press.

Kosslyn, S.M., & Kagan, J. (1981). "Concrete thinking" and the development of social cognition. In J.H. Flavell & L. Ross (Eds.), *Social cognitive development.* Cambridge: Cambridge University Press.

Kurdeck, L.A., & Rodgon, M.M. (1975). Perceptual, cognitive and affective perspective taking in kindergarten through six-grade children. *Developmental Psychology, 11,* 643-650.

Labov, W. (1966). *The social stratification of English in New York City.* Washington D.C.: Center for Applied Linguistics.

Labov, W. (1972). *Sociolinguistic patterns.* Philadelphia: University of Philadelphia Press.

Ladd, G.W. (1981). Effectiveness of a social learning method for enhancing children's social interaction and peer acceptance. *Child Development, 52,* 171-178.

Landwehr, K. (1988). Environmental perception: An ecological perspective. In D. Canter, D. Stea, & M. Krampen (Eds.), *New directions in environmental research.* London: Gower.

Leahy, R.L. (1985). The costs of development. In R.L. Leahy (Ed.), *The development of the self.* New York: Academic Press.

Leahy, R.L., & Shirk, S.R. (1985). Social cognition and the development of the self. In R.L. Leahy (Ed.), *The development of the self.* New York: Academic Press.

Lee, D.N. (1976). A theory of visual control of braking based on information about time-to-collision. *Perception, 5,* 437-459.

Lee, D. N., & Lishman, J.R. (1977). Visual control of locomotion. *Scandinavian Journal of Psychology, 18,* 224-230.

Lee, D.N., Lishman, J.R., & Thomson, J.A. (1982). Regulation of gait in long jumping. *Journal of Experimental Psychology: Human Perception and Performance, 8,* 448-459.

Lee, D.N., & Reddish, P.E. (1981). Plummeting gannets: A paradigm of ecological optics. *Nature, 293,* 293-294.

Lee, D.N., Young, D.S., Reddish, P.E., Lough, S., & Clayton, T.M.H. (1983). Visual timing in hitting an accelerating ball. *Quarterly Journal of Experimental Psychology, 35A,* 333-346.

Leekam, S. (1991). Believing and deceiving: Steps to become a good liar. In S.J. Ceci, M.D. De Simone, & M. Putnick (Eds.), *Social and cognitive factors in preschool children's deception.* Hillsdale, N.J.: Lawrence Erlbaum Associates Inc.

Lefebvre-Pinard, M. (1982). Questions about the relationship between social cognition and social behaviour: The search for the missing link. *Canadian Journal of Behavioural Science, 14,* (4), 323-327.

Leslie, A.M. (1987). Pretense and representation: The origins of "theory of mind". *Psychological Review, 94,* 412-426.

Leslie, A.M. (1988). Some implications of pretense for mechanisms underlying the child's theory of mind. In J.W. Astington, P.L. Harris, & D. Olson (Eds.), *Developing theories of mind.* Cambridge: Cambridge University Press.

Levinson, S. (1983). *Pragmatics.* Cambridge: Cambridge University Press.

Locke, J. (1690). *An Essay concerning human understanding.*

Liddell, C., & Collis, G. (1988). Second-order effects: Number or nature of companions. *Journal of Genetic Psychology, 148,* 237-247.

Light, P. (1983). Social interaction and cognitive development: A review of post-Piagetian research. In S. Meadows (Ed.), *Developing thinking:Approaches to children's cognitive development.* London: Methuen.

Lindsey, P.H., & Norman, D.A. (1977). *Human information processing. 2nd Edition.* New York: Academic Press.

Lloyd, B., & Goodwin, R. (1990). Let's pretend: Casting the characters and setting the scene. Abstracts of the 1990 Child Language Seminar. *First Language, 10,* 255-270.

Mackie, D. (1980). A cross-cultural study of intra and inter-individual conflicts of centration. *European Journal of Social Psychology, 10,* 313-318.

Mahalingam, K. (1984). Naming strategies in child language. *Psycho-Lingua, 14,* (2), 123-133.

Mantel, N., & Haenszel, W. (1959). Statistical aspects of the analysis of data from retrospective studies of disease. *Journal of National Cancer Institute, 22,* 719-748.

Marr, D. (1982). *Vision.* Cambridge, Mass.: M.I.T. Press.

Mays, W. (1982). Piaget's sociological theory. In M. Modgil (Ed.), *Jean Piaget, consensus and controversy.* London: Holt, Rhinehart, & Wilson.

McArthur, L.Z., & Baron, R. M. (1983). Toward an ecological theory of social perception. *Psychological Review, 90,* (3), 215-238.

McConvell, P. (1988). MIX-IM-UP. Aboriginal code-switching old and new. In M. Holler (Ed.), *Code-switching: Anthropological and sociolinguistic perspectives.* Mouton: De Grugter.

McFall, R.M. (1982). A review and reformulation of the concept of social skill. *Behavioural Assessment, 4,* (1), 1-33.

McGarrigle, J., Grieve, R., & Hughes, M. (1978). Interpreting inclusion. *Journal of Experimental Child Psychology, 26,* 528-550.

McGillicuddy-DeLisi, A.V. (1982). The relationship between parents beliefs about development and family constellation, socioeconomic status and parents' teaching strategies. In L.M. Laosa & I.E. Sigel (Eds.), *Families as learning environments for children.* New York: Plenum.

McGregor, G. (1983). Listener's comments on conversation. *Language and Communication, 3,* 271-304.

McHoul, A. (1978). The organization of turns at formal talk in the classroom. *Language in Society, 7,* 183-213.

McLaughlin, B. (1971). *Learning and social behaviour.* California: Free Press.

McNeill, D. (1966). Developmental psycholinguistics. In F. Smith & G. Miller (Eds.), *The genesis of language.* Cambridge, Mass.: M.I.T. Press.

McTear, M. (1985). *Children's conversation.* Oxford: Basil Blackwell.

Mead, G.H. (1934). *On social psychology.* Edited by A. Strauss. Chicago: University of Chicago Press, 1977.

Messer, D.J. (1983). In R. Golinkoff (Ed.), *From Pre-linguistic to Linguistic Communication.* Hillsdale, N.J.: Lawrence Erlbaum Associates Inc.

Messer, D.J., & Turner, G. (1992). *Critical influences in language development.* London: MacMillan.

Messer, D.J., & Vietze, P.M. (1988). Does mutual influence occur during mother-infant social gaze? *Infant Behaviour and Development, 11,* (1), 97-110.

Michaels, C.F., & Carello, C. (1981). *Direct perception. Century psychology series.* Englewood Cliffs, N.J.: Prentice-Hall and Wiley.

Miller, P.J., & Sperry, L. (1988). Early talk about the past: The origins of conversational stories about the past. *Journal of Child Language, 15,* 293-315.

Montague, R. (1970). English as a formal language. In B. Visenti (Ed.), *Linguaggi: nell societa e enllatechnica* (pp. 189-222). Milan: Edizioni di communita.

Morton, J., 1969. Interaction of information in word recognition. *Psychological Review, 76,* 165-178.

Morton, J. (1979). Word Recognition. In J. Morton & J.C. Marshall (Eds.), *Psycholinguistics Series 2,* London: Elk.

Mowrer, O.H. (1960). *Learning theory and the symbolic process.* New York: Wiley.

Mueller, E. (1972). The maintenance of verbal exchanges between young children. *Child Development, 43,* 930-938.

Mueller, E., & Lucas, T. (1975). A development analysis of peer interaction among toddlers. In M. Lewis & L.A. Rosenblum (Eds.), *The origins of behaviour (Vol. 4). Friendship and peer relations.* New York: Wiley.

Mugny, G., & Doise, W. (1978). Socio-cognitive conflict and structuration of individual and collective performances. *European Journal of Social Psychology, 8,* 181-192.

Mugny, G., Perret-Clermont, A.N., & Doise, W. (1981). Interpersonal co-ordinations and sociological differences in the construction of the intellect. In G. Stephenson & G. Davies (Eds.), *Applied social psychology.* Chichester: Wiley.

Murray, L., & Trevarthen, C. (1986). The infant's role in mother-infant communications. *Journal of Child Language, 13,* 15-29.

Neisser, U. (1976). *Cognition and reality.* New York: M.I.T. Press.

Nelson, K. (1981). Social cognition in a script framework. In J.H. Flavell & L. Ross (Eds.), *Social cognitive development.* Cambridge: Cambridge University Press.

Nelson, K., & Greundel, J.M. (1979). At morning it's lunchtime: A scriptal view of children's dialogues. *Discourse Processes, 2,* 73-94.

Nelson, K., & Seidman, S.J. (1984). Playing with scripts. In I. Bretherton (Ed.), *Symbolic play: The development of social understanding.*

Newman, D. (1986). The role of mutual knowledge in the development of perspective taking. *Developmental Review, 6,* 122-145.

Newport, E.L., Gleitman, H., & Gleitman, L. (1977). Mother I'd rather do it myself. In C. Snow, & C.A. Ferguson, *Talking to Children.* Cambridge: Cambridge University Press.

Ochs, E. (1982). Talking to children in Western Samoa. *Language in Society, 11,* 77-105.

Ochs, E., & Schiefflein, B. (1979). *Developmental pragmatics.* London: Academic Press.

Olson, D. (1988). On the origins of beliefs and other intentional states in children. In J.W. Astington, P.L. Harris, & D. Olson (Eds.), *Developing theories of mind.* Cambridge: Cambridge University Press.

Oppenheimer, L., & Rempt, E. (1986). Social-cognitive development with moderately and severely retarded children. *Journal of Applied Developmental Psychology, 7,* 237-249.

Orsolini, M. (1988). Information exchange in classroom conversation: Negotiation and extension of the focus. *European Journal of Psychology of Education, 3,* (3), 341-355.

Oshima-Takane, Y. (1988). Children learn from speech not addressed to them: The case of personal pronouns. *Journal of Child Language, 15,* 95-108.

Parker, I. (1989). *The crisis in modern social psychology.* New York: Routledge.

Parker-Rhodes, F. (1978). *Inferential semantics.* Sussex: Harvester Wheatsheaf.

Payne, G., & Hustler, D. (1979). Teaching the class: The practical management of a cohort. *British Journal of the Sociology of Education, 1,* 49-56.

Perner, J. (1988a). Developing semantics for theories of mind: From propositional attitudes to mental representation. In J.W. Astington, P.L. Harris & D. Olson (Eds.), *Developing theories of mind.* Cambridge: Cambridge University Press.

Perner, J. (1988b). Higher-order beliefs and intentions in children's understanding of social interaction. In J.W. Astington, P.L. Harris, & D. Olson (Eds.), *Developing theories of mind.* Cambridge: Cambridge University Press.

Perret-Clermont, A.N. (1980). *Social interaction and cognitive development.* London: Academic Press.

Piaget, J. (1929). *The child's conception of the world.* New York: Harcourt Brace Jovanovich.

Piaget, J. (1954). *The construction of reality in the child.* New York: Basic Books.

Piaget, J. (1966). *Mathematical epistemology and psychology.* Trans. W. Mays. Berlin: Reidel.

Piaget, J. (1932/1977). *The moral judgement of the child.* Harmondsworth: Penguin.

Piaget, J. (1936/1952). *The origin of intelligence in the child.* London: Routledge and Kegan Paul.

Piaget, J. (1965/77). *Etudes sociologiques* (1965). Geneva, 1977: Librairie Droz.

Pick, H.L. (1987). Information and the effects of early perceptual experience. In N. Eisenberg (Ed.), *Contemporary topics in developmental psychology.* New York: Wiley.

Pimm, D. (1987). *Speaking mathematically: Communication in mathematics classrooms.* London: Routledge & Kegan Paul.

Pinker, S. (1984). *Language learnability and language development.* Cambridge, Mass.: M.I.T. Press.

Plunkett, D. (1990). *Language acquisition in a parallel distributed processing system.* Paper presented at the 1990 Child Language Seminar, University of Kent, Canterbury. (Abstract in *First Language, 10,* 255-270.)

Pomerantz, J.R. (1981). Perceptual organization in information processing. In A.M. Aitkenhead & J.M. Slack (Eds.), *Issues in cognitive modelling.* Hove, U.K.: Lawrence Erlbaum Associates Ltd.

Poole, J. (1985). Coming into social being: Cultural images of infants in Bimin-Kuskusmin Folk Psychology. In G.M. White & J. Kirkpatrick (Eds.), *Person, self and experience.* Berkeley: University of California Press.

Potter, J., & Weatherall, M. (1987). *Discourse and social psychology: Beyond attitudes and behaviour.* London: Sage.

Pratt, M. W., Kerig, P., Cowan, P.A., & Cowan, C.P. (1988). Mothers and fathers teaching 3 year olds: Authoritative parenting and adult scaffolding of young children's learning. *Developmental Psychology, 24,* (6), 832-834.

Premack, D. (1983). The codes of man and beast. *Behaviour and Brain Sciences, 6,* (1), 125-167.

Premack, D., & Woodruff, G. (1978). Does the chimpanzee have a theory of mind? *Behavioural and Brain Sciences, 1,* 515-526.

Putallaz, M. (1983). Predicting children's sociometric status from their behaviour. *Child Development, 54,* 1417-1426.

Putallaz, M., & Gottman, J.M. (1981). Social skills and group acceptance. In S.R. Asher & J.M. Gottman (Eds.), *The development of children's friendships.* Cambridge: Cambridge University Press.

Radziszewska, B., & Rogoff, B. (1988). Influence of adult and peer collaborators on children's planning skills. *Developmental Psychology, 24,* (6), 840-848.

Reason, D. (1984). *Generalisation from the particular case study: Some foundational considerations.* Occasional paper, Keynes College, University of Kent.

Reschley, D.J., & Gresham, F.M. (1981). *Use of social competence measures to facilitate parent and teacher involvement and non-biased assessment.* Unpublished manuscript. Iowa State University.

Roberts, M.C. (1986). *Pediatric psychology: Psychological interventions and strategies for pediatric problems.* New York: Pergamon Press.

Rogoff, B., Ellis, S., & Gardner, W. (1981). Adjustment of adult-child instruction according to child's age and task. *Developmental Psychology, 20,* 193-199.

Rogosch, F.A., & Newcomb, A.F. (1989). Children's perceptions of peer reputations and their social reputations among peers. *Child Development, 60,* (3), 597-610.

Romaine, S. (1989). *Bilingualism.* Oxford: Basil Blackwell.

Rosch, E. (1975). Cognitive reference points. *Cognitive Psychology, 7,* 532-47.

Ross, H.S. (1982). Establishment of social games amongst toddlers. *Developmental Psychology, 18,* 509-518.

Ross, L. (1981). The "intuitive scientist" formulation and its developmental implications. In J.H. Flavell & L. Ross (Eds.), *Social cognitive development.* Cambridge: Cambridge University Press.

Rubin, K.H., & Ross, H.S. (1982). (Eds.), *Peer relationships and social skills in childhood.* New York: Springer-Verlag.

Rumelhart, D.E., & McClelland, J.L. (1986). (Eds.), *Parallel distributed processing: Explorations in the microstructure of cognition, (Vol. 1).* Cambridge, Mass.: M.I.T. Press.

Russell, J. (1981). Why socio-cognitive conflict may be impossible: The status of egocentric errors in the dyadic performance of a spatial task. *Educational Psychology, 1,* 159-69.

Russell, J. (1982). Propositional attitudes. In M. Beveridge (Ed.), *Children thinking through language.* London: Edward Arnold.

Russell, J. (1983). Piaget's theory of sensorimotor development: Outlines, assumptions and problems. In G. Butterworth (Ed.), *Infancy and epistemology.* London: Routledge and Kegan Paul.

Russell, J. (1987). (Ed.), *Philosophical perspectives on developmental psychology*. London: Basil Blackwell.

Rutter, D.R. (1987). *Communication by telephone*. New York: Pergamon Press.

Ryan, J. (1974). Early language development: Towards a communicational analysis. In M.P.M. Richards (Ed.), *The integration of a child into a social world*. Cambridge: Cambridge University Press.

Sachs, J., Brown, R., & Salerno, R.A. (1976). Adults' speech to children. In W. von Raffler-Enger & Y. Lebrun (Eds.), *Baby talk and infant speech*. Lisse, Netherlands: Swets and Zeitlinger.

Sacks, H. (1980). "Button, button, who's got the button?" *Social Enquiry, 50*, 3-5.

Sacks, H., Schegloff, E., & Jefferson, G. (1974). A simplest systematics for the organization of turn-taking in conversation. *Language, 50*, 696-735.

Saussaure, F. de (1966). *Cours de Linguistique Générale*. New York: McGraw-Hill.

Savic, S. (1980). *How twins learn to talk*. London: Academic Press.

Schaffer, H.R. (Ed.). (1977). *Studies in mother-infant interaction*. London: Academic Press.

Schaffer, H.R. (1980). *Mothering*. Glasgow: Collins.

Schaffer, H.R. (1984). *The child's entry into the social world*. London: Academic Press.

Schaffer, H.R., & Crook, C.K. (1978). Maternal control techniques in a directed play situation. *Child Development, 50*, 696-735.

Schaffer, H.R., & Emerson, P.E. (1964). The development of social attachments in infancy. *Monographs of the Society for Research in Child Development*, (3. Serial No. 94).

Schaffer, H.R., & Liddell, C. (1984). Adult-child interaction under dyadic and polyadic conditions. *British Journal of Developmental Psychology, 2*, 33-42.

Schank, R.C., & Abelson, R. (1977). *Scripts, plans, goals and understanding: An inquiry into human knowledge structures*. Hillsdale, N.J.: Lawrence Erlbaum Associates Inc.

Schegloff, E.A. (1988). Goffman and the analysis of conversation. In P. Drew & A. Wootton (Eds.), *Ervin Goffman: Exploring the interaction order*. Polity Press: Cambridge.

Schegloff, E.A., & Sacks, H. (1973). Opening up closings. *Semiotica, 8*, (4), 289-327.

Schiefflein, B. (1981). A developmental study of pragmatic appropriateness of word order and case marking in Kaluli. In W. Deutsch (Ed.), *The child's construction of language*. New York: Academic Press.

Schmidt, R.C., Carello, C., & Turvey, M.T. (1990). Phase transitions and critical fluctuations in the visual co-ordinations of rhythmic movements between people. *Journal of Experimental Psychology: Human Perception and Performance, 16*, (2), 227-247.

Schober, M.I., & Clark, H.H. (1989). Understanding by addressees and overhearers. *Cognitive Psychology, 21*, 211-232.

Schutz, A. (1962). *Collected papers II. Studies in social theory*. The Hague: Nijhoff.

Scotton, C.M., & Ury, W. (1977). Bilingual strategies: The social functions of code switching. *Linguistics, 193*, 5-20.

Searle, J.R. (1969). *Speech acts: An essay in the philosophy of language*. Cambridge: Cambridge University Press.

Selman, R. (1981). The child as a friendship philosopher. In S.R. Asher & J.M. Gottman (Eds.), *The development of children's friendships*. Cambridge: Cambridge University Press.

Selman, R. (1985). The use of interpersonal negotiation strategies and communicative competencies: A clinical developmental exploration in a pair of troubled adolescents. In R.A. Hinde, A.N. Perret-Clermont, & J. Stevenson-Hinde, (Eds.), *Social relationships and cognitive development*. Oxford: Clarendon Press.

Shantz, C.U. (1975). The development of social cognition. In E.M. Hetherington (Ed.), *Review of child development research*. Chicago and London: University of Chicago Press.

Shantz, C.U. (1983). Social cognition. In J.H. Flavell & E.M. Markman (Eds.), *Handbook of Child Psychology. 4th Edition, (Vol. 3)*. New York: Wiley.

Shatz, M., & Gelman, R. (1973). The development of communication skills: Modifications in the speech of young children as a function of listener. *Monographs of the Society for Research in Child Development*, 38 (5. Serial No. 152).

Shatz, M., Wellman, H.M., & Silber, S. (1983). The acquisition of mental verbs: A systematic investigation of the first reference to mental state. *Cognition, 14,* 301-321.

Shure, M.B. (1985). Interpersonal problem-solving: A cognitive approach to behaviour. In R.A. Hinde, A.N. Perret-Clermont, & J. Stevenson-Hinde (Eds.), *Social relationships and cognitive development*. Oxford: Clarendon Press.

Shute, R., & Paton, D. (1990). Childhood illness: The child as helper. In H.C. Foot, M.J. Morgan, & R.H. Shute (Eds.), *Children helping children*. Chichester: Wiley.

Sigel, I.E., Dreyer, A.S., & McGullicuddy-DeLisi, M. (1984). Psychological perspectives of the family. In L. Lhosa & I.E. Sigel (Eds.), *Families as learning environment for children*. London: Plenum Press.

Sinclair, J. McH., & Coulthard, R. M. (1975). *Towards an analysis of discourse: The English used by teachers and pupils*. London and New York: Oxford University Press.

Sinha, C. (1988). Language and representation. London: Harvester Wheatsheaf.

Slaby, R.G., & Guerra, N.G. (1988). Cognitive mediators of aggression in adolescent offenders. *Developmental Psychology, 24,* (4), 580-588.

Smith, P., & Connolly, K. (1980). *The ecology of pre-school behaviour*. Cambridge: Cambridge University Press.

Snow, C., & Ferguson, C. (1977). *Talking to children*. Cambridge: Cambridge University Press.

Snow, C., & Galbraith, K. (1983). Comments on the volume. In R. Golinkoff (Ed.), *From pre-linguistic to linguistic communication*. Hillsdale, N.J.: Lawrence Erlbaum Associates Inc.

Sperber, D., & Wilson, D. (1986). *Relevance: Communication and cognition*. Oxford: Blackwell.

Stamback, M., Ballion, M., Breaute, M., & Rayna, S. (1985). Pretend play and interaction in young children. In R.A. Hinde, A.N. Perret-Clermont, & J. Stevenson-Hinde (Eds.), *Social relationships and cognitive development*. Oxford: Clarendon Press.

Stein, N.L., & Goldman, S.R. (1981). Children's knowledge about social situations: From causes to consequences. In S.R. Asher & J.M. Gottman (Eds.), *The development of children's friendships*. Cambridge: Cambridge University Press.

Stern, D. (1974). Mother and father at play: The dyadic interaction involving facial, vocal and gaze behaviours. In M. Lewis & L. Rosenblaum (Eds.), *The effect of the infant on its caregiver.* New York: Wiley.

Stitch, S. (1983). *From folk psychology to cognitive science.* Cambridge, Mass.: M.I.T. Press.

Stoffergen, T.A., Schnuckler, M.A., & Gibson, E.J. (1987). Use of control and peripheral optical flow in stance and locomotion in young walkers. *Perception, 16*, 113-119.

Stokes, T.F., & Osnes, P.G. (1986). Programming the generalization of children's social behaviour. In P.S. Strain, M.J. Guralnick & H.M. Walker (Eds.), *Children's social behaviour: Development, assessment and modification.* New York: Academic Press.

Stotland, E., & Canon, L.K. (1972). *Social psychology: A cognitive approach.* Philadelphia: Saunders Press.

Strain, P.S., Guralnick, M.J., & Walker, H.M. (1986). (Eds.). *Children's social behaviour: Development, assessment and modification.* New York: Academic Press.

Strayer, F.F. (1983). Social ecology of the preschool peer group. In W.A. Collins (Ed.), *Development of cognition, affect, and social relations.* Hillsdale, N.J.: Lawrence Erlbaum Associates Inc.

Strayer, F. F., & Strayer, J. (1980). Pre-school conflict and the assessment of social dominance. In D.R. Omark, J. Strayer, & D.G. Freedman (Eds.), *Dominance relations.* New York: Garland Publications.

Strayer, J. (1977). *The development of personal reference in the language of two-year-olds.* Unpublished PhD dissertation. Simon Fraser University.

Tajfel, H., & Forgas, J.P. (1981). Cognitions, values and groups. In J.P. Forgas (Ed.), *Social cognition.* London: Academic Press.

Tanz, C. (1980). *Studies in the acquisition of deictic terms.* Cambridge: Cambridge University Press.

Taylor, T.J., & Cameron, D. (1987). *Analysing conversation: Rules and units in the structure of talk.* Language and Communication Library (Vol. 9). Oxford: Pergamon Press.

Trevarthen, C. (1977). Descriptive analysis of infant communication behaviour. In H.R. Schaffer (Ed.), *Studies in mother-infant interaction.* London: Academic Press.

Trevarthen, C., & Hubley, P. (1978). Secondary intersubjectivity: Confidence, confiding and acts of meaning in the first year. In A. Lock (Ed.), *Action, gesture and symbol: The emergence of language.* London: Academic Press.

Turiel, E. (1982). *The development of social knowledge.* New York: Cambridge University Press.

Turiel, E. (1983). Interaction and development in social cognition. In E.T. Higgins, D.N. Ruble, & W.W. Hartup (Eds.), *Social cognition and social development.* Cambridge: Cambridge University Press.

Turner, R. (1972). Some formal properties of therapy talk. In D. Sudnow (Ed.), *Studies in social interaction.* New York: Free Press.

Turvey, M. T., & Kugler, P.N. (1984). An ecological approach to perception and action. In H.T.A. Whiting (Ed.), *Human motor actions—Bernstein reassessed.* North-Holland: Elsevier Science Publishers B.V.

Ullman, S. (1980). Against direct perception. *Behaviour and brain sciences, 3,* 373-415.

Vaughen, B.E., & Waters, E. (1980). Social organisation among pre-school years. In D. Omark, F. Strayer, & D.G. Freeman, (Eds.), *Dominance relations.* New York: Garland Publications.

Vaughen, B.E., & Waters, E. (1981). Attention structure, sociometric status, and dominance. *Developmental Psychology, 17,* 275-288.

Von Cranach, M., & Vine, I. (Eds.). (1973). *Social communication and movement.* London: Academic Press.

Von Hofstein, C. (1983). Foundations for perceptual development. In L. Lipsett & C.K. Rovee-Collier (Eds.), *Advances in infancy research. (Vol 2).* N.J.: Ablex.

Vygotsky, L.S. (1934). *Thought and language.* Cambridge, Mass.: M.I.T. Press.

Vygotsky, L.S. (1978). *Mind in society: The development of higher psychological processes.*

Vygotsky, L.S. (1981). The genesis of higher mental functions. In J. Wertsch (Ed.), *The concept of activity in Soviet psychology.* New York: M.E. Sharpe Inc.

Wales, R. (1979). *Deixis.* In P. Fletcher & M. Garman (Eds.), *Language acquisition: Studies in a first language development.* Cambridge: Cambridge University Press.

Wales, R., Colman, M., & Pattison, P. (1983). How a thing is called: A study of mothers' and children's naming. *Journal of Experimental Child Psychology, 36,* (1), 1-17.

Walkerdine, V. (1982). From context to text: A psychosemiotic approach to abstract thought. In M. Beveridge (Ed.), *Children thinking through language.* London: Edward Arnold.

Walkerdine, V. (1988). *The mastery of reason.* London: Methuen.

Walkerdine, V., & Sinha, C. (1978). The internal triangle: Language, reasoning and the social context. In I. Markova (Ed.), *The social context of language.* Chichester: Wiley.

Wellman, H.M. (1985). A child's theory of mind: The development of conceptions of cognition. In S.R. Yussen (Ed.), *The growth of reflection in children.* New York: Academic Press.

Wellman, H.M. (1988). First steps in the child theorizing about the mind. In J.W. Astington, P.L Harris, & D. Olson (Eds.), *Developing theories of mind.* Cambridge: Cambridge University Press.

Wells, G. (1979). Variation in child language. In P. Fletcher, & M. Garman (Eds.), *Language acquisition.* Cambridge: Cambridge University Press.

Wells, G. (1983). Language and learning in the early years. *Early Child Development and Care, 11,* (1), 61-77.

Wertsch, J.V. (1985). *The social formation of mind.* New York and London: Routledge and Kegan Paul.

Wertsch, J.V., McNamee, G.D., McLane, J.B., & Budwig, N.A. (1980). The adult child dyad as a problem-solving system. *Child Development, 50,* 1215-1221.

Wertsch, J.V., & Sammarco, J.G. (1985). Social precursors to individual cognitive functioning: The problem of units of analysis. In R.A. Hinde, A.N. Perret-Clermont, & J. Stevenson-Hinde (Eds.), *Social relationships and cognitive development*. Oxford: Clarendon Press.

Wexler, K., & Cullicover, P. (1980). *Formal principles of language acquisition*. Cambridge, Mass: M.I.T. Press.

Whiten, A. (1991) (Ed.), *Natural theories of mind: Evolution, development and simulation of everyday mindreading*. Oxford: Basil Blackwell.

Whorf, B.L. (1956). Science and linguistics. In J.B. Carroll (Ed.), *Language, thought and reality: Selected writings of Benjamin Lee Whorf*. Cambridge, Mass: M.I.T. Press.

Williams, M. (1989). Vyotsky's social theory of mind. *Harvard Educational Review, 59*, (1), 108-126.

Wilson, E.O., (1975). *Sociobiology: The new synthesis*. Cambridge, Mass.: M.I.T. Press.

Winner, E., & Leekam, S. (1991). Distinguishing irony from deception: Understanding the speaker's second-order intention. *British Journal of Developmental Psychology, 9*, 257-270

Wimmer, H., & Perner, J. (1983). Beliefs about beliefs: Representation and constraining function of wrong beliefs in young children's understanding of deception. *Cognition, 13*, 103-128.

Wimmer, H., Hogrofe, J., & Sodian, B. (1988). A second stage in children's conception of mental life: Understanding informational accesses as origins of knowledge and belief. In J.W. Astington, P.L Harris, & D. Olson (Eds.), *Developing theories of mind*. Cambridge: Cambridge University Press.

Wittgenstein, L. (1953). *Philosophical investigations*. Oxford: Basil Blackwell.

Wood, D. (1988). *How children think and learn*. London: Blackwell.

Youniss, J. (1978). The nature of social development: A conceptual discussion of cognition. In H. McGurk (Ed.), *Issues in childhood social development*. London: Methuen.

Youniss, J., & Volpe, J. (1978). A relational analysis of children's friendship. In W. Damon (Ed.), *New directions for child development (Vol. 1)*. San Francisco: Jossey-Bass.

Zajonc, R. (1980). Feeling and thinking: Preferences need no inferences. *American Psychologist, 35*, 151-175.

Zimmerman, D.H., & West, C. (1975). Sex-roles, interruptions and silences in conversation. In B. Thorne & N. Henley (Eds.), *Language and sex: Difference and dominance*. Rowley, Mass: Newbury House.

Zukow, P.G. (1986). Interactions with the caregiver and the emergence of play. *British Journal of Developmental Psychology, 4*, 223-231.

Author Index

Sachs, J., 117
Sacks, H., 52, 56, 68, 69, 70, 71, 72,
    80, 89, 134, 164, 165
Salerno, R.A., 117
Salvador, F., 93
Sammarco, J.G., 41
Saussure, F. de, 7
Savic, S., 73
Schaefer, E.F., 42
Schaffer, H.R., 3, 4, 5, 49, 54, 73, 87,
    102
Schank, R.C., 18, 29
Schegloff, E.A., 52, 69, 70, 71, 72, 74,
    89, 165
Schiefflein, B., 48
Schmidt, R.C., 62
Schnuckler, M.A., 62
Schober, M.I., 92
Scotton, C.M., 96
Searle, J.R., 123
Seidman, S.J., 19
Selman, R., 17
Shantz, C.U., 2, 3, 12, 155
Shatz, M., 3, 28, 72, 93, 135
Shirk, S.R., 45
Shure, M.B., 20
Shute, R., 6
Silber, S., 22
Sinclair, J. McH., 68
Sinha, C., 8, 23, 37, 54, 65, 79, 80,
    158, 160, 161, 166, 172
Slaby, R.G., 53
Slaby, R., 53
Smith, P., 98
Snow, C., 49, 51, 85, 117
Sodian, B., 24
Spelke, E., 20
Spendberg, C., 73
Sperber, D., 30, 83
Sperry, L., 41
Stamback, M., 17
Steffan, J.J., 154
Stein, M.R., 54,
Stein, N.L., 20, 21
Stern, D., 51, 69, 84, 141
Stephenson, G.M., 46
Stevenson-Hinde, J., 55
Stitch, S., 8, 29
Stoffergen, T.A., 62

Stokes, T.F., 27, 53
Stotland, E., 3
Strain, P.S., 53, 161
Strayer, F.F., 73, 118
Strayer, J., 73
Swann, D., 56

Tajfel, H., 7
Tanz, C., 47, 122
Taylor, S.E., 18
Taylor, T.J., 56, 69, 71, 83
Thomson, J.A., 62
Trabasso, T., 15
Trevarthen, C., 28, 52, 69, 141
Tucker, H., 120
Turiel, E., 3, 5
Turner, G., 50
Turner, R., 68
Turner, T.J., 18
Turvey, M.T., 62, 66

Ullman, S., 62
Ury, W., 96

van Dijk, T., 21
Vaughen, B.E., 98
Vietze, P.M., 78
Vine, I., 154
Volpe, J., 15
Von Cranach, M., 154
Von Hofstein, C., 64
Vygotsky, L.S., 36, 37, 38, 48, 159

Walden, T.A., 19
Wales, R., 97, 112
Walker, H.M., 53, 161
Walkerdine, V., 42, 51, 80
Washington, J.A., 34, 93, 136
Waters, E., 98
Weatherall, M., 162
Wellman, H.M., 22
Wells, G., 130
Wells, T., 20, 21
Wertsch, J.V., 37, 38, 40, 41, 48, 160
West, C., 71
Wexler, K., 49
Whatley, J.L., 55
White, G.M., 27
Whiten, A., 159

Subject Index

KNOWING CHILDREN

Experiments in Conversation and Cognition

MICHAEL SIEGAL (University of Queensland)

It has been often maintained that young children's knowledge is limited to perceptual appearances; in this "preoperational" stage of development, there are profound conceptual limitations in that they have little understanding of numerical and causal relations and are incapable of insight into the minds of others. Their apparent inability to perform well on traditional developmental measures has led researchers to accept a model of the young child as plagued by conceptual deficits. These ideas have had a major impact on educational programs. Many have either accepted the view that the young are not ready for instruction, especially in subjects such as mathematics and science.

However, this essay provides evidence that children's stage-like performance on the many tasks that have been used to demonstrate their limitations can be reinterpreted in terms of the language used in experiments. In many specialized experimental settings, children may inadvertently perceive adults' well-meaning questions as redundant, insincere, irrelevant, uninformative, or ambiguous. Under these conditions, there is a clash between the conversational worlds of children and adults. Children do not share an experimenter's purpose in questioning and how his or her words are intended. They do not disclose the depth of their understanding and may respond to an experimenter's questions incorrectly even when they are certain of the right answer.

In this light, a different model of development emerges. It proposes that young children have abstract knowledge that can be examined through attention to their conversational experience. The implications for instruction in subjects such as mathematics and science are significant.

0-86377-158-0 1991 154pp. $31.95 £19.95 hbk.

0-86377-159-9 1991 154pp. $15.95 £8.95 pbk.

Lawrence Erlbaum Associates Ltd

Please send USA & Canadian orders to: Lawrence Erlbaum Associates Inc., 365 Broadway, Hillsdale, New Jersey 07642 USA. For UK & Rest of World, please send orders to: Lawrence Erlbaum Associates Ltd., Mail Order Department, 27 Church Road, Hove, E.Sussex, BN3 2FA, England. Note, prices shown here are correct at time of going to press, but may change. Prices outside Europe may differ from those shown.

Other Titles in the Series
Essays in Developmental Psychology
Series Editors: Peter Bryant, George Butterworth, Harry McGurk

SOCIAL INTERACTION AND THE DEVELOPMENT OF LANGUAGE AND COGNITION

ALISON F. GARTON
(Health Department of Western Australia)

This book identifies important research areas where social interaction has been considered in relation to children's language development and children's cognitive development. By incorporating research from major areas in developmental psychology, a unique conceptual contribution is made by the author. Further, an integrative analysis of the various theoretical positions considered provides the basis for unification of the different perspectives.

The author sets the scene by describing theories of development that have had a major impact on research concerned with the influence of social interaction on linguistic and cognitive development. Subsequent chapters critically discuss and evaluate research, firstly on social interaction and language development through an examination of how specifically linguistic input facilitates language development, and then more generally how social aspects of the interaction process assist language development. Broad social explanations of cognitive development are then followed by an account of how conflict, collaboration and communication facilitate cognitive development. An argument is developed that permits the postulation of social mechanisms in interaction that mediate to facilitate both linguistic and cognitive growth during development from infancy to middle childhood.

This book differs from others in the field by integrating in a unique way a diverse range of contemporary developmental research. Traditional demarcation between areas of research studies is ignored in an attempt to reconcile both empirical evidence and theoretical perspectives. In addition, a synthesising position is developed, incorporating aspects of the research and theories presented throughout the book, which advocates the facilitary role of active social interaction in both language and cognitive development. Recent research extensions of social interaction as applied to the realm of academic learning are highlighted.

ISBN 0-86377-227-7 1991 176pp. $25.50 £14.95 hbk.

Lawrence Erlbaum Associates Ltd

Please send USA & Canadian orders to: Lawrence Erlbaum Associates Inc., 365 Broadway, Hillsdale, New Jersey 07642 USA. For UK & Rest of World, please send orders to: Lawrence Erlbaum Associates Ltd., Mail Order Department, 27 Church Road, Hove, E.Sussex, BN3 2FA, England. Note, prices shown here are correct at time of going to press, but may change. Prices outside Europe may differ from those shown.

Other Titles in the Series
Essays in Developmental Psychology
Series Editors: Peter Bryant, George Butterworth, Harry McGurk

LANGUAGE EXPERIENCE AND EARLY LANGUAGE DEVELOPMENT

From Input to Uptake

MARGARET HARRIS (University of London)

This book is about one of the most fundamental debates on language development, namely the relationship between children's language development and their language experience. This issue is not only of theoretical interest: understanding how a child's language development is related to experience, has important implications for children whose early language development is giving cause for concern. If there are no environmental influences on early development then little can be done to help the child whose first steps into language are faltering. But, if the speed with which children develop language is subject to some external influence, then there are likely to be opportunities for successful intervention and grounds for optimism rather than pessimism in this area. This book argues that there are grounds for optimism.

The first chapter provides an overview of some of the theoretical controversy relating to fundamental questions about the nature of language development. The second chapter presents a review of research into parental speech to young children and considers whether there is any evidence for a causal link between parental speech and child language development. The third chapter discusses the methodological problems inherent in investigations of the relationship between language development and language experience, and chapter four considers the wider social context of the child's language experience and the work of Halliday and Bruner.

Chapter five examines the relationship between young children's socio-linguistic experience and their early language development. Chapter six discusses early vocabulary development and chapter seven describes a detailed study of the relationship between early vocabulary development and maternal speech. Chapter eight explores the language development of deaf children and considers how deaf children learn sign language. The final chapter discusses language development in blind children and ideas of innate constraints. It also provides an overview of the issues discussed in the book and draws out some of the practical implications of the research findings.

ISBN 0-86377-231-5 forthcoming 1992 176pp. $24.95 £14.95 hbk.

Lawrence Erlbaum Associates Ltd

Please send USA & Canadian orders to: Lawrence Erlbaum Associates Inc., 365 Broadway, Hillsdale, New Jersey 07642 USA. For UK & Rest of World, please send orders to: Lawrence Erlbaum Associates Ltd., Mail Order Department, 27 Church Road, Hove, E.Sussex, BN3 2FA, England. Note, prices shown here are correct at time of going to press, but may change. Prices outside Europe may differ from those shown.

CHILDREN'S SAVING

Studies in the Development of Economic Behaviour

EDMUND J.S. SONUGA-BARKE (Southampton University)
PAUL WEBLEY (Exeter University)

This book presents an alternative approach to the study of the emergence of economic awareness during childhood: a new developmental economic psychology! In the past, attempts to study the emergence of children's economic consciousness have failed to take account of the practical nature of the "economic" in the history of western cultures. Economic socialization has been seen as the acquisition of abstract knowledge about the institutions and agents of adult economic culture. The child has been seen as a spectator, acquiring knowledge of that culture, but never really part of it.

Economic actions, in essence, are directed not towards the attainment of knowledge but rather towards the practical solution of problems of resource allocation imposed by constraint. Children, just like adults, are faced with practical problems of resource allocation. Their response to these problems may be different from those of adults but no less "economic" for that. This realization forms the heart of this book. In it children are seen as both inhabitants of their own "playground" economic sub-culture and actors in the wider economic world of adults, solving, or attempting to solve, practical economic problems.

In order to highlight this "child centered" approach the authors studied the way children tackle the particular problems posed by limitations of income. How do children learn, a) the relationship between choices available in the present and the future, b) to spread their limited financial resources over time into the future and c) about the strategies, such as banking, that allow them to protect those resources from threats and temptations? In short, how do children learn to save? This volume goes some way to answering these and related questions and in so doing sets up an alternative framework for the study of the emergence of economic awareness.

0-86377-233-1 forthcoming 1992 176pp. $26.95 £14.95 hbk.

Lawrence Erlbaum Associates Ltd

Please send USA & Canadian orders to: Lawrence Erlbaum Associates Inc., 365 Broadway, Hillsdale, New Jersey 07642 USA. For UK & Rest of World, please send orders to: Lawrence Erlbaum Associates Ltd., Mail Order Department, 27 Church Road, Hove, E.Sussex, BN3 2FA, England. Note, prices shown here are correct at time of going to press, but may change. Prices outside Europe may differ from those shown.

Other Titles in the Series
Essays in Developmental Psychology
Series Editors: Peter Bryant, George Butterworth, Harry McGurk

LANGUAGE LEARNING

A Special Case for Developmental Psychology?

CHRISTINE J. HOWE (University of Strathclyde)

The starting place for this book is the notion, current in the literature for around thirty years, that children could not learn their native language without substantial innate knowledge of its grammatical structure. It is argued that the notion is as problematic for contemporary theories of development as it was for theories of the past. Accepting this, the book attempts an in-depth study of the notion's credibility, arguing that it runs into two major problems. Firstly, proponents of the innateness hypothesis are too ready to treat children as embryonic linguists, concerned with the representation of sentences as an end in itself. A more realistic approach would be to regard children as communication engineers, storing sentences to optimize the production and retrieval of meaning. Secondly, even when the communication analogy is adopted, it is glibly assumed that the meanings children impute will be the ones adults intend.

One of the book's major contentions is that a careful reading of contemporary research suggests that the meanings may differ considerably. Identifying the problems, the book considers how development should proceed, given learning along communication lines and a more plausible analysis of meaning. It makes detailed predictions about what would be anticipated given no innate knowledge of grammar. Focusing on English but giving full acknowledgement to cross-linguistic research, it concludes that the predictions are consistent with both the known timescale of learning and the established facts about children's knowledge. Thus, the book aspires to a serious challenge to the innateness hypothesis via, as its final chapter will argue, a model which is much more reassuring to psychological theory.

0-86377-230-7 forthcoming 1992 176pp. $26.95 £14.95 hbk.

Lawrence Erlbaum Associates Ltd

Please send USA & Canadian orders to: Lawrence Erlbaum Associates Inc., 365 Broadway, Hillsdale, New Jersey 07642 USA. For UK & Rest of World, please send orders to: Lawrence Erlbaum Associates Ltd., Mail Order Department, 27 Church Road, Hove, E.Sussex, BN3 2FA, England. Note, prices shown here are correct at time of going to press, but may change. Prices outside Europe may differ from those shown.

Other Titles in the Series
Essays in Developmental Psychology
Series Editors: Peter Bryant, George Butterworth, Harry McGurk

ANALOGICAL REASONING IN CHILDREN

USHA GOSWAMI (University of Cambridge)

Analogical reasoning is a fundamental cognitive skill, involved in classification, learning, problem-solving and creative thinking, and should be a basic building block of cognitive development. However, for a long time researchers have believed that children are incapable of reasoning by analogy. This book argues that this is far from the case, and that analogical reasoning may be available very early in development. Recent research has shown that even 3-year-olds can solve analogies, and that infants can reason about relational similarity, which is the hallmark of analogy.

The book traces the roots of the popular misconceptions about children's analogical abilities and argues that when children fail to use analogies , it is because they do not understand the relations underlying the analogy rather than because they are incapable of analogical reasoning. The author argues that young children spontaneously use analogies in learning, and that their analogies can sometimes lead them into misconceptions. In the "real worlds" of their classrooms, children use analogies when learning basic skills like reading, and babies can be shown to use analogies to learn about the world around them.

Contents: Reasoning by Analogy. Structural Theories of Analogical Development. Testing the Claims of Structural Theory. Information-Processing Accounts of Classical Analogical Reasoning. Problem Analogies and Analogical Development. Analogies in Babies and Toddlers. Analogies in the Real World of the Classroom.

ISBN 0-86377-226-9 forthcoming 1992 176pp. $26.95 £14.95 hbk.

Lawrence Erlbaum Associates Ltd

Please send USA & Canadian orders to: Lawrence Erlbaum Associates Inc., 365 Broadway, Hillsdale, New Jersey 07642 USA. For UK & Rest of World, please send orders to: Lawrence Erlbaum Associates Ltd., Mail Order Department, 27 Church Road, Hove, E.Sussex, BN3 2FA, England. Note, prices shown here are correct at time of going to press, but may change. Prices outside Europe may differ from those shown.